Far East RAF Liberators

Attacking the Japanese: Roy Andrews and 215 Squadron

Far East RAF Liberators

Attacking the Japanese: Roy Andrews and 215 Squadron

Matt Poole

AIR WORLD

First published in Great Britain in 2025 by
Pen & Sword Military
An imprint of
Pen & Sword Books Ltd
Yorkshire - Philadelphia

ISBN 978 1 03613 168 5

A CIP catalogue record for this book is available from the British Library.

Typeset in INDIA by IMPEC eSolutions
Printed and bound in England by CPI Group (UK) Ltd, Croydon, CRO 4YY

The Publisher's authorised representative in the EU for product safety is Authorised Rep Compliance Ltd., Ground Floor, 71 Lower Baggot Street, Dublin D02 P593, Ireland.
www.arccompliance.com

For a complete list of Pen & Sword titles please contact

PEN & SWORD BOOKS LIMITED
47 Church Street, Barnsley, South Yorkshire, S70 2AS, England
E-mail: enquiries@pen-and-sword.co.uk
Website: www.pen-and-sword.co.uk

or

PEN AND SWORD BOOKS
1950 Lawrence Rd, Havertown, PA 19083, USA
E-mail: uspen-and-sword@casematepublishers.com
Website: www.penandswordbooks.com

FSC
www.fsc.org
MIX
Paper | Supporting responsible forestry
FSC® C013604

Contents

Acknowledgements

I've benefitted from the knowledge and generosity of too many people to thank on this page. I'm especially grateful to: the Air Force Museum of New Zealand; Peter ARNOLD; the Australian War Memorial; Rod BEATTIE; John BIK; Colin BRUGGY; Joe CARBERRY (air bomber, 356 Squadron RAF, and later in the Cocos Islands the Squadron's Adjutant, then its Commanding Officer); Steve FOGDEN; Laurie FRAZER (daughter of Wally Frazer, pilot, 215 Squadron RAF); Dick GONSALVES; John GREHAN; Richard HAKANSON; Joe HALL; Adam HAMBURGER; Mike HERNANDEZ (grandson of Frederic Hernandez, bombardier, US 492nd Bombardment Squadron); the Imperial War Museum (London); Simon JERVIS; Brian JOHNSON (son of Jack Johnson, W/Op/AG, 215 Squadron RAF); Amy JORDAN; Paul KIGHTLEY (son of Eric Kightley, nose gunner, 355 Squadron RAF); Ian KIKUCHI; Richard LEWIS; Bob LIVINGSTONE (son of R. Murray Livingstone, navigator, 160 Squadron RAF); Ann LYONS (niece of Ken Brailsford, pilot, 90 Squadron RAF, then 159 Squadron RAF, then 358 Squadron RAF); Martin MACE; Terry MANTTAN; Paul MCMILLAN; National Archives and Records Administration; Garth O'CONNELL; Matthew O'SULLIVAN; Tony O'TOOLE; Colin PATEMAN; Ken PATTERSON; James PAYNE; Jagan PILLARISETTI; Air Chief Marshal Sakpinit PROMTHEP (Royal Thai Air Force, retired); Robert QUIRK; Andy RENWICK; the Royal Air Force Museum; the Royal Air Forces Association; Thansawath 'Alex' SARANYATHADAWONG; Tom SHARRAD (grandson of Stan Sharrad, air gunner, 355 Squadron RAF, then 159 Squadron RAF); Clarence SIMONSEN; Squadron Leader Tim SINDALL (son of Wing Commander James Sindall DSO, pilot, Commanding Officer, 215 Squadron RAF); Geoff SMITH (son of Alan Smith, bomb aimer, 215 Squadron RAF); Phillip THOMAS (son of David Thomas, W/Op/AG, 159 Squadron RAF, then 355 Squadron RAF); Kiran TOOR; Pavel TURK; Tony VINE (son of Ronald Vine, W/Op/AG, 355 Squadron RAF); Angus WALLACE; Jeremy WALSH (son of Benjamin Walsh, pilot, 418 Squadron RCAF, then 27 Squadron

RAF, then 45 Squadron RAF); Jon WILKINSON; Andy WRIGHT; Edward M. YOUNG; Andy ZIMNY and Stefan ZINGG.

I also wish to thank Roy's son, Greg ANDREWS, and daughter, Sue SILVESTER, for trusting me with the challenge of presenting an accurate review of their father's life, as often as possible by using Roy's own words.

Matt Poole

Maps

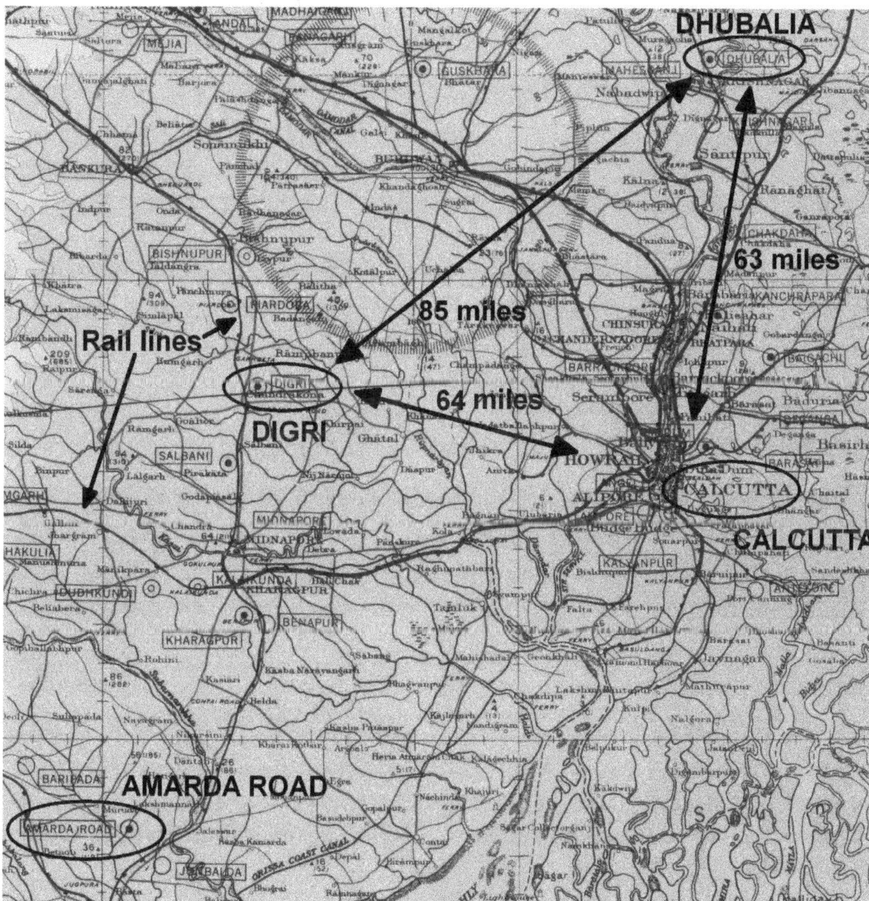

On a 1944 map can be seen the locations of Digri and Dhubalia, 215 Squadron's Royal Air Force bases in Bengal, India, during the time period when Roy Andrews flew on the unit. Also noted is Amarda Road airfield, where Roy received some training in 1944 prior to flying his first op with 215. After completing his 215 Squadron tour of ops Roy served with the Communication Flight at 231 Group Headquarters in Calcutta. (*Matt Poole*)

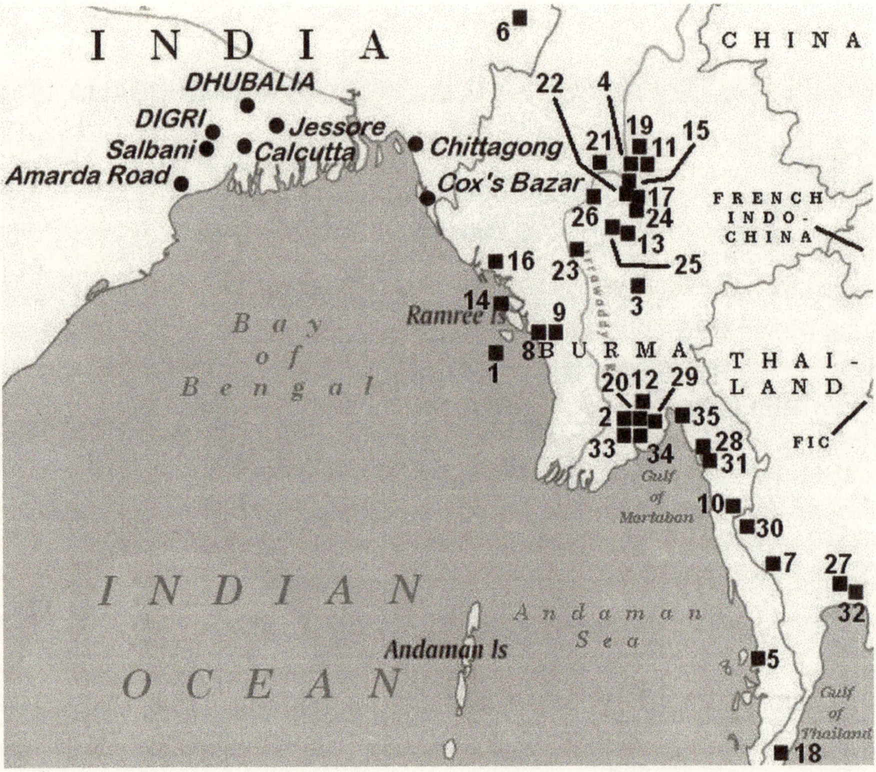

This map chronologically plots the locations of all thirty-five of Roy's 215 Squadron operational flights. In italicised ALL CAPS black type Roy's two 215 Squadron bases are noted: DIGRI and DHUBALIA. (*Matt Poole, edited from a page 129 graphic in Edward M. Young's book*, DEATH FROM ABOVE, *subtitled* The 7th Bombardment Group in World War II)

Introduction

The text is the memoir of B-24 Liberator veteran Roy Stuart Andrews, a Royal Australian Air Force (RAAF) wireless operator/air gunner (W/Op/AG), supplemented by additional material covering the Liberator's use by his operational unit in India, 215 Squadron, Royal Air Force (RAF) and by my further analysis and opinion. Roy accomplished his operational flying, all on 215 Squadron, between 11 October 1944 and 8 April 1945. He died in 2011.

I was fortunate to have learned much about his experiences directly from him.

No. 215 Squadron's operational usage of the four-engine Liberator coincided with the entire length of Roy's tenure on the squadron. The unit flew twin-engine Wellingtons on India-based bombing ops between 1942 and 1944, before Roy's posting, until it converted to Liberators and flew its first B-24 sortie when Roy was a squadron member. Then after 8 April 1945 (215 Squadron's final Liberator bombing op and Roy's thirty-fifth and last op), the unit became a twin-engine Dakota transport squadron. Having completed his tour of ops on Liberators, Roy departed 215 Squadron and did not fly Dakota missions.

Because Roy's association with 215 and the squadron's Liberator use essentially covered the same time frame, I decided to summarise every Liberator sortie, not just Roy's, flown by 215 Squadron, including all long training exercises. They flew the Liberator from Jessore, Digri, and Dhubalia airfields in Bengal, India. Liberator conversion training began at Jessore, before Roy's arrival on the squadron. Digri was where the unit relocated in September 1944, Liberator conversion training continued, Roy joined the squadron and the unit began its Liberator operational bombing campaign. A move by 215 Squadron to Dhubalia followed in December 1944. Roy flew op numbers ten through thirty-five from there.

Thus, while this book isn't a full review of 215 Squadron's war record, it does completely cover the unit's operational Liberator period.

Besides incorporating some of what I learned from Roy into the book, I've based the text upon his self-published 1993 memoir, *TALES OF A LIBERATOR SQUADRON*; the OPERATIONS RECORD BOOK (ORB) documents of each RAF Liberator squadron flying from India; selected US records; other book references and my own knowledge. I only present what I've determined to be the correct and most logical detail; many sources contained errors I have unscrambled. Excerpts of other sources, such as newspapers, books and ORBs, have been reproduced verbatim, including misspellings, punctuation anomalies, capitalisation errors and things (like the use of numerals, not text, for mileage figures under 100) that did not follow Pen & Sword style guidelines.

Each B-24 Liberator on an RAF squadron was assigned a unique letter code that was painted onto both sides of the fuselage. I sometimes refer only to this letter, not to the full two letter/three number serial.

Some readers may be distracted by my 'in the weeds' detail, but many who crave such information would be disappointed and frustrated by its exclusion.

All of the headings, subheadings and the appendices are my own writing. I've written all photo captions.

Because the book contains segments of writing by both Roy Andrews and myself, and because I added much supplemental information not found in Roy's memoir, it is essential that the authorship of any piece of writing be easily understood. To make this happen in every chapter (but not in the acknowledgements, introduction, epilogue, headings, subheadings and appendices) I have introduced each block of Roy's writing with '**ROY:**' in bold text, and my own writing has always been introduced with '**MATT:**' in bold text. There is also a blank space between Roy's writing and my own at the point of change.

On Roy's ops, the subheadings introducing the flights only refer to the targets his individual aircraft bombed. Mostly these were the same destinations as attacked by other 215 Squadron Liberators on the same ops, but sometimes his specific targets were uniquely attacked just by his Lib or weren't bombed by all of 215's aircraft. The text below each subheading, however, reveals the entire squadron's assigned objective or objectives for that op.

For example, on Roy's seventh op (10 December 1944) his Liberator, KG831, bombed and strafed locomotives and rolling stock at Milestones 174, 175 and 176½ of the Thailand-Burma Railway (all in Thailand), while the other 215 Squadron Liberators struck different Thai targets along an even longer stretch of the same railway. So, then, although Roy's aircraft attacked targets along the Thailand-Burma Railway like the other 215 Squadron Libs, only KG831's specific targets are given in the 10 December 1944 subheading. However, 215

Squadron's assigned bombing sector (Ban Wang Yai to Kanchanaburi, both in Thailand) is given in the text below the subheading.

I refer to the Death Railway in Burma and Thailand as the Thailand-Burma Railway, not as the Burma-Thailand Railway or Burma-Siam Railway, per the opinion of noted Death Railway historian Rod Beattie. Note that 'Thailand', not 'Siam', was the country name at the time.

Place names are as spelled during the war and are taken mainly from wartime maps. Official records, such as squadron ORBs, sometimes misspelled such names and were unreliable as name/spelling sources. Where a specific name differed on contemporary wartime maps I consistently use one spelling.

Chapter 1

Roy's life before joining the air force: SEPTEMBER 1924 to NOVEMBER 1942 *(Part 1)*

Roy's earliest years in Hong Kong

ROY: I was born a British citizen in Hong Kong on 20 September 1924 of parents Arthur Albert Andrews and Edith Ruth Andrews (called Ruth), but my lineage is traced to Suffolk, UK.

My brother, Donald Eric Andrews, followed my birth with his 1926 entrance into the world, also in Hong Kong.

My first memory was of falling into a boating pond back in England. Mother and Father had gone back there on leave. I know it was in the middle of winter because I was wrapped up in coats and scarfs. People were sailing little boats there. My fall caused such consternation and excitement that it impressed itself on my 3-year-old mind. I still have small flashes of memory of it today, more than sixty-five years later.

Another memory is also hardly pleasant. Having gone into hospital for tonsil removal, subsequent to the operation I had a violent haemorrhage, to the point where the doctors told my parents that they didn't think I'd survive. The medical experts were going to give me one last type of treatment, and I wouldn't live if there was no improvement after that. Obviously, the therapy worked. I still remember that terrible time when I kept coughing over everybody, and I recall an image of red and the smell of blood.

Then came kindergarten, when I disgraced myself by wetting my pants because I was too shy to mention that I needed to go to the toilets. Mother, phoned by the school, had to come and fetch me.

We lived at 15 Bowen Road on Hong Kong Island, halfway up The Peak, overlooking the harbour.

Father was employed by Peak Tramways Company Limited as Traffic Superintendent, a position that afforded him a company house. This was a two-storey brick structure with a flat roof, and with a terrace out front. Built on a steeply sloping hillside, the home had a magnificent view of the harbour and today would probably be worth millions of Hong Kong dollars. When somebody came to stay or visit once, he or she nearly fell over from the sheer beauty of the view. To me, however, it was just part of my everyday life, and I thought nothing of its magnificence.

While its physical location was alluring to many, unfortunately it was far removed from everybody else, specifically my playmates. We were about a mile from the nearest Peak Tram station, so the distance was detrimental to visits with friends, where tram journeys were needed.

My sole nearby playmate was a fellow who lived next door (about 100 yards away) only for two years.

In a way having few friends living close by made me a fairly solitary person. I didn't get along well with my brother, so I did a lot of reading, even when very young.

My education began at the Garrison School, where the majority of students were children of the regular British Army regimental soldiers guarding Hong Kong. The soldiers were in barracks not far away from the Lower Peak Tram station. I had two ways of getting to school, firstly by walking the mile to the Bowen Road station and going down the hill by tram, or else by running or walking on the diagonal downward to school. This made me very skilful at traversing steep hillsides. I remember I had well-developed legs compared with the rest of my body.

At the Garrison School I showed no particular academic prowess. I enjoyed my time there, for the most part. While at this school I fell deeply in love for the first time with a girl named Pauline Buchanan. I cannot remember how old I was.

Because of always getting into trouble, principally for talking and not paying attention, I was occasionally disciplined with corporal punishment. One was caned on the hands with a stick, and it was imperative that the offender be extremely stoical. If the student should show even the remotest sign of pain, it was considered most undignified and weak. I recall getting four or five cuts per hand and maintaining a most impassive face on returning to my seat, revealing no sign of pain, while my hands felt as if they'd been dipped in boiling water. Caning did me no permanent harm, but today a teacher who was to cuff a boy's head would face assault charges. Discipline is lacking nowadays, really.

It's very difficult for teachers to administer their classes when being unable to punish anybody.

The courts are similarly inclined. Kids up to sixteen aren't properly disciplined. However, I'm getting off track.

Roy's young life continues in England

In the late 1930s when I was in the second form at school, Mother, my brother and I went to England. That was Depression time. I'm only conscious that this was so because I went to Father and asked him if I could have fifty cents a week more pocket money than I was getting. He said, 'Just sit down for a minute. I want to talk to you.'

'The world is in a Depression, and I'm very lucky to be working. There are millions of people who are out of work, and some of them are starving,' he explained, before going on about soup kitchens. He then told me about my Uncle Cyril, who'd gone to England on 'leave'.

'Leave' in Hong Kong at the time meant that every five or six years a nine-month holiday on full pay was granted, including paid passage. Within a week of Uncle Cyril returning from leave in England he was sacked. I remember Father telling me that because Cyril and family knew they were coming back to Hong Kong they'd spent all their holiday money. But my uncle's return to Hong Kong didn't end so well.

At the end of this talk I said to Father, 'I can do without that fifty cent raise.'

He said, 'No, I think we can handle fifty cents a week, but I just want you to realise that things are very difficult.'

Moreover, he decided that he was too nervous to leave the colony at the time, but that Mother, Donald and I would go to England.

We went on a German passenger ship, a very fine boat called *Gneisenau* (not to be confused with the German battlecruiser of the same name).

There was quite a lot of ill feeling between the German and English adults. Even at that stage it was quite noticeable. I remember, even at my young age, hearing people talking about it, but that didn't bother me, as it wouldn't most children.

I was told in later years that Mother was taken aboard ship on a stretcher. She suffered from phlebitis, an inflammation of her leg veins, and any blow on the legs, even something like a dog's tail striking her, would produce a haematoma. However, I don't remember a stretcher. If she was, indeed, on a stretcher, that brain cell has died, because I don't recall it. However, I do remember arriving in England.

When we reached the UK we rented a house in Brighton with my grandmother, whom we called Danny, but she was also known as Lill. I really enjoyed living with her. I later discovered that Father didn't, or at least they didn't get on very well; their relationship entered into his thinking when he opted to remain in Hong Kong. I remember saying once, when I was in Hong Kong, how much I liked her, but he didn't think highly of his mother-in-law.

She used to write to me a lot. I was her favourite grandchild. Father told me that they didn't get on, which I couldn't understand, because I found her very pleasant. Before travelling, she'd promised to gift me a bicycle soon after my arrival in England. Sure enough, almost at the first opportunity she bought me a really fine bicycle. I was rapt about that.

Crystal Palace, Buckingham Palace, Hampton Court, Tower Bridge and all those touristy things were terrific, of course, but the school part of my stay in England was quite awful. I went to the Council school (the public school), where there were some very tough kids. They gave me hell! I suppose it was understandable. I was a white bear in a brown pack of bears. I spoke differently. I suppose that I'd have spoken similarly to how I do now, with a seemingly slight American accent.

Because Hong Kong was very cosmopolitan, especially American, I stood out as being different at school in England. I used to be beaten up all the time, and I wasn't sufficiently strong enough to do much about these boys. They were a very hardened gang. I remember being burned on my stomach with a magnifying glass a few times while being held down on the ground. I did everything I could not to go out into the schoolyard. I hid in the library. I did anything I could think of to avoid being out there, but I couldn't hide all the time. Sometimes it was awful.

I remember that one day I burst into tears right before leaving to go to school, prompting my mother to say, 'Right, I'm going up to the school.' I finally told her what I was being subjected to; until then, I'd been too terrified to tell her, in case she'd do the very thing she then threatened to do. 'I'm seeing the headmaster this morning,' she said. I knew that if she did that, I might as well commit suicide.

However, time passed, and at the end of the nine months I was able to leave that school and those bullies, and we got on the ship and went back to Hong Kong.

Hong Kong again

By the time I returned to live in Hong Kong Father's circumstances must have changed for the better because I was allowed to go to the Central British School (CBS). That was the 'white' school in Hong Kong. I'm referring to Imperial times when the white occupying power didn't have anything to do with the other part. It was like that. Nobody was allowed to go to CBS except Europeans and Eurasians, really. It was a terrific school, a lovely school, and, enjoying every minute of it, I stayed there until I was in the fifth form. I went through all the love affairs and things that a boy has when growing up at such a school, and it was very nice.

Academically I was ahead of other students my age. I was doing the fifth form (year eleven) when I was fifteen, and most of the other kids in the class were a year older than me, which meant that their physical development was a year more advanced than mine. That made things a little difficult for me. For example, my classmates were on the cricket team when I was just on the edge of being selected. They were on the football team when I was almost being chosen. They could run faster, and they were heavier, too. I suppose I could say that I was their intellectual equal, as I didn't ever fail to be promoted, and one was only promoted by results, but I never did any work if I could help it, and I used to do my homework on the way to school.

Bowen Road, where we lived, was a very narrow street above a water viaduct, and because of the viaduct only small cars, like Austin 7s, with special permits, were allowed to drive along this road. Father, with a motorbike and sidecar, was allowed to use Bowen Road.

To get to school I'd walk down to the Star Ferry after reaching the Lower Peak tram station.

I was never any good at athletics. I entered the mile once because nobody from our house had entered that race. Only one boy was skilled enough to win, and he did. (Hosegood, I think his name was.) He was a star athlete and had won some very prestigious race in the colony as a schoolboy.

I came in last in the mile, but it didn't matter; at least somebody from our house was in it.

I did excel at swimming. I won the sprinting races for two or three years until a boy who became my friend arrived in Hong Kong from Reading College, or somewhere in England. He then proceeded to humiliate me in the pool. I think he took something like two seconds off my times. To recover my status I switched to diving, which I subsequently won. It had been a bad time for me, because until then swimming had been my only sporting success.

CBS was co-educational, which for me wasn't an advantage. The presence of the girls was a constant distraction, and often an inhibiting factor. If the teacher asked if everything was clear, and no girl put her hand up to register that it wasn't, then there was no way Andrews was going to put up his hand! So, while it was lovely having my girlfriend in the class, it actually worked against me.

Because I wasn't interested in what was being taught, I was only an average student, not a scholar. I just wasn't motivated. It wasn't the school's fault. As mentioned before, I was a voracious reader, but I didn't read the sort of stuff presented in school. I was very keen about astronomy and also all medical matters; anything medical that I could get in an encyclopedia I read and learned.

Also among my interests were rocketry, radio and science generally, including anatomy, but chemistry especially appealed to me. Peter Seats, a friend in class, was a very clever young lad at chemistry. My memory is that he was hopeless at anything else, but at chemistry he was brilliant. The master was quite nervous about him, because Peter would ask him questions that were quite difficult to answer. We had our own laboratories in our houses, where all sorts of accidents occurred.

I remember that once we made some caustic soda – quite pure, and clear like water. On this hot day I came back from outside with a beaker of water to drink. I placed it on the table, but later I picked up the wrong beaker and took a mouthful of caustic soda, burning my mouth very badly! Fortunately, we had enough sense to use diluted acids. Another time we could have died when making cyanide. We were very ill for about a day, which caused my parents to utter all sorts of threats like, 'It's all going in the rubbish bin tomorrow' and 'You're never to see Peter again,' but eventually it all blew over.

Though I don't remember how, I became a choirboy at St. John's Cathedral. Strangely, nobody ever teased me about it. Over the years I steadily worked my way up to be Head Boy. We were paid an amount to be choirboys, and I needed the money. Payment wasn't the only motivating factor, because I loved the music and singing, and I guess also the importance in the church.

I wasn't aware of that at the time, but reflecting now, I think it was in the back of my mind.

When I became one of the Head Boys I was granted a singing scholarship, which paid for my last two years at school. Father must have been pleased about that.

Life was quite good until war was declared between England and Germany on 3 September 1939; we thought the war was only going to last a month. How could Germany handle Great Britain's might? I mean, here I was, overlooking a harbour that was filled with destroyers, submarines and cruisers. There were Gurkha soldiers, the Gloucester Regiment and all sorts of other units nearby, and to me we were in an impregnable position. It came as an awful shock to find that Britain had allowed itself to be so lacking in arms that soldiers coming into the service were drilling with broomsticks and were being armed with pitchforks to fight enemy parachutists.

Australia, Roy's new home

Schoolboy life still went on fairly normally for me, and then in 1940 the Hong Kong Government, realising that the Japanese were becoming very threatening, knew that the Japanese were going to do something.

It was eventually decided that all women and children would be evacuated. This was quite a decision to make, and there was a bit of fuss about it. However, the first lot was sent to Manila, but the conditions the evacuees were placed in over there caused quite an outcry. I'm not sure, but I think they were put into army barracks. Wherever it was the women had to shower altogether as did men in the army, all undressed in one room, all under showers together. In those days this was considered objectionable. There was enormous outcry. Mother, my brother and I were in the next lot, and they shipped us down to Australia.

When we landed in Sydney I was dressed in my school uniform of brown shoes, grey slacks and a chocolate brown blazer with brass buttons. On the breast pocket was a blue badge with a rampant yellow lion at centre. Being quite a nice badge, it caused a lot of interest wherever we went. People would look at me and say, 'What school could that be?' I remember, because I became quite self-conscious about it. However, I don't really recall any more particulars of the journey, such as coming down to Melbourne on the train from Sydney. On our very first night there we were billeted in two bedrooms above a nightclub at Black Rock, a beachside suburb in Melbourne on the south-eastern side of the metropolitan area.

Mother soon decided that staying there would be the bitter end of us, because when the band was playing, and most people were singing, dancing and shouting, other patrons were trying the door handles of our bedrooms, presumably in search of a place to indulge in a little fooling around.

After two days that was it. Having decided to leave this den of iniquity, Mother found us half a house to rent at 26 Edward Street, Sandringham. It was run by a woman, Mrs Rhodes, whom I thought of as old, but she was probably only about fifty-five! The living arrangement there was much better than in the club, and Mother was happy. Though it wasn't the conditions under which we were used to, it was okay. We shared a bathroom, I think, but we had our own kitchen, sitting room and bedrooms, and that was fine.

I'd long been a swimmer and a beach lover, and now living within a quarter mile of the beach fronting Port Phillip Bay seemed too good to be true! Fairly soon after my arrival in the area I met this crowd of boys, probably in the street. I remember the first time we all went down on the beach, on a lovely hot day. This was probably in September, though September in Melbourne is typically cool, being late winter or the beginning of spring. Unlike now, Australians were very tough in those days. Back then they were bigoted, united and strong – very strong – people.

Down on the beach someone enthusiastically suggested, 'Let's go for a swim.' I had my togs on, and another boy said something like, 'Okay, last one in's mad.' We all ran towards the bay, but when we got to the water's edge they stopped. I plunged on in. They had to help me out of the water; I was so cold I couldn't walk! Because of the frigid water my legs just wouldn't work. That was a good introduction to my new gang of Aussies – each with a twinkle in his eyes. They were good lads, though, even if I had to warm up to them after my cold plunge that day.

Black Rock is adjacent to an ocean cliff outcrop called Red Bluff. Immediately to the south of the bluff is Half Moon Bay (a small body of water in the larger Prince Phillip Bay) and its sandy beach. A little over 300 yards off of Half Moon Beach there was a breakwater shipwreck, HMVS *Cerberus*, which had served as part of the Victorian Naval Forces when Australia was still a British colony and then as part of the Royal Australian Navy (RAN) until 1924.

Though the *Cerberus* was, by World War I, one of the jewels of the RAN, after having been on active duty for over half a century her usefulness had passed. In 1924 the ship was sold for scrap and was scuttled in 1926 as a breakwater. Ten years later I saw the *Cerberus* off the beach every day, rusting in the mud. It's a protected site today.

Working at Australian Iron & Steel, and the Air Training Corps

Mother decided that I had to go back to school to get my matriculation, the university entrance exam. I was just sixteen as of 20 September 1940. I said, 'No way, I'm not going back,' and she said, 'You're going to school.' Then a battle ensued for a couple of weeks, but in the absence of my father Mother lacked enough strength to force me to go. So I went looking for a job.

I applied to Australian Iron & Steel in South Melbourne. Looking back, I think that would have been the last place to go, but in those days, being very competitive, I wanted to get the first job I'd applied for. No matter where it was, I wanted it.

So I went down for an interview, after which the fellow told me I didn't get the job, and I should leave. After walking about 150 yards back up the street I heard yelling behind me. The interviewer, despite his dismissal moments earlier, shouted for me to come back. He'd apparently been given an earful for letting me go. I returned, was hired and stayed there for two years while waiting to get into the air force; I knew it would be relatively short-term employment, as joining the Royal Australian Air Force (RAAF) was all I was interested in at that time.

I worked as a costing clerk. We were costing every piece of steel that left the factory, based upon the calculated weight of each item. I did quite well, but I was still just filling in time until my eighteenth birthday, after which I planned to enter the RAAF.

In anticipation of the future, I set about preparing for air force life. I'd joined the Air Training Corps (ATC) in April 1942 at seventeen; ATC members had to be between sixteen and eighteen. I started in 5 Squadron as a cadet, was advanced to a corporal's rank in just over a month and then shot up to sergeant in early August.

In the ATC I learned to march/drill properly; this activity was a standard evil forced upon the membership as one means by which discipline was instilled into young minds. I was also taught important communication skills that would transfer into the RAAF: Morse code, semaphore (waving flags) and Aldis lamp messaging (transmission by light). Aircraft recognition training enabled me to instantly identify, from every angle, all Japanese and British aircraft that were available at the time. Other subjects relating to the air force were also practised.

In early September 1942 when approaching my eighteenth birthday I requested papers at an RAAF recruiting centre. The fellow said to me, 'Australian Iron & Steel. You won't be allowed to join up because you're in an essential industry.' Imagine what that did to me! It had never occurred to me that I'd not be allowed to join up. Obviously, somebody had to stay home to make the instruments of war, but, no, I didn't think they'd ever keep me from joining the air force.

Chapter 2

Roy's preliminary air force career: NOVEMBER 1942 *(Part 2)* to NOVEMBER 1943 *(Part 1)*

No. 4 Initial Training School, Victor Harbour *(NOVEMBER 1942 to FEBRUARY 1943)*

It took a huge effort on my part, including subterfuge, but in the end, after about the fifth manpower officer had rung him up, an Australian Iron & Steel accountant summoned me to his office and said, 'Get out and don't ever come back.' What beautiful words!

And so, I resigned to join the Royal Australian Air Force. My 'Oath or Affirmation' papers for enlisting in the RAAF were signed on 21 September 1942 at No. 1 Reception Centre (1 RC) in Melbourne the day after I turned eighteen.

I entered as aircrew. I wasn't called up until 6 November when, officially, my RAAF enlistment began at No. 4 Initial Training School (4 ITS), located 385 miles north-west of Melbourne at Victor Harbour, South Australia. When entering the RAAF one was sent to various destinations, usually in other states, probably because it was felt that a typical recruit could be better handled if he was away from his family support.

By this time Father had joined Mother in Australia, where they resided at 9 Carew St in Sandringham. I listed him as my next of kin.

The next three months were incredible. The Drill Instructors to whom we raw recruits were handed had to make soldiers out of us. In three months. There were no excuses; in that short time a recruit had to be a trained soldier and able to run something like five miles while toting all of his equipment, strip his rifle to pieces and put it back together again, clean. He had to be able to march in concert with fellow trainees, with impeccable style and precision in response to the DI's commands. Unreal!

As I said, I was an indifferent pupil at school; I just didn't care about studying, really. I was hardly a poster boy for the merits of co-education. My attitude changed rapidly now that I was in the RAAF. Admittedly, I'd started to come around while in the ATC, having begun to realise that there was a purpose to what I was studying: to be accepted into the RAAF in order to fly.

In a lecture during my first week at 4 ITS an officer said, 'At the end of three months you'll sit for an examination. If you don't pass you'll be dismissed from aircrew, to become part of ground staff.' To me that would have been utterly humiliating; I couldn't think of anything more demoralising than that, let alone it being the loss of what I'd been working towards with a sharpened focus. Suddenly my motivation at 4 ITS went from ten miles an hour to ninety. I started studying every night, and I was successful. I passed all of my exams.

When going before the Categorisation Board I was marched in to face an officer seated at a table before me. I saluted. I was then asked questions, including what it was I hoped to be. I answered, 'Pilot, sir.' The officer then asked what I wanted to be if I couldn't be a pilot. 'Pilot, sir,' I responded. 'No, but if you can't be a pilot?' 'Pilot, sir,' I again replied.

He said that was fine and asked if I'd been a sportsman. I offered that I was very good at swimming. I left the rest out. He then said, 'Just a minute…Errr…,' before uttering, 'Look, I'm sorry, but I've a medical report here saying that your eyesight isn't absolutely perfect. I'm afraid that you can't be a pilot.'

I thought of my lack of academic prowess and, thus, that I'd never make it as a navigator. I couldn't afford to fail, so I replied, 'I'll be a wireless operator/air gunner, sir.' He said, 'Right, about turn. Quick march.' Nobody I knew volunteered to be a W/Op/AG, but having done that, the die was cast, and off I went.

Men were there at initial training from all walks of life. Some were slovenly and unshaven, looking as if they'd just arisen from bed. Others were smartly dressed in suits, and there was everything in-between. At the end of three months this Drill Instructor had to have everybody working together, capable of moving in any direction he ordered, and to do so with impeccable timing and form. Anything that airmen might have to know to accomplish this was forced upon us by the DI.

It was an amazing transformation. We all hated our DI. I mean, if a lad did anything slightly wrong he might have to run 400 metres with his rifle at high port, i.e., held in both hands above his head. Not really being athletic, I found it unbelievably hard. However, after three months I ran with everybody else, not up at the front of the pack, but I was there, and we did all our work.

No. 1 Wireless Air Gunners School at Ballarat *(FEBRUARY to JULY 1943)*

After completing the 4 ITS course and having been granted an opportunity to become a W/Op/AG, I was next sent in early February 1943 to join Course 35 at No. 1 Wireless Air Gunners School (1 WAGS) at Ballarat, west of Melbourne in the Central Highlands of Victoria. The facility was the first school in Australia to train wireless operators. The course also provided air gunnery training at No. 3 Bombing and Gunnery School (3 BAGS) located in West Sale, Victoria, but first came the W/Op training at Ballarat.

While at Ballarat for five and a half months I had to reach proficiencies of twenty words per minute (WPM) in receiving Morse code and twenty-five WPM in sending Morse. I did. I also became well-practised in using the wireless apparatus available at the time and in mastering the transmission methods, such as using Q-code words that shorten certain phrases (and that are still employed today). Most of the training was ground-based, even in 'outstations' set up at fair distances from the main buildings, but in the latter stage of the W/Op portion of the course we trainees were finally sent aloft.

Flying aboard single-engine Commonwealth Aircraft Corporation Wackett trainers, I logged fourteen hours and thirty-five minutes of airborne wireless training – requiring transmitting and receiving messages – during my tenure at 1 WAGS. Being the first flying most of us had ever done, the process weeded out a few more of us who suffered airsickness, or who just couldn't handle flying. I loved every minute of it!

One big hang-up marked my experience. I reported to sick bay with a cold so bad that I was admitted to hospital...and placed in the measles ward, though I was measles-free. Two or three weeks later I returned from hospital with the measles, interrupting my training.

In spite of being off course I still managed to finish thirty-first out of the 175 students who started, and I thusly earned my W/Op's shoulder badge – a fist holding lightning bolts. To this day I'm proud of my accomplishments at Ballarat, despite physical adversity.

No. 3 Bombing and Gunnery School at West Sale *(JULY and AUGUST 1943)*

After Ballarat's W/Op training, my course continued at 3 BAGS at West Sale, Victoria, starting on 26 July 1943. This school was 180 miles to the east of Ballarat and also east of Melbourne. My trade called for dual wireless and gunnery training, and West Sale offered a suitable setting where aerial firing could be practiced at no threat to the local population. At 3 BAGS I learned the rudiments of gunnery, including air-to-air and air-to-ground firing. Though I recall being aboard Fairey Battles, my RAAF personnel file says I flew seven hours and fifty-five minutes aboard twin-engine Airspeed Oxfords; Battles weren't mentioned. I don't have my logbook to clarify matters, but I believe a simple clerical error was made in noting Oxfords instead of Battles on one document.

Firing exercises were quite interesting. We students fired machine guns at drogues flown past our aircraft, and we also shot at targets on the ground. A single machine gun was mounted about halfway down the aircraft. From a standing position, with his helmet on, a student fired at the drogue being towed behind another plane.

Two students plus the pilot occupied each aircraft. Between the students and the pilot there was a huge hole in the floor, i.e., a hatchway; it was difficult – almost impossible – to speak to the pilot, who flew an assigned course.

At the moment one fellow completed his firing exercise one day the pilot suddenly realised that he was on a collision course facing an oncoming aircraft. He flung the stick forward to pass underneath the approaching aircraft, and the student, who'd just finished firing, promptly flew out of the aircraft because we weren't strapped in.

As he went out a foot hooked onto the gun mounting, and here was this fellow lying back along the fuselage and flapping in the breeze, almost like a flag. The second student, crouched down because there was insufficient room for both trainees to stand up, and having nearly passed out from shock, initially thought that the other student had fallen out. Then, standing up, he saw the fellow flapping in the slipstream and tried desperately to alert the pilot.

With this biggish floor hatch acting as an obstacle, it took a long time before the second student could get the pilot's attention. Imagine the pilot's reaction when he looked over his shoulder and saw what was happening! He landed very gently, I imagine. The second student was unable to help the poor victim while in the air, fearing that any attempt at rescue might dislodge his leg and send him plunging to his death.

Afterwards I didn't see the victim back on the ground, but I was told that he couldn't walk. He was transported to hospital, where he wasn't able to speak for a few days.

The course included ground instruction in turrets, weapons, aircraft recognition and tactics. We learned how to assemble, disassemble, clean and oil machine guns, set a gun into position in the aircraft, load magazines and clear blockages. For some tests we were blindfolded. Little did I know at the time how valuable this training would be when I was in India on Liberators.

We had to know how the turrets worked, including an understanding of the valves, the piping for oil and the motors driving the turrets.

For aircraft recognition the instructor would project an aircraft image, such as a head-on view of a German Ju88, onto a screen, and we trainees would be prodded to make an accurate split-second identification. 'Come on, boys, what is it?' asked the instructor. 'Quick!' he'd implore, 'Your lives depend on it!' With such language we got the message. I was quite skilled in the task, having had some aircraft recognition training while in the ATC.

My gunnery assessment at West Sale was 'average'. I felt I was better than average, but a higher rating was hard to come by. I ranked seventh at the end of this course, and I really never looked back after that. What I knew I needed at any school was motivation. I had potential, but it had never been brought out before. Motivation now was the key. I was honoured to have been awarded my air gunner's badge as of the end of the course on 19 August 1943.

My fellow students and I took turns at taking the routine parades that were part of our ongoing training. Once, when a friend and I were the 'officers' of the day (though neither was yet a commissioned officer), the other students asked that we two protest something. Having been granted a meeting with the CO, we explained that we represented our group as their 'officers' of the day. The CO tore strips off of us. Replying, I remember saying to him, 'We're giving the views of the men we represent, not our views.'

We must have impressed him because three weeks later, on 19 August, my friend and I graduated with commissions; we were two of only seven on our course to be granted commissions, meaning that we were now promoted from the rank of warrant officer to pilot officer – making us commissioned officers; a warrant officer was non-commissioned. Along with the bump to officer's status came a little more money for each of us (and added responsibilities).

I'm telling this because I feel it's so important to motivate people when they're young.

The big day came when we graduated in August 1943. My fellow newly minted officer mate and I managed to get one of the Women's Auxiliary Australian Air Force (WAAAF) members to tape our little strips of blue officer braid onto our sleeves. We waited to see if the guard would salute us as we walked out the West Sale gate, but he acted very busy and looked the other way when we passed! But it was all very exciting, and I expressed it in my letters to my parents.

Thus, my basic training concluded. Posted back to Melbourne, I first took a fortnight's leave to stay with a girl with whom I'd become friendly in Adelaide. Then I arrived in Melbourne. I took out Paddy Hare, my next-door neighbour, several times and also a couple of other girls I knew in Sandringham.

No. 1 Air Observers School at Cootamundra, then No. 1 Embarkation Depot, Melbourne *(SEPTEMBER to NOVEMBER 1943)*

My next assignment, much to my disgust and humiliation, was at a training establishment, No. 1 Air Observers School (1 AOS) at Cootamundra, New South Wales, where navigators were being trained. I couldn't believe that I'd trained for over half a year in the ATC and nearly a year in the RAAF to go to war, but then I'd been sent to train others to go to war.

I constantly whined and cursed about being at Cootamundra. All the while in performing my duties I accumulated sixty-six hours and fifty minutes of flying aboard Avro Ansons. While the time aloft was to my liking, and resultingly I honed my W/Op's skills even further, I just didn't want to be at 1 AOS. I appealed for a fresh duty assignment to every appropriate officer I could talk to, each time asking if he'd assist in getting me moved.

I thought I was doomed to be stuck in Cootamundra, a posting that had commenced on 2 September 1943. Then suddenly a posting came through on 28 October to No. 1 Embarkation Depot (1 ED), situated at the Melbourne Cricket Ground (MCG). The MCG had been taken over by the military, and presumably the RAAF, since I encountered only RAAF personnel there. I was held at the MCG until such time as a position became available on a ship.

At the MCG I was billeted at the top of the members' stand, where I slept upon a wire mesh bed. I was now with fellow officers, and we were treated well. By then, having received my proper officer's uniform and cap, I apparently looked quite smart.

The day came for Australians to go down to the former luxury ocean liner SS *Lurline.* Taken over by the US Government, it had been converted to a troopship. There were many Americans aboard.

The Aussies had a reputation for being unruly, contemptuous of authority, uncontrollable and very difficult to handle. We marched down to the ship impeccably (I was in charge). When we reached the dock, in front of these other troops, my group promptly turned into 'Australians'. It became almost impossible to manage them. Everybody seemed to have taken delight in looking as unkempt as possible.

They didn't answer properly when spoken to. It was unbelievable how they'd changed from precision soldiers to an unruly, boisterous gang, as they reverted back to being stereotypical Australians.

Chapter 3

Travel to the USA, then to England and initial service in the UK: NOVEMBER 1943 *(Part 2)* to MAY 1944

Roy departs Australia for San Francisco

The SS *Lurline* embarked Melbourne for the US on 17 November 1943.

Two interesting events marked the voyage. I was at lunch when, suddenly, the plates started sliding across the table. The SS *Lurline* was on its own in crossing the Pacific, as it was said she was too fast for submarines. Because the ship was heeling over we knew something was up, and everybody raced upstairs to witness a 180-degree turn to get back onto our wake.

To their great credit the crew found an American who'd jumped overboard. He was returning to the US to his new wife with, rumour had it, genital injuries, so he decided to commit suicide by leaping from the ship and drowning. We'd been warned that if anybody fell overboard the ship wouldn't stop to pick him up, as it would endanger the lives of the 3,000 troops on board. However, the captain did just that.

There we were, stopped in the middle of the Pacific with thousands of troops on board. A boat was lowered. The poor fellow grabbed hold of the first oar within reach, and his rescuers had great difficulty in prying his hands off the oar once he was in the boat. It was incredible that they found the tiny little dot of a man's head in the sea. We were all nervous, because Japanese subs were reported in the area, so it was a relief to be underway again and taking an unpredictable zigzag course.

Another incident, the memory of which I'll never forget, was when the SS *Lurline* fired up a small parachute that hung in the sky above us, and all the ship's anti-aircraft guns opened fire. The result was incredible. The volume of fire from those guns! It was something I recalled later when, on 215 Squadron, we were sent to try to find some warships.

In the United States

After safely reaching San Francisco, California, I was billeted on Treasure Island in San Francisco Bay, but I managed to see the city. It was a very exciting time to be in the USA. America was at war, and everything was jumping. I went to one or two of the troop dances with entertainment, where film stars occasionally were in attendance, but I didn't see any stars.

We rode in Pullman railway carriages right across the country to New York; the Americans travelled in style even in wartime. In New York City a friend and I managed to stay with a very popular society hostess, Mrs Stevie Hafner, who lived in a beautiful penthouse on Park Avenue. We were allowed to stay out of barracks as long as our whereabouts were known.

We lived with the incredibly generous and influential Hafner family for about ten days. During the days we guests used to go on our own sightseeing excursions to different places, and then every second night our hosts brought us somewhere special, such as to restaurants and then nightclubs, including the legendary Stork Club. Very exciting! On Christmas Eve 1943 they took us to some famous hotel, maybe the Waldorf Astoria, where Xavier Cugat, a noted bandleader, was entertaining. What a time that was!

Then the night came when Bill Wright – my future 215 Squadron crewmate – and I went to see Tommy Dorsey and his orchestra playing at a venue similar to California's Hollywood Palladium. After the show we went backstage to see if we could maybe meet Tommy Dorsey. The doorman told us that Mr Dorsey went out with the regular crowd wearing a hat, and no fans expected to see him there.

While we were talking a singing group came up a staircase with a man who'd been entertaining with them. He asked us about ourselves and then invited us to a party. It would be great, he assured us. I must be the only person who refused to party with Frank Sinatra! All I wanted to do that evening was to go to some stupid cafe I'd heard about. Later, in England, after I'd commented on how great this singer Frank Sinatra was my friend said, 'You didn't feel that way in New York.' I guess he was correct!

A sea voyage to the UK

Soon we were put onto a troopship that sailed for England in a sizeable convoy that stretched from horizon to horizon. We saw destroyers around the edges, though occasionally they came nipping through the convoy.

There were two significant incidents. Once, an enemy submarine's torpedo just missed us. There was no gunfire or anything else related to it, because the pursuing U-boat stealthily escaped.

Onboard this ship we were packed in bunks. The quarters were nothing as luxurious as on the SS *Lurline*, where we'd been in staterooms with stewards. We were fed twice a day on our transatlantic troopship. There was a canteen where one could buy food; everybody was young and hungry.

Initial period in the UK

After arriving safely in England I disembarked on 8 January 1944. The Australians aboard were sent to No. 11 Personnel Despatch and Reception Centre (11 PDRC) in Brighton, the town where the Australian military headquarters were located, and where Australian airmen were seemingly everywhere.

The pebbly Brighton beaches were mined and isolated with barbed wire. Supposedly, on occasion dogs were blown up after wandering onto the beach.

Never before had we seen any substantial wartime defensive works.

As a commissioned pilot officer I was billeted in a small hotel near the landmark Brighton Pier. The non-commissioned officers (NCOs, which included warrant officers) were in the Grand Hotel. We didn't have to do much. There was our morning parade, which was the usual scruffy procession, but that was all.

There were a couple of air raid alerts while I was stationed in Brighton. One night, after I'd been there about a week, the air raid alarm went off while I was standing in the bar of the Officers' Mess in the hotel. This was the first time I'd heard it. Everybody just went on drinking and talking. I looked at the others and wondered why they were waiting and where we should go.

Because nobody was taking notice, I eventually asked, 'When do we go to the shelter?' 'We don't bother about the shelters,' came the reply. I was the new boy; that's how it was when you were new!

I was a bit edgy because I could hear aircraft, and they were low. Afterwards I worked out that these were our fighters on their way to France skimming over the water to avoid enemy radar.

On 14 January 1944, after a visit to the dentist and a night vision test, I was issued my flying suit and battle dress. I spent the rest of the day sewing my pilot officer's braid and various other patches, including my air gunner's half-wing brevet, onto my newly issued clothing.

On the seventeenth I went with some Aussie mates to the Theatre Royal to see a ballet performed by an Anglo-Polish group, but the show wasn't very good. I was now told that I could take leave with mates to visit a family in Castle Garth in Wetherby, Yorkshire.

After arriving in London by train from Brighton we dropped two of our party at the Boomerang Club, a welcoming environment for Australians far from home. Following a long rail trip from Kings Cross station to Leeds we grabbed something to eat at the Queens Hotel before ringing our host, the charming Mrs Colley. We then caught a bus to Wetherby and arrived at Castle Garth in time for dinner. Mrs Colley had a young son and two girls of fifteen and eighteen. An old nurse, Nanny, also resided there.

After dinner we visitors went down into town to a dance, but it was overcrowded with servicemen from a Halifax bomber Operational Training Unit nearby. There were too many oversexed men and too few ladies!

Following breakfast the next morning my fellow RAAF friends and I went for a stroll around the extensive grounds bordering on the River Wharfe. It was lovely going for a walk with the dogs through the village and along the riverbank.

We were told that Mary, the Princess Royal (King George V's daughter), would be inspecting the local canteen, and Mrs Colley had received permission for us to be inside, in our hope to meet Mary. After lunch on Friday, 21 January 1944 we went down to attend the canteen's opening.

After the workers and staff had been presented to the Princess Royal, she came over and spoke to my mate Alec and me for at least five minutes.

I asked if I might photograph her and was given permission. When outside she asked where I'd like her to stand. That absolutely threw me, and it was all I could do to get it right. I only had a cheap camera that I'd picked up in the States, and I was a bit ashamed to produce it.

Following dinner Alec and I said that we were thinking of going to a dance in town, but it was pointed out to us that it wasn't one that officers would attend.

Instead, we walked along the riverbank to view the raging waters, followed by a visit to Frank, Mrs Colley's brother-in-law, who was a maltster, a maker of alcoholic malts. It was all so very interesting.

On the twenty-fourth we went by bus to see the inspirational York Minster. It was a beautiful cathedral on the outside and just as beautiful inside. We climbed the Central Tower, which was only 235 feet tall, but it seemed to be 500 feet in height.

It was back to London the next day, 25 January 1944. On the train we met Sergeant David Stokes, who'd lunched with the King and Queen in Devon. A journalist, he told us that we could make a broadcast back to Australia about our meeting with the Princess Royal. He took our names for a broadcast.

Then from London we returned to Brighton. When I was getting a haircut the barber asked where I was from, guessing South Africa. South Africa! I couldn't believe it.

Back at 11 PDRC, in the afternoon I had a swimming test. I had no problem, of course, swimming 100 yards.

An attachment to RAF Filey

Granted was a request from my future crewmate Bill Wright and me to be posted together. Rumour had it that we were to go to the East Coast near Scarborough. Indeed, in late February 1944 about one hundred of us, including Bill and myself, were posted to take an officers' course at RAF Filey, located at a peacetime holiday resort eight miles south-east of Scarborough on the North Sea near Hunmanby in East Riding of Yorkshire. We were once again handed over to Drill Instructors, who proceeded to turn Australian officers into what the English would call officers and gentlemen.

When I went into the air force the DI barked, 'What a miserable lot they've handed me! Look at you! What a collection of ugly specimens!' In stark contrast, at the RAF Filey officers' school our DI said, 'Righto gentlemen, smarten up. Shoulders back. Head up.' It was a completely different attitude, given that we trainees were officers.

Nevertheless, we still had work to do. We went on long runs, probably two or three miles, carrying kit. We were in good shape. I won't say I was as fit as when I finished my 4 ITS course back in Australia; I could never be fitter than when I came out of that.

We learned to do officers' things. Everybody had a turn at taking the early morning parade, when all the squadrons were lined up. The officers reported to whomever of us was in charge that the parade was all present and correct, and then the officer in overall command turned about and reported to the CO. Being taught to command was really something.

Air force officers weren't really like officers in the army and navy. In the air force officers and NCOs were often combined in the same aircraft, and crewmen called each other by Christian names. In fact, a sergeant or flight sergeant in the skipper's seat could actually be outranked by a crewmate such as an air gunner, yet the pilot was absolutely in command despite his inferior rank. There wasn't that strict officer-NCO differentiation until back on the ground, where there were different Messes, different social groups, different privileges, etc.

Some days at Filey were taken up with lectures on the Hispano cannon, Bofors gun and Sten gun. As usual, much of the time we were left on our own. We did an awful lot of smoking.

In our Mess were men from England, Canada, Australia, New Zealand and South Africa, and the behaviour at times was disgusting. Each evening a line of staff emerged from the kitchens carrying trays, just above their shoulders, holding plates of cakes and sandwiches and things for supper. Rowdy officers would surge forward and grab food from the trays before the stewards could reach the tables to put them down. It was unseemly and embarrassing. I refused to take part; it wasn't the way officers were supposed to behave.

Snow compounded the difficulty in performing outdoor activities. The second of March was particularly freezing. During bayonet practice, due to the miserable cold, I couldn't properly bend two swollen fingers of my right hand. It added to the burden of participating in grenade trials, too.

I was the flight commander that day, and Bill Wright was the parade's adjutant. In the afternoon we played rugby in the snow. At Filey, in fact, I played my first game of rugby, on a team of Australians opposing a squad of RAF men. It was hard to believe, but we won! There was great rivalry between the Australians and the Poms. Aussies had a high opinion of themselves and generally thought they were better than the English. Considering myself from Down Under, I was one of those arrogant Aussies.

On 10 March 1944 I received a letter from David Stokes saying that he'd written a story about us meeting the Princess Royal, and that it should soon be published in Australia. I was thrilled, hoping that my parents would read it in the local newspaper.

I spent a lot of my free time writing letters home, including to my girlfriends in Australia.

In addition to gunnery lectures, we learned how to throw dummy hand grenades. I endured bayonet practice, as well. When, I wondered, was I going to bayonet somebody? We were given some rifle range firing opportunities, and

I was one of the top shots in the Aussie squadron. I'd always been a good shot, probably because I'd had a Daisy air rifle when in Hong Kong.

My camera's film was developed around this time. The print of Mrs Colley was fine, but the one of the Princess Royal was just OK.

When each of us was required to give a short talk to our fellow officers, I spoke on a topic my classmates seemed to find intriguing – the Japanese conquest of Hong Kong. I commanded the squad at another point, but the squadron leader overseeing the course reprimanded me mildly. I saw it all as a game, really, and didn't cower under the criticism; overall the experience was worthwhile.

It was our good fortune to be entertained by quality ENSA talent on some nights.

MATT: ENSA (Entertainments National Service Association) was a British service organisation – similar to the American United Service Organizations (USO) – that put on shows for those in uniform far and wide.

ROY: I was rapt to get the highest score in pistol shooting, which seemed appropriate, as I was both an air gunner and a wireless operator.

I was impressed by the explosions and the whistling of shrapnel during live, not dummy, grenade throwing one day. However, when it was our turn in the trench I made sure that I'd be in the corner in case anything went wrong. And it did! When one of my classmates named Cassidy raised his arm up to toss the live grenade, he hit his helmet, and the grenade went up in the air instead of out to where it should have gone. Instantly I dived for the corner where I'd planned to be should trouble arise. I saw the grenade go up in the air and start falling back downward. Fortunately, it hit the built-up edge of the trench's rim, rolled outside...and exploded. Phew! It seemed to take forever falling down. Time can go very slowly in those instances.

The highlight of the rest of my stay in Filey was being declared on the noticeboard as a crack shot. I admit to having enjoyed the recognition and congratulations which followed.

Back in Brighton and 11 PDRC

Having finished our latest officers' training in late March 1944, a gang of us Australians endured myriad train changes as we travelled back to 11 PDRC in Brighton.

On my first full day back in Brighton our group had to form up for morning parade. I think that I must have been at the back of the parade, where people couldn't see me. We lined up on the command, 'Markers!' The lads acting as markers would run out and stand in their designated positions, and then the call would come, 'On your markers. Go!' We'd fall in on the left of the markers, raise the right arm to the shoulder of the man on one's right to get the correct distance and stand at attention. Our group's fellows did what they'd been doing up at Filey – making a proper job of it, initially. Every line was dead straight.

Each group in the parade marched past the CO who was taking the parade and, upon hearing the command 'Eyes right!' collectively turned their heads. When it was our turn, we Aussies then reverted to the antics performed back at dockside in Melbourne with the Americans watching – going from impeccable marchers to a group giving only a fifty per cent effort. That's what Aussies did.

However, despite this poor showing we must have impressed the CO, because the next day we were made to march as an example to the watching parade, and even though the fellows tried not to be too good, we were still sensational. Our personal pride took over.

Then it was back to the ordinary routine stuff as we waited to be posted onward. We went to a few dances at night. In a town overrun by lads in the military, surprisingly there were few men at these dances, presumably because of leave restrictions back at the nearby camps and local men being away on war duty. The typical ratio was probably about five girls to each man.

I remember on one occasion being invited with my mates to a Women's Auxiliary Air Force (WAAF) establishment. When we got there we saw about fifty women, but there were just the three of us lads in uniform. No other men. We just couldn't take it; it was just too much, and we had to leave after about an hour. Imagine that!

The usual dances we attended in the town, though, were really terrific fun. We had a marvellous time at such gatherings in England. I remember meeting a girl and walking her home, only to find that she lived in Hove, several miles west of Brighton. That was a long way on foot in the middle of the night, but it was worth the effort.

No. 6 (Observers) Advanced Flying Unit, RAF Staverton

After 11 PDRC it was decided that rather than leave us fiddling our thumbs in Brighton some additional training elsewhere would do us good. On 21 March

1944 I was posted to Staverton, an RAF station opposite the Gloster Aircraft Company factory and on the north-east side of the town of Gloucester, in Gloucestershire. Staverton was the home of No. 6 (Observers) Advanced Flying Unit, or 6 (O)AFU for short.

I had to get thirty-six sergeants and eighteen officers to 6 (O)AFU. I marched them up to the Brighton rail station, called the roll and saw them loaded onto the train. At London's Victoria station I had a helluva job getting their kit loaded into the vans to transfer to Paddington station, where we'd catch the next train out to Gloucester. I had to ensure that nobody left the station. In order to feed the men I sent a sergeant to buy some buns to keep the lads satisfied. When we arrived at Gloucester at 1400. I handed the men over to the Training Adjutant 'all correct'. Phew!

At 6 (O)AFU we, the trainee W/Op/AGs, flew around the area aboard Avro Ansons, joined by trainee navigators. We were all learning technique and communication. All told, I accumulated twenty-five hours and fifty minutes of flying time at 6 (O)AFU – all of great value in preparing me for my future tour of ops against the Japanese in the Far East, though I didn't then recognise its value. It was a strange atmosphere for us, because we'd not yet seen action. It was just more training, as we waited to get into the fight. And more training, being so close to war action, could be frustrating.

Once we were forced to hide in clouds for a time because supposedly an enemy aircraft was in the area.

I never saw any Allied bombers, probably because we were so far west of the operational airfields of RAF Bomber Command and the US Eighth Air Force. Naturally, these bases were much closer to German-held Europe.

At 6 (O)AFU I saw my first jet aircraft. Or, rather, I heard my first jet aircraft. I perceived a whistle, and then a propellerless aircraft shot across the aerodrome; it was thrilling! Of course, we were sworn to secrecy.

On Sunday, 9 April 1944 some of the lads and I decided to go fishing in the local river, but we were warned that in response to some Americans fishing on the Sabbath villagers had threatened to stone them. We had no problems… except in catching fish; it was harder than it seemed.

On Thursday, 25 May when having breakfast with Bobbie Eldrid, a senior WAAF officer on the station, I was invited to go down to her family's house in Chard for a few days; Chard was seventy-nine miles south-west of 6 (O) AFU. After meeting her at the Gloucester railway station, we changed trains at Bristol and Taunton on our way to Chard. Bobbie's parents, super people, met us in their car.

The countryside was the most beautiful I'd seen in England.

On the following day Bobbie woke me up for breakfast. After the meal we knelt down in prayer at our chairs, joined by the staff. Bobbie had to go back to RAF Staverton after lunch, but I stayed on. I had a long talk with Bobbie's mum, Mrs Eldrid, about my ambitions. She'd heard from Bobbie that I'd love to do medicine but could never afford it, and she made a wonderful offer – someone who would help with my fees. After prayers Mr Eldrid and I walked through the fields to the village.

When the time came for me to depart a prayer in the kitchen was offered up for my safety in the war.

I spent the last days of my leave in late May 1944 poking around London, and I even took communion at St Paul's Cathedral. The devastation in the vicinity caused by the German Luftwaffe was shocking, but the mighty St Paul's stood out in defiance. I certainly felt inspired by this symbol of strength despite adversity.

Chapter 4

Further duties in the UK and sailing to India: JUNE 1944

To Blackpool

After the short leave it was back to RAF Staverton, where I learned that in preparation to go overseas we were posted to No. 5 Personnel Despatch Centre (5 PDC) at Blackpool, Lancashire, north of Liverpool by twenty-eight miles. Fantastic news!

I was put up in Blackpool's Astoria Hotel. Our group was bound for either the Middle East or India, but we were kept in the dark about our ultimate destination, perhaps so that spies wouldn't catch wind of it.

There were things to do before I sailed. For example, one of the girls in Blackpool cut the tail off my shirt, made a couple of epaulets and sewed them on my uniform.

I spent the rest of my final day in the UK doing the town, as this was my last opportunity before departing. It was 6 June 1944, and the huge news was that, at long last, the second front had begun with the D-Day invasion of Normandy, France. We listened intently to radio reports of the intense action. The weather had been dreadful in the lead-up to D-Day, but the gamble was taken; conditions weren't ideal for our landings, but ultimately Allied forces succeeded.

Roy sails to India from Glasgow, Scotland

We arrived by train in Glasgow, Scotland, reached the King George V Dock at 0500 on 7 June and boarded the ship, soon to depart. We lay down on our bunks until breakfast, when we saw white bread for the first time in ages. I wasn't sure that I liked it.

There were 4,000 men on board, and a lot of women – Wrens (Women's Royal Naval Service, or WRNS), Red Cross members, etc. A line drawn on the top deck separated the men and women. As one of our fellows said about crossing the boundary and mixing with the ladies, 'Fat chance!'

At 1500 the next day, 8 June 1944, we pulled up the gangway and headed seventeen miles down the River Clyde to Greenock. People on the shore waved furiously, possibly thinking we were second front troops. If the flattops (aircraft carriers) that were here were going with us, then, I thought, it could be an eventful voyage.

At 2200 we upped anchor and sailed through the boom gates bound for Bombay, India.

We were awakened on our first day at sea, 9 June, by the batman of one of our officers, Flight Lieutenant Dixon. Then up on deck we performed compulsory physical exercise, which, fortunately, wasn't too strenuous. Each day was the same routine: initial PT, sitting on deck chatting up the girls and trying to stay out of the very cold wind. There were also boat drills, and lectures on security attended by the officers aboard.

Our ship fell back, unable to keep up with the others, but the problem must have been solved, as we caught up after a surge.

The lamp signals between ships made for interesting reading, and analysing the blinking lights was a practical way for W/Ops to hone their skills, too.

After a drill we were informed that the next time we heard alarm bells it would be the real thing.

I saw a Fairey Swordfish biplane land on a carrier. This aircraft, dubbed 'the Stringbag', was legendary in military history for its successful torpedo attack on the Italian fleet in Taranto harbour, Italy, in November 1940 and then on the German battleship *Bismarck* in May 1941. I wouldn't have liked being in the open back seat of the Stringbag I witnessed landing. The kite stopped very quickly once it snagged the tripwire. So, as cold as it must have been in that aircraft; at least the two occupants were out of the aircraft and probably plied with mugs of hot tea in no time.

On Monday, 19 June, we passed into the Mediterranean Sea through the Straits of Gibraltar. Later in the day trouble of some sort was obviously expected. Frigates dashed around the convoy laying smoke screens, and there was also a burst of ack-ack fire from our ship, but I saw nothing.

It was now very hot. Wearing shorts up on deck we soaked up the rays, trying to avoid sunburn. Sunbathing was the most common pastime.

When we passed Bizerte, Tunisia, we saw war-damaged ships piled up on the beaches to save their cargos.

We amused ourselves watching a tug of war contest between two groups of ladies: Wrens and Voluntary Aid Detachment (VAD) nurses. The Wrens were great.

We passed beleaguered Malta at 0400. Why hadn't we made our way past such an inspiring place in the daytime? Although we later sailed by Benghazi, Libya, at 1500, in daylight, we were too far away to see anything, unlike when we journeyed past Bizerte, the northernmost town in Africa.

On 25 June we turned into line with other ships to enter Port Said, Egypt, on the northern end of the Suez Canal. When we halted the natives kept everybody amused by diving for coins, just as I'd seen them do when I was here on my way to England in the late 1930s.

Wonderful sights greeted us as we transited the Suez Canal on 27 June. We watched camels moving along in the sand, and we passed wizard little groves of palm trees. Lots of natives swam in the canal, including one fellow who was starkers, which amused the girls.

One couple married onboard, and we showered them with rice when they returned from the ceremony.

Our boat dashed off to Aden alone at 18½ knots. It was thrilling to see the ship all lit up at night as it ploughed along; there was no blackout in the Red Sea. To add to my sense of anticipation Indian music was played over the loudspeakers.

In the Red Sea target practice commenced with the 3-inch gun when a smoke float was dropped. After that, parachute flares were launched, and every gun on the ship fired at them.

Soaked with perspiration, I'd never been so bloody hot in all my life. Prickly heat, a common malady for those of us fair-skinned lads not brought up in such a climate, raised its ugly head as we travelled. So many of us would be cursed by prickly heat while in the Far East.

Of great interest was a huge shark sighted at one point.

Someone stole my Mae West and my torch. 'What could be gained by such thievery?' I wondered.

We W/Ops, trained in sending and receiving Aldis lamp signals, were much in demand for reading light messages from the shore.

A lounge steward was buried at sea after he'd died one night. Death came not only in training or in battle!

I was on an RAAF deck hockey team versus the Kiwis. We won the first game but lost the second.

On the night before we reached Bombay we all packed up our kit in preparation for disembarking.

Chapter 5

In India Roy's sojourn begins: JULY 1944

To Worli Transit Camp, India

We didn't disembark in Bombay until Tuesday, 11 July 1944. Then we were whisked straight into vans and out to nearby Worli Transit Camp. I was drenched, as it was raining and there were no sides to the van. Put up in barracks that leaked when it rained, even one's bed was wet. After being issued mosquito netting and blankets my mate Les and I went down to the army and navy store to each buy sheets, a pillow, a pillow case and a pair of drab trousers. The shop tailor altered the trousers while we waited. The hibiscus, palms and flowers reminded me of Hong Kong.

I learned that an old friend from Hong Kong, Noel Booker, was here as well. Chang, they called him.

The Mess wasn't bad.

The grog was Indian, but at least it was alcohol, and the effects were welcomed. I got blind drunk with two ladies, Joan and Eileen, and a male friend Mick, and I finished up in a girl's flat – until we got turned out about 0100. Back to the transit camp!

This wasn't the end of our fun with these girls. We saw them again when we could get a break, and together we went to dinner and the pictures.

When I woke up the morning after my partying with Mick and the girls my bedding was drenched. We got coolies to bring down the rest of our kit from the luggage dump.

It was pouring when I went down to breakfast. I had a helluva job getting what I wanted to eat. The waiter seemed to forget what we ordered before he reached the end of the table.

We were lectured on security and postings, and we learned that ten crews would depart the next weekend, bound for an assignment on Liberator bombers. I guessed that I'd be in this draft. When the morning came there were no drafts posted, so I went into Bombay to look at the shops and market and enjoyed a most satisfying dinner at the magnificent Taj Mahal Hotel.

No. 1673 Heavy Conversion Unit at Kolar, India

On 18 July 1944 I found that I'd been posted to No. 1673 Heavy Conversion Unit (HCU) just outside of Kolar.

Those of us being sent to 1673 HCU left the Worli camp at 0600 to catch a train to Bangarapet, via Bangalore. Bangalore was 530 miles south-east of Bombay, and Bangarapet railway station was an additional thirty-eight miles by rail east of Bangalore's railway station. Kolar town was an additional eleven miles north of Bangarapet's station, while 1673 HCU was situated on the north-east fringe of Kolar.

For our journey we officers secured First-Class railway carriages with four bunks plus a bathroom in each. The NCOs and ORs (other ranks) had to ride in terrible Third-Class carriages. All of our luggage came with us. Our carriage had two fans, and over the windows there was steel netting, ostensibly so that we could leave the window open yet keep the riff-raff – beggars and thieves – out.

Our train travelled very quickly between stations, but at these stations I'd never seen such disorganisation, with crowds of yelling and gesticulating natives.

In advance of any mealtime and before we departed a station the guard wired ahead to the next station and ordered meals. The food at these little stations was awful and was probably water buffalo or something. Most of the boys had the trots and didn't seem to be getting rid of them; food was suspected as the cause. So far I'd avoided this uncomfortable condition.

I amused myself by taking an occasional shot out of the window with my pistol, and at one spot I nearly shot a native. The stupid things we do when we're young!

We saw a few monkeys in the trees along the way.

We pulled into Bangalore at 0700 on the day after our rail journey began. There was a helluva panic in one carriage, as they'd only just awakened to find natives swarming in through the windows and piling up the luggage on the platform; either the lads failed to secure the steel netting over their windows, or there was no netting such as on my windows. We only had time for a quick breakfast, and we were on our way to Bangarapet, arriving at 1300. There were lots of monkeys about, with young often hanging onto their mothers.

There was no transport arranged by the RAF to move us from Bangarapet north-east fifteen or so miles to the airfield. Apparently, the transmission lines were down, disrupting communication, so an army truck was borrowed.

Before the truck arrived an Anglo-Indian kindly served us each an egg with bread and a cup of tea in the waiting room.

1673 HCU's aerodrome seemed spacious. I was initially put up in a tent in the camp and had to use my portable kit for washing; there was then no ablutions block. Our lavatories were just holes in the ground – pit latrines.

We were told that our course would be for six weeks, with lectures beginning in five days.

On our first evening at 1673 HCU we had a few drinks followed by dinner with Liberator fellows from 215 Squadron. I found this interaction quite valuable, as most of these lads had operational experience against the Japanese aboard Wellington bombers.

The next morning we sent our bearer into Kolar to buy some sheets and oddments, but he never returned. His brother said that our bearer would come back and look after us, but as he was nowhere to be found we had to fend for ourselves. That night, with no lamp, it was difficult getting to bed.

We still had no bearer on the following day, so getting water for washing was our own responsibility. I didn't shave because of this.

I went with pilot Ian Hyndman for a walk to explore the bush outside the camp area. There were lots of beautifully coloured lizards, but the orange ones predominated. There were also frogs in a pool.

I'd noticed how particular the Indians were with their women, whose bodies were covered as we approached. The headman of one group of stone breakers sent a little girl away because she wasn't properly dressed.

I usually went to a movie in the camp every night.

Not being trained as expected at 1673 HCU, I was fed up with doing nothing and wanted to know if I'd really be on the course or not. One day the CO reassured us that we were definitely on the course, and that after completing the course we'd join 215 Squadron at Jessore in East Bengal, India, flying four-engine Liberator bombers.

After hearing this I went down with pilot Reginald 'Jackson' Grouse to try and change over to his crew. Jackson, my fellow RAAF mate from Randwick, New South Wales, had significant operational experience flying Dakotas on transport duties with 62 Squadron in the Imphal Valley and then on bombing ops aboard 215 Squadron Wellingtons. For his skill and dedication he was later awarded the Distinguished Flying Cross.

Now he'd become a Liberator skipper at 1673 HCU, and I hoped that I could fly with him. The CO wasn't overly optimistic, but I had my fingers crossed.

The next morning the Chief Ground Instructor (CGI) gave a talk, and even the Chiefs of Station turned up. We were lectured on the equipment and layout of the Mk. VI Liberator – the model in which I flew at 1673 HCU and the only model Lib on 215 Squadron – followed by an intelligence lecture on Burma. In the afternoon we had two and a half hours of solid signals organisation. Bags of sand flies were everywhere, however, and they nearly drove us mad.

More lectures the following morning focused upon radio communication (intercom) equipment on the Liberator. That topic continued for the whole day and the lecture continued the next day. The trick with such equipment was to speak slowly, one person at a time.

The layout of the Mk. VI Liberator

In the Mk. VI Liberator the skipper (the aircraft captain) sat in the left-hand seat, and the second pilot (called the 'co-pilot' by the Americans) occupied the right-hand seat. Behind the second pilot sat the W/Op, in front of his equipment at a table.

More or less behind and above the W/Op was the mid-upper gunner in a turret holding twin .50-calibre Browning machine guns.

MATT: The turret was installed in the centre of the fuselage roof, aligned more or less with the four engines. This position and an upgrade in this turret's firepower had been introduced in the Mk. III Liberator; the earlier Mk. II's mid-upper turret, holding four inferior .303-calibre Browning guns, was further back, poking out of the fuselage spine at a point closely in line with the trailing edge of the wings.

ROY: In the nose of the plane was the front gunner's power turret, holding dual .50-calibre guns. In front of and just below the two pilots were the navigator and bomb aimer.

MATT: The earlier Mk. II and Mk. III Liberators each had a 'greenhouse' nose, with no turret, affording the navigator – who was then also typically the bomb aimer – a sweeping frontal view. With the arrival of the Mk. VI, however, its front turret significantly reduced this forward visibility. The nose was even more cramped than before, now that it held a nose turret (and gunner) and a navigator and sometimes a separate bomb aimer.

Behind the mid-upper turret and the W/Op's station was the bomb bay, which held the bombs stacked in racks, one bomb above the other.

ROY: There was a forward bomb bay and a rear bay, each with its own set of doors that opened by rolling up the fuselage sides. This was unlike bombers like the B-17 Flying Fortress, which had far less aerodynamic clamshell-like bomb bay doors opening outwards. On the Liberator a narrow catwalk only nine inches wide bridged the forward and rear halves of the bomb bay, allowing passage from the front of the aircraft to the rear.

Aft of the bomb bay was the rear fuselage section, where one came upon the Sperry ball turret (with twin .50-calibre guns) protruding through the floor of the kite. Above this turret was the mechanism to raise and lower it; naturally in the lowered position – needed in order to properly fire the weapons – drag degraded the Liberator's flight characteristics and petrol consumption increased, so the turret was raised within the fuselage much of the time. Behind the ball turret were the beam guns, one .50-calibre Browning per side. Each could be swung into position to protrude out the side of the fuselage from its open window.

MATT: The second W/Op/AG manned one of the beam guns. Usually, an air gunner with no further training manned the other side's weapon, but on Roy's crew there was no such air gunner at that position; instead, his flight engineer (there was no specific Liberator flight engineer station) handled this second beam gun.

Each beam hatch, or window cover, hinged at the top and opened upwards and inwards.

ROY: Lastly, at the very tail of the aircraft was the rear gunner's turret. The British specification had initially called for four .303-calibre Brownings in a turret manufactured by Boulton Paul.

MATT: The .303-calibre bullet lacked the sting of a more powerful .50-calibre projectile, and ultimately Boulton Paul rear turrets were replaced by separate American-built turrets armed with twin .50-calibre weapons. This switch didn't happen all at once. Occasionally, 215 Squadron ops flown into 1945 included some aircraft still retaining four .303-calibre Brownings in the rear turret, while the majority of the participating Liberators flew with the replacement turrets, holding twin .50-calibre Brownings.

Thus, the Liberators carried either ten .50-calibre Brownings or else eight .50-calibre and four .303-calibre Brownings. Undeniably, each aircraft, even those without the upgraded rear guns and turret, packed a potentially deadly punch.

Roy's time on No. 1673 HCU continues

ROY: To my delight I found out that my request to be transferred to Jackson Grouse's crew had been granted. My crew, for now, was set at:

Pilot	Reg 'Jackson' Grouse
Second pilot	J.D. 'Bing' Bingham
Navigator	John 'The Boong' Campbell
Bomb aimer	Freddy 'Pissy' Houghton
First wireless operator	W.G. 'Bopp the W/Op' Abbott
Second wireless operator	Me (mostly manning a beam gun, as I trained as both a W/Op and an AG)
Nose turret gunner	'Paddy' McCartney
Mid-upper turret gunner	Bill Wright
Ball turret gunner	'Jock' Smith
Tail gunner	Joe Marsh
Flight engineer	'Smithy' Smith (also responsible for manning a beam gun)

The Boong and Bopp the W/Op had crewed with Jackson on 215 Squadron Wellington ops, where Pissy also flew, but with another Wellington crew. When the squadron converted from Wellingtons to Liberators, Jackson was able to retain The Boong and Bopp the W/Op on his new crew, and Pissy was snatched up, too. I was thrilled to have been made a part of Jackson's crew.

A tailor told me that material I'd bought was unsuitable for bush jackets, so instead I had it made into two shirts.

I finally fell victim to the dreaded trots around this time. The forces that ruled us mere mortals proved too powerful, and my resistance had been overcome. Everybody seemed to have them, so it was probably coming from the kitchen.

Jackson was rapt, as his promotion to flight lieutenant came through. Not only was it satisfying for him to jump in rank – with advancement came justifiable gratification – but it also meant more pay, more recognition and more prestige in the overall pecking order, as I'd learned from experience. Occasionally a promotion to an officer's rank was unwanted, because of pressure to associate even more with fellow officers when many best mates were NCOs. Some men were known to have turned down promotions in order to continue to primarily socialise with their NCO mates. Jackson, though, was already an officer, and his promotion to flight lieutenant was, for him, positive all around. We, his crewmates, were happy for him, whatever our ranks.

In the evening, before dressing for socialising and a meal in the Officers' Mess, one sat in a collapsible canvas bath, which was part of each officer's kit. His Indian bearer, hired relatively cheaply, would heat up some water over a small wood fire and then pour hot water into the bath. One would sit cross-legged in about four inches of water, soap himself all over, and then the bearer would pour some water over the bather to rinse off the soap.

We officers quite often shared a bearer, who acted pleased and honoured to be one's personal batman. He was smartly dressed in a white uniform consisting of a coat that buttoned up the front, white trousers, a turban, a wide belt of air force colours and sandals. In the Officers' Mess (and in other Messes, too; an Indian was subservient to all whites) he'd attend to his man and purchase anything needed from the commissary.

Chapter 6

In India: AUGUST 1944

At 1673 HCU there was fun, too

One night in the bar a debagging session started, and in no time everybody was standing at the bar in underpants. Yet we professed to be military men who trained to wage the most no-nonsense kind of war against our brutal enemy! It was quite the dichotomy – myself and my friends being silly to the max in the bar, yet ultra-focused upon our professional duties, as need be.

We also played a wild and wonderful two-team game called 'saddle-me-nag', which put our spines at risk – but taking a Liberator filled with petrol and explosives skyward to face potential opposition seemed a far greater risk. To play the game the first man of Team A placed his back against the wall. The next man put his head between the first man's legs, with his arms around that man's thighs. Then the next did the same, until a 'line of humps' was formed.

A participant from Team B, after as long a run as possible, leapfrogged over the last member of Team A. Picking what he thought was the weakest member of Team A, the leaper landed with a ferocious thump onto someone's back. Then, one after the other, further Team B individuals tried to land on the same perceived weak link in Team A's line of humps. It was murderous, as Team A, swaying under the onslaught, tried to withstand Team B's assault. The idea of Team B was to make the 'hump team' buckle under the combined weight. If – usually when – Team A collapsed, they lost, and the penalty was payment for Team B's drinks.

Perhaps it was goofy, but with a few drinks in us it was a fabulous game! After a while, with alcohol taking hold, most of us saw double.

Returning to our billets that night my crewmates, the Medical Officer and I played a trick on Pissy Houghton. Pissy was told that the MO – naturally, we called him 'Doc' – needed to give him a morphine injection in his stomach, right then and there. Pissy struggled like hell when we rubbed some unction on his tummy. Then The Boong poured a bucket of water over a very jovial-spirited Doc, and that was that! It was great fun at the time.

The next morning we laughed over the events of the previous night. Reality couldn't be avoided, however, and I went down to the Station Sick Quarters for a required, and not painless, vaccination.

Training and experiences at 1673 HCU continue

More training characterised my dad's birthday, 4 August 1944, inching me along the path to being posted to 215 Squadron. We started with lectures on baling out. I was pleased to discover that I'd be the first one out in an emergency. Then it was down to the dinghy section to run through the drill after a water ditching. We followed that with a trip to the kite to see where the dinghies were stored. Ours were stowed in special compartments at the top of the fuselage just aft of the top turret, along with the radio to generate and transmit a signal. One released these from inside the aircraft.

We were lectured the following day, 5 August, on trekking back to Allied territory if our aircraft went down. From behind enemy lines the odds of escaping were slim. White men stood out in the Far East, and a justified fear of brutal Japanese punishment often led the locals to turn over Allied flyers.

I passed the written exams administered to keep us on our toes.

The lectures, mostly informative and worthwhile, continued. First a British Army major spoke on the topic of army operations, and then an RAF wing commander lectured us on navy ops and showed us secret films of landing barges. Later, I did participate on 215 Squadron ops in support of the army ground war, and I also witnessed the navy in action during Operation MATADOR, the 21 January 1945 invasion of Ramree Island.

We reported in crews to the Watch Office on 8 August for an official reception into Flights. My crew was assigned to 215 Squadron's 'A' Flight.

On 11 August, Jackson, our skipper, was screened – mentored in flight – by a senior pilot. The MO, Doc, held me up for an hour by not showing on time when I needed medical clearance, so I missed our Liberator's take-off. I still had a sore arm from my recent vaccination (plus the trots, as did most of the others – and typically flying duties weren't dismissed just because of the trots). Due to Doc's tardiness I had to race down to the end of the strip and hop aboard my crew's Liberator after they touched down following a set of practice landings and take-offs (then called 'circuits and landings' and now called 'touch and goes').

Once aboard, I did some air-to-ground wireless communicating with the aerodrome's wireless section. At 1500 Jackson went solo for the first time on a Liberator – without one of the experienced instructor pilots hanging over his shoulders. I was needed as the W/Op in the aircraft, and that day, despite joining late, I still accumulated three hours of flying.

Later that day, because I'd refused to take one of Doc's remedies for gastro issues, castor oil was forced down my throat as I was held down.

We tried to fly the next day despite some heavy rain. However, we sprung an oil leak in an engine, so back we came.

On 13 August the *gharry* (truck) coming to take us to our Liberator crashed into a tree, and one of our gunners, Joe Marsh, cut his head. I took him to the Station Sick Quarters for treatment. A Tiger Moth biplane pranged, too, but neither the pilot nor the W/Op aboard was killed.

We learned on 14 August that just before midnight the previous night Liberator EV851 crashed while taking off on a night training exercise and burned after hitting a tree. All six of the crew were killed. The experienced instructor pilot, Warrant Officer Arthur Denton, had completed a tour of ops on 159 Squadron. The two pilots under instruction were from New Zealand (Flying Officer Ernest McConnel) and Canada (Flying Officer Noel Moysey).

The navigator had tossed up with the bomb aimer to see who would go. The nav lost the toss, and yet he won! Some of my crew and I went to look over the charred remains of the kite. What a mess; little remained after the fire. I found a fellow's keys lying there. It was doubtful that any of the six airmen were alive when the Liberator burned, but how would this be known?

MATT: In his online memoir ex-159 Squadron navigator Sam Bourque RCAF wrote of fulfilling a promise while in London during his post-op tour's return to Canada:

> My only means of contact with the Denton family was with a daughter [Arthur Denton's sister] who was employed at Canadian army headquarters in London. When I arrived at headquarters and requested to see Miss Denton, the soldier on duty did not believe my story: that I did not know Miss Denton, that she had probably never heard of me,

that I did not want to make a date and that I really wanted to meet her family. I finally suggested to the soldier that he be present while I talked with Miss Denton. He agreed and I was able to make arrangements to meet her parents. The meeting went well. The family, although sad, did not cry and were very proud that their son had died for the cause of democracy and for his country.

ROY: With another I practiced on the mid-upper gun turret, while others worked on the beam guns. After that came more dinghy practice.

Though not the only sufferer, I sure was tired of my ordeal to rid myself of the trots. I tried to acquire some human cement to regain normal stomach and intestinal function.

One chore all gunners had to master was the cleaning of Browning machine guns. We air gunners had performed this task as part of the syllabus leading to winning our AG badges, but practice, practice, practice, improved our skills. My role as second W/Op/AG required that I man one of the two beam guns at times, while the flight engineer, Smithy Smith, took the other gun. I tossed up with Smithy to see which gun would be handled by which airman; the starboard gun would be mine.

Among the subjects drilled into us was the proper use of the parachute harness; we were told that needless death resulted when an airman failed to secure himself safely in his harness before jumping. The simplest things could kill a man!

On 19 August my crew made a practice cross-country flight. I fired bursts from my beam gun, which admittedly was fun, and the rest of the time I spent on the wireless. We also stopped in Madras, India, to pick up two new instructors.

I journeyed to Bangalore on the following day. Despite the *gharry* being heavily overloaded we made it there. I managed to get swimming trunks for the boys, and together we enjoyed a dip at a club in town. We followed that outing with a meal at Victory Chinese Restaurant. I told the proprietor that I was from Hong Kong and asked him to choose the meal for us, which he did. It was most satisfying, and a step up from the usual RAF fare.

When we returned from flight training one day we learned that fellow trainee Walter Clements had turned the wrong way when exiting his Liberator and had walked into a propeller. The prop broke his arm and severely wounded his head. He died two hours later. Apparently, in the aircraft in which he'd previously flown with regularity one had to exit a certain way to avoid the spinning props. Clem had lost concentration for a fatal moment. It was a very bad show, especially as he was a wizard type.

We made a five and a half hour cross-country flight on 23 August. Pissy toggled sixteen bombs over the sea, and we also engaged in some fighter affiliation training. During Spitfire mock attacks we attempted evasive action, while also practicing fighter control among the crew over the intercom. I was nearly thrown out of the beam hatch when Jackson took sudden evasive action.

On 24 August I was the Duty Wireless Operator, but really I acted as both the Duty W/Op and the Duty Pilot. It was the Duty W/Op's job to land incoming Libs and send Libs off. I fired a green flare from a Very pistol to those kites whose W/Ops weren't communicating with me.

I didn't have to go when my crew flew that evening, but it was good to get the flying hours in. Jackson flew solo on three circuits and landings, and then we carried on until 2300. Afterwards, we ate a late supper.

Airborne the next night at 2300, we headed for the east coast, and everything that could go wrong with the wireless did. I couldn't get any readings for The Boong to determine a 'fix' for identifying our location, so he had to take us round the sky by astronavigation fixes derived from his sextant's star sightings.

These were taken through the small Perspex dome on the aircraft's upper spine forward of the cockpit windscreen. The navigator would plot the aircraft's positions using the sextant to register the angle of the sun during the day and stars at night. He'd then determine the Liberator's latitude and longitude by consulting a table, and corrections in flight characteristics would be made by the pilot as needed.

MATT: Normally, radio signals transmitted from ground stations and picked up by the W/Op were plotted by the navigator, and the intersection of two or more signals would yield a 'fix' – a map location, sometimes within a small triangle. In lieu of such fixes, such as when static from electrical storms was overwhelming, a navigator took sun or star readings, called celestial or astronavigation fixes, to establish position.

When cloudy or where air turbulence was excessive, making celestial reading impossible, and if radio fixes were out of the question, the navigator made his best Dead Reckoning calculations.

Via in-flight wind drift analysis the navigator also determined the wind's effect upon course and speed – as the wind could substantially impact even a behemoth Liberator's track and timing. To obtain a wind drift reading the rear gunner would centralise his turret and look through his illuminated sight with the guns pointing downward. When a released smoke flare passed through the centre of the sight the gunner would track it with the sight until he no longer had to move his turret to keep the object central. He'd then look at the rim of the turret to his left or right and give the navigator the reading – so many degrees red or so many degrees green – thus revealing the amount the aircraft was drifting to port or starboard. The navigator, in turn, would give the pilot a correction on the course being flown.

Navigation was an art form, though sometimes it seemed like a crapshoot.

ROY: Another cross-country exercise of six hours' duration occupied our time soon thereafter. From the end of the second hour to the end of the third hour we were in an electric storm. However, it wasn't too bad. This time, fortunately, I was able to get bearings for The Boong. We came down to about 500 feet for the last twenty to thirty miles, no doubt frightening the hell out of villagers.

1673 HCU training is completed

With this trip we finished our training at 1673 HCU; my flight time added up to thirty-two hours and ten minutes. A huge celebration in the Sergeants' Mess ensued, and the officers were invited there to celebrate with our crew's NCOs. Consuming too much rum and Coke, I passed out. I'm afraid that I'm a lousy drinker; maybe I have a small liver. The boys carried me home and laid me on my bed. Later that night they came into my tent and tried to wake me but finally gave up.

I'm deeply ashamed to say that when I eventually came to, I found that I'd been sick during the night. I refused to let the bearer in until I'd done some cleaning up.

With our training completed the crew was granted a short break. A typical leave day for us involved doing very little – just eating, swimming and sunning. The other boys got terribly burned, but as I was already fairly dark, I just got a bit darker. There were lots of girls at the club we frequented, but we didn't converse much with them, not for lack of trying. I asked one married woman to come to a dance with us, and she agreed, but when the time came for her to go home at the dance's conclusion Jackson got in front of me; I wasn't pleased about that.

On the following day a fish bone got caught fairly far down my throat. I wouldn't go to hospital because I was nervous about an MD trying to get the bone out from so far down. Instead, I kept working my throat muscles for a day until the bone finally snapped, and I swallowed it.

A street photographer took a crew photo, which was an incredible procedure. After snapping the picture the photographer worked under a black cloth at the camera's rear to develop and print the photo. Amazing!

Chapter 7

In India Roy joins 215 Squadron and is sent to 22 APC for training: SEPTEMBER 1944

215 Squadron becomes a reality for Roy

On 4 September, the day after returning from leave, I was Range Safety Wireless Operator at the bombing range, while our second pilot, Bing Bingham, was the Range Safety Pilot.

As my gastrointestinal issues just wouldn't dissipate, I ultimately had to go to hospital for treatment. Additionally, I suffered from sore eyes. I got into trouble for leaving the hospital without permission after three days, done because I was afraid I'd miss my posting. Officially I was posted from 1673 HCU to 215 Squadron RAF with effect from 8 September.

While in hospital I was reminded of an evening at Mrs Colley's in Yorkshire in January 1944. After our dinner's soup course the maid brought in the next serving. A plate with a piece of Yorkshire pudding was placed in front of each of us. Because of the paucity of food due to rationing, both my friend and I immediately assumed that this was the main course. I laughed uncontrollably when I realised that roast beef and fixings would soon follow, and so did he.

Mrs Colley asked what the joke was, and another bout of hysteria erupted. Then, after we'd eaten our delicious Yorkshire pudding, the main course came out. More mirth resulted. We knew it was rude, but we lacked the confidence to tell her. We apologised, and that was that.

Months after my embarrassing bout of the giggles in England I was in India and on the verge of departing 1673 HCU to join 215 Squadron. However, I lacked clean clothes, and I was concerned that a *dhobi wallah* – a local Indian who physically laundered our gear – hadn't finished with my clothing yet.

My bearer had taken my soiled clothing down to the *dhobi wallah*, who was sometimes a man, sometimes a woman. I never set eyes on the actual person doing the washing. The laundering process was done by soaping the article of clothing and then repeatedly beating the cloth against a stone on the banks of a creek or river. It worked, as my freshly laundered clothes were always clean. However, not only did this pounding reduce the life of the fabric, but also the waistband in a pair of underwear lost its elasticity over time.

On this occasion the *dhobi wallah* alleviated any worry I harboured when the wrapped package of clean clothes turned up. My bearer carted the package over to the guardroom, where it was picked up by a *gharry* for onward delivery to me prior to my departure from 1673 HCU.

Journeying to Digri and 215 Squadron

Very soon the time had come to travel, in early September 1944. Despite a septic toe, I managed to load my stuff and to see it secured. I was with Pissy and two warrant officers in a Second-Class rail carriage.

When we reached Madras and exited the train I had trouble dressing because of my toe. I went straight to the nearby British military hospital, where the doctor drained the pus and dressed the toe. I then had a lovely hot bath, followed by a shave and shampoo at the barbers.

On 10 September 1945, when our train stopped for the night, we found that we had to sleep at the station. On the floor outside the First-Class waiting room I woke up often during the night wary that our kit would be stolen; it wasn't. For breakfast I bought a tin of sardines, a bottle of ketchup and some bread. Off again early, the train departed the station at 0715.

We saw some pitiful sights at the rail stations we passed. At one point, while eating my lunch, I looked out the window to see some hungry kids following every move of my fork to my mouth, and it tore at my heart. I caught one kid's eyes and motioned with my head for him to come to the carriage door. He did, and when I thought that none of the others were looking I threw him a bread roll. I soon wished that I hadn't, because a hundred kids appeared from nowhere and dived atop him. I couldn't watch, so I went inside, pulled down the blinds and felt awful.

The food was inedible at some stops, so we ate army-type rations of bully beef with some of my tomato sauce. At one stop we were eaten alive by mosquitoes, but we avoided malaria, thankfully.

At Kharagpur, Bengal, a Railway Transport officer told us to disembark and switch trains to catch one travelling northward towards Digri, our new squadron's base, located sixty-four miles west-north-west of Calcutta's Howrah Bridge.

MATT: From Jessore, Bengal (sixty-six miles north-east of the Howrah Bridge), 215 Squadron had been flying bombing ops over Burma aboard Vickers Wellingtons. However, in mid-1944 the squadron converted to four-engine Liberators. The ability to carry a large bombload over a great distance was the Liberator's forte, and the distances to targets in the Far East had increased. The Liberator was the best option at the time. As more Libs became available their presence on RAF bomber squadrons in India grew.

In September, as Roy was finishing up Liberator training at Kolar, 215 Squadron began relocating from Jessore to Digri, Bengal, 118 miles to the west-south-west. Consequently, those like Roy destined for 215 Squadron duty were rerouted to Digri. Roy was excited to be part of this change, which he equated with favourable progress in the struggle against Japan. His wide-eyed naiveté would be tempered given time, and his mindset would also be influenced at the end of 1944 by another major 215 Squadron move, in which he actively participated, yet he remained enthused about his role in fighting the enemy and proud of his service.

ROY: We arrived at Chandrakona Road station, the nearest stop to Digri, where *gharries* awaited to take us to our billets several miles further north.

At last, a member of 215 Squadron at Digri

MATT: Roy's new squadron wasn't the only Lib unit located at Digri; 159 Squadron had been flying on Liberators out of Digri since October 1944, except for about a month spent at Dhubalia, north of Calcutta, from March into April 1944. The unit had been on Liberator bombing ops in the Middle East in 1942 before relocating to Salbani (also spelled 'Salboni'), India – about sixty-seven miles west of Calcutta – in the latter part of that year. In October 1943 159 Squadron moved thirteen miles northward to Digri.

A Special Duties unit, 357 Squadron formed at Digri in February 1944. It flew Liberators from there before 215 Squadron's tenure on the aerodrome began, but by 15 September 1944 357 had departed Digri. Thus, of the RAF Liberator units then in India, only 159 Squadron called Digri home when 215 moved there.

On Friday, 15 September 1944, Liberators posted to 215 Squadron flew in to Digri from Jessore with all the ground staff. Roy's crew learned that their Liberator would be given the fuselage letter designation 'B', unique from any other 215 Squadron Liberator.

ROY: There were no required activities for our first three days on 215 Squadron at Digri, as the main relocation from Jessore to Digri was in progress, so we spent time reading, playing darts, sunbaking, eating and drinking. We also got cracking addressing administrative matters, like our next of kin forms. I found out that I'd be due for a promotion to flight lieutenant in May 1945, a mere eight months away! It was something to look forward to, and the extra pay accompanying the promotion was a bonus. And I'd no doubt enjoy added creature comforts.

On 215 Squadron there was a mix of seasoned veterans and those, like me, who'd never faced combat. Some of the men who would either join 215 Squadron anew or who were veterans of the squadron's Wellington ops received Liberator training at Kolar, similar to my experiences there, while many others already on the squadron continued training at Digri that had begun at Jessore. Some crews, like mine, were sent to RAF Amarda Road for armament training prior to 215's first operational flying.

MATT: Roy likely didn't make any training flights from Digri in September 1944. His flight logbook, containing the proof, disappeared long ago, and the 215 Squadron ORB is of no help.

ROY: My living quarters at Digri were in a *basha*, a structure measuring 20x14x20 feet. It contained four or so bedrooms, each separated from another by a concrete wall. I'm guessing that the design was basically the same at all RAF stations. There was a concrete floor and wooden poles for supports, and the roof and outer walls were rattan; other *bashas* had solid external walls, but not mine. A man slept on a *charpoy*, a wooden rectangle-shaped bed sitting on four legs. The legs stood in either saucers or small tins, like cigarette tins, in which was some kerosene to keep out bedbugs, ants and anything else that came crawling around. Bedbugs typically infested a man's *charpoy* initially and had to be eliminated. The foundation of the bed itself was a series of thick crisscrossing strings, making a sort of hammock. Sitting immediately atop the strings was a 'biscuit' – a mattress – and then blankets and sheets we'd bought ourselves completed the bedding.

Atop the *charpoy* was anchored a mosquito net. Due to the threat of mosquito-transmitted malaria, it was absolutely necessary at night to wear long trousers, long-sleeved shirts, socks and shoes when out and about. Also, it was absolutely necessary to have a mossie net for sleeping; the netting would be unfurled and secured to protect a man when lying down.

We each went to sleep protected by a mosquito net, and one had to be quick in getting under the net to avoid taking mossies into the immediate sleeping area with him; otherwise, the winged bastards would feast all night. A man would lift the net just enough to slide in and then reach over and tuck in. But getting out in the middle of the night to go to the toilet, especially after a big night of drinking, could be hazardous. Some men forgot that the net was there, and more than once the result was to finish up in a complete mess on the floor. Further entanglement routinely followed when trying to make things right afterwards.

On the occasion of moving into my *basha*, I lay down on the *charpoy* for my first night's rest. I hadn't been in bed long before the bedbugs attacked. I awoke to find blood spots all over the sheet and bedbugs moving around. I killed as many as I could and tried to sleep, but what with bedbugs and mossies attacking me (I'd not yet properly set up my mosquito netting), it was a long night. On the following day I treated the *charpoy* for the bugs by spraying the strings supporting the biscuit, and I made certain that there was kerosene in each leg to stop bedbugs and other insects from climbing up onto the bed. I also ensured the proper hanging of my mossie netting, so necessary for protection from the little monsters. That's all it took.

My *basha* mates and I prioritised acquiring furniture for the room and taking ownership of the space.

As a safeguard against debilitating illness we took our Atabrine, an anti-malarial drug available to us at the time.

We often inhabited our *basha* when not away on other duties, like flying or attending briefings. There was a toilet attached per so many rooms, and one's ablutions were performed in a portable canvas washbasin.

Our *basha* at Digri had Jackson, The Boong, Pissy, Bing and me, because we were all officers in the same crew.

Jackson was a devil. Sometimes he'd wake us up after a real Officers' Mess piss-up by playing a recording of an oboe solo on his gramophone. Jackson, a classical music lover, knew nothing could be worse for us than to be awakened with an oboe solo. We threatened to dismember him, but, of course, we didn't mean it; we were all mates.

Instruction begins at No. 22 Armament Practice Camp at RAF Amarda Road

My crew was sent for instruction to No. 22 Armament Practice Camp (22 APC), a subsidiary of the impressive Air Fighting Training Unit (AFTU) located at Amarda Road airfield, seventy miles south-south-west of Digri in Orissa, India.

MATT: The AFTU schools were formed by Hurricane fighter ace Frank Carey. When sent to the Far East after his Battle of Britain exploits, he again proved to be a highly successful Hurricane pilot, this time against the Japanese over Burma. Wing Commander Carey set up AFTU to teach various aerial tactics and leadership principles needed in facing the Japanese. He was the CO when Roy attended AFTU.

Roy was likely open to the wisdom of teachers at 22 APC who'd previously been on ops. Roy and those of his crewmates who were untested in combat had already benefitted from such insight at 1673 HCU, where most of their instructors had flown at least one tour of combat, and at 22 APC Roy was offered another superb opportunity before entering action himself.

ROY: Squadron Leader Clive 'Zoot' Beadon of 215 Squadron, who'd just transited to Digri from Amarda Road, told us that it was a difficult course. 'Good,' I said, 'we'd be that much better because of it.' At Digri Zoot gave me a lift down to Flights in his *gharry* and found Jackson and The Boong – still my skipper and my navigator – already waiting there. All told, four crews would be going to Amarda Road from Digri. My crew would get a lift down to 22 APC aboard another Liberator, because our kite, 'B', was already there. However, the Liberator in which I'd been assigned as a passenger started spitting bits of engine when the ground crew warmed it up, so our flight was cancelled.

My crew and I occupied ourselves with more sunbathing and reading that day.

The Boong woke me up on Wednesday, 20 September, wishing me a happy birthday, and before we went to breakfast all the boys wished me many happy returns. This was a most appropriate offering to somebody going to war!

Jackson had promised not to reveal my age, yet he then promptly announced that I was only twenty! I was teased incessantly, being such a babe in the woods yet also an officer, and I was duly dubbed 'Chico', a nickname I still have today.

I collected mikes and headsets to take down to Amarda Road. We packed up our luggage and loaded it onto the *gharry* shuttling us to the kite. I was supposed to fly with Keith Palmer as my skipper, but the weather turned bad, and, additionally, the kite was again declared in need of servicing. More waiting around was on the menu.

I shared a cake that Mother had sent, and it sure was appreciated; everybody complimented her baking skills.

After Jackson woke us at 0545 the following morning, 21 September, we managed to pack our gear, have breakfast, and be back at the billet by 0700. Later that day we flew to Amarda Road aboard skipper Athol Graham's Liberator. Our kite, next to Athol's on the Amarda Road tarmac, looked fine.

We soon met our Gunnery Leader instructor, Flight Lieutenant Bruce Copp, and our legendary CO, Wing Commander Frank Carey. Not bad! Copp had flown air gunner ops with Bomber Command over Europe and then on a 159 Squadron Liberator tour.

By Friday, 22 September, Jackson and Pissy's bearer was down with cholera. We were never far from health challenges in India: cholera, malaria, dengue fever, dysentery and prickly heat, to name a few.

We had our first air gunnery practice at Amarda Road on Saturday, 23 September. Keith Palmer's flight engineer held us up for thirty minutes because he didn't wake up on time. Squadron Leader Doug Connor, chief instructor in the AFTU Bomber Wing, tore a strip off of him. It was unpleasant enough that we had to arise at 0430, but to have been forced to wait for one tardy airman added to our discomfort.

The first exercise was designed to give us sighting and range estimation experience while being 'attacked' by American-built P-47 Thunderbolt fighters, whose pilots were also taking an AFTU course. Unlike actual combat, however, our Liberator took no evasive action. The Thunderbolts came right up our tail before breaking away about twenty-five yards from the rear turret.

The exercise went very well, and I got off some good 'shots'.

After lectures from 0930 to 1100 we saw the first gun camera films of our shooting efforts against the incoming Thunderbolts. I was pleased to receive a very good assessment for my gunnery.

We went aloft after lunch with a 'screen gunner' aboard; similar to a mentoring screen pilot, a screen gunner was an experienced airman who oversaw and assessed each individual gunner and offered his valuable opinions. Our gunners on the whole were good.

Then there was time for an hour of formation flying with other Liberators, followed by mock attacks upon us by Thunderbolts, when we did take evasive action. We felt the air getting hotter as we descended.

Pissy and The Boong were scheduled to fly on a bombing exercise in the morning with pilot Athol Graham, but Pissy turned up so tight and Athol had piles so badly he couldn't fly, so Jackson cancelled the exercise. Instead, he flew as screen pilot for Athol's crew.

In another training flight we were airborne at 1430 for two hours of fighter control and bombing exercises. Pissy could only drop eight bombs before the weather closed in, and the error was about 120 yards. Bill Wright had registered some exceptional mid-upper shooting during our exercise; I hoped he'd always be that good.

Bruce Copp, already seen as a good type by my crew and myself, lectured on the .50-calibre guns. Again, my gun camera films were pretty good, nearly as good as yesterday.

Although I'd bounced around India, the mail continued to reach me. At 22 APC I received lots of lovely mail from Paddy Hare and Pauline Buchanan.

I had to censor letters whenever there was a break, and it could be very tiring.

On Thursday, 28 September, the fighter boys showed us their own gun camera films of their mock attacks on our aircraft. Upon viewing these films more than a few dubious frowns were draped across the faces of us Liberator men, especially rear gunners, but the cinema footage didn't lie. We had to realize that fighters were serious adversaries.

I was informed at 0430 on Friday, 29 September, that I'd been appointed the Range Officer on the bombing range for the day. Tony Stoddard drove Bopp the W/Op and me out to the range and left us there, to the north-west of the Amarda Road airfield by three miles. I took the left-hand quadrant and Bopp the W/Op the right.

The Liberator practice bombing seemed to worsen with every bomb dropped. The last bomb was only twenty yards from my tower, shaking me up a bit.

The following day, 30 September, was one of continuous rain, resulting in the cancellation of all flying – but also the dismissal of assignments like Range Officer. I wasn't complaining! There was little to do except censoring.

Chapter 8

In India 215 Squadron activities and its first operational Liberator flights, Roy's 22 APC training ends and he flies his first 215 Squadron op: OCTOBER 1944

Sunday, 1 OCTOBER 1944 and Thursday, 5 OCTOBER 1944
(Roy does not fly on these sorties; he is still at Amarda Road's 22 APC)
From Digri operational Liberator flights of significantly longer duration than on previous training sorties begin on 215 Squadron with two weather reconnaissance flights to Bentinck Island, BURMA

MATT: Before Liberator ops began 215 Squadron flew thirteen separate long distance training sorties, first from Jessore and then Digri, to hone formation flying and bombing skills and also to defensively prepare for fighters. (In his memoir Roy had previously mentioned 215 Squadron training flights at Digri in September 1944, although his participation is doubtful.) Seven of the thirteen flights were staged out of Jessore and ranged in length from three hours and thirty minutes to four hours and forty minutes. After 215 relocated to Digri the first four training flights spanned up to three hours and fifty minutes in duration, and then the final three September flights, lasting from six hours and thirty minutes to seven hours, increased the length of time spent airborne.

As October began, while Roy was still at Amarda Road, two 215 Squadron crews back at Digri were sent out on the unit's first operational Liberator sorties, on 1 October and again on 5 October. Each was a one-aircraft weather reconnaissance flight of significantly longer duration than any previous pre-operational sortie, and spanning thirteen hours and fifty minutes and then ten hours and twenty minutes. The flights, into enemy airspace, extended across the Bay of Bengal and onward over the Andaman Sea (far to the south of Rangoon, Burma) to different destinations off of the southern coast of Burma.

The Liberators then safely returned to Digri. No enemy ships were sighted, or aircraft, for that matter.

Friday, 6 OCTOBER through early Wednesday morning, 11 OCTOBER 1944

(Roy does not fly on these sorties)

Twelve one-aircraft Air-Sea Rescue search flights

On 6 October, Liberator BZ978 'W' of 159 Squadron, unable to reach the safety of Cox's Bazar or Chittagong, India, ditched near Cheduba Island in the Bay of Bengal just off of the west coast of Burma after sustaining serious fighter damage over Thailand. This crew had flown from Digri. The Liberator, with wings high up the fuselage and with flimsy bomb bay doors, was a notoriously poor ditching aircraft, often resulting in loss of life and/or serious crew injuries.

BZ978's skipper, Warrant Officer John 'Jock' McKinnon – on the last scheduled op of his combat tour – was so close to earning a rest from ops! The irony of McKinnon's disappearance on his final required op wasn't lost on anyone.

A major effort to find ditching survivors was undertaken by various India-based RAF Liberator squadrons, but they didn't include aircraft or men, like Roy and his crew, who were training at Amarda Road.

On the night of 6 October, roughly twelve hours after the ditching, one 215 Squadron crew sighted a bright light on the sea flashing 'S.O.S.' The Lib remained in the area for one hour after the light had been extinguished, but in darkness and with petrol low it finally departed for Digri.

Then on 9 October a 215 Squadron Liberator sighted the greyish-coloured dinghy containing three men, but for only three or four minutes. A second 215 Squadron Lib may have also seen the dinghy but couldn't maintain contact.

A dinghy was spotted by Liberators from other squadrons more than once through the evening of 9 October, and an Air-Sea Rescue (ASR) launch in the area was sighted numerous times, but in sometimes difficult atmospheric conditions the launch couldn't reach the dinghy. The aerial search continued.

Liberators from 215 Squadron flew twelve individual ASR search sorties from Digri through the early morning of 11 October. The twelve 215 Squadron

ASR searches varied in duration from nine hours and eight minutes to twelve hours and fifty-four minutes.

Finishing up at 22 APC

ROY: My crew faced an early morning practice bombing detail on Sunday, 1 October. We were dragged out of bed to catch the 0600 *gharry* down to Flights and were airborne by 0700. We had a lot of trouble with the bomb rack and with clouds closing in and obscuring the target. By the end of the detail The Boong was dropping bombs by hand on Pissy's command.

Nothing marked the afternoon's syllabus, so we took advantage of the break for sunbaking, reading and later card playing. We'd engage in poker on most nights, though I didn't do well.

Flying was varied and usually exciting, although formation flying could be nerve wracking, as it wasn't easy to hold Liberators in tight formation in unstable air.

Gunnery with intense evasive maneuvering was a favourite of mine. When I wasn't on the wireless, but was back at a beam gun, violent Liberator movements were like terrific amusement park rides at the rear of the aircraft. Whenever we made a seventy-degree turn or we corkscrewed to escape a fighter I found that I couldn't get up from the crouch I'd adopted to fire my beam gun.

Call me crazy for mostly loving the ride's thrill, though I was generally spooked far more readily by things when I was on the ground. For example, in my billet one night I was terribly frightened when a huge bat flew in. My first recognition of its presence was when a wing hit my cheek, but, fortunately, that was the extent of the trouble. It escaped the room at the next opportunity.

Bats would fly around at night, feeding on the many bugs flitting about, and that was good. Only once, as mentioned above, was I scared silly by a bat in the *basha*. They occasionally entered the billet, but generally we thought little of it! Typically, a man sitting at the desk in his room would suddenly sense movement in the air. He'd look up to see this bat racing around the room at very high speed, just missing his head, inevitably pursuing insects. Except for that one incident when the bat actually made contact with my face, the flying didn't worry us much, because I knew that bats had incredible internal radar for manoeuvring about any space. Yet I was always glad when one of these flying mammals had departed the *basha* again, although in India I never heard of even one case of a bat attacking a human!

Lectures were the norm in the mornings if we weren't flying then. There was always more to be taught. The Sperry ball turret was our focus one morning, as it was a type carried in a Liberator's belly. We were also lectured on different types of ammo (especially what we used in our machine guns: .50-calibre bullets in most guns, but also an ever-lessening amount of .303-calibre ammunition for the remaining rear turret guns of that inferior size).

Our gun camera films were both fascinating and useful; after all, we were at 22 APC to hone our skills in gunnery, and though there wasn't enough footage gathered, these films were practical and helpful tools.

An aircraft recognition exam sprung upon us certainly caught me flat-footed; I didn't do well on that one, though normally I was ace at making identifications.

In typically frustrating RAF fashion five crews, including mine, had to catch the *gharry* at 0645 down to the Liberators one morning, yet only two crews – not mine – flew. Being awakened early for no good reason was such an annoyance.

On an afternoon flight in our final week Bopp the W/Op did all the work while I read on the flight deck. We took some pretty violent evasive action on that trip, too. Bing made a big faux pas by banking our Liberator into a ninety-five degree turn – five degrees over the vertical! The wings didn't fall off, though, and Bing recovered control.

We had another exam on the Friday towards the end of the course. Though it should have been a pushover, I ashamedly confess that Ned Kelly and I, the only officer W/Op/AGs, didn't do well. However, our gunnery films were good, showing attacking Thunderbolts, good defensive gunnery action and violent evasive action by our Liberator.

My crew was airborne again the following day, heading out to sea and back westward towards Cuttack, south of Amarda Road. Picked up by radar, we were bounced by Hurricanes sent out to catch us. After their good interception they mock shot us up properly. We dived down to low level – very low level, skimming over paddy fields. Only one Hurricane followed us.

After the exercise was over we beat up the Amarda Road aerodrome, but as fate would have it a Thunderbolt was taking off, so our Liberator's showing off was considered potentially disastrous. Jackson was grounded until he'd seen Wing Commander Carey.

In a required check I found that three crews had not turned up to clean their guns, so I put them on a detail that night. It didn't benefit my popularity, but duty assignments from officers weren't designed to make friends!

When our course at 22 APC concluded we received a farewell talk from Wing Commander Carey, and we viewed our films for the last time. Some showed very low flying! I accrued twenty-seven hours and twenty minutes of Liberator flight time at 22 APC.

Back to 215 Squadron at Digri

On 9 October 1944 we flew back to Digri and reoccupied our old billets on 215 Squadron. In a fearful mess, papers were strewn all over the floor and there was evidence of rats having been everywhere. Rodents had eaten through some of The Boong's clothing and a tablecloth. One huge rat made its presence known, but we couldn't catch it.

My crew was excused from flying duties on that Monday, our first day back on the squadron.

I was tasked with an assignment that took me twenty-five miles from Digri. Zoot Beadon, our Flight Commander, called Jackson and myself into his office to tell us that we were to sit on a Court of Inquiry over a man's death by drowning in his bath at Midnapore, south of Digri.

We took a *gharry* over there and were interviewed by a lieutenant colonel in charge of the Indian General Hospital. He suggested a ruling of suicide as a possibility, but he still thought that it might have been an accidental death.

The Court couldn't sit, because no officer could be found to represent the British Army. It seemed obvious to Jackson and me that there was some sort of cover-up.

Wednesday, 11 OCTOBER 1944
(Counting as the first op of Roy's combat tour)
Near BURMA – Air-Sea Rescue search *(daylight)*

MATT: It was hoped that Roy or a crewmate, back from Amarda Road and again settled in with 215 Squadron at Digri, would make a difference in saving the lives of three of his brethren from BZ978, spotted in a dinghy. Consequently, Roy and his crew flew an 11 October ASR search.

ROY: Having returned to Digri, my crew joined in on the multi-squadron dinghy search, with our independently flown sortie. Though the nature of our

ASR work was sad, one aspect pleased us: getting our first operational hours in the books to begin our 215 Squadron tours.

MATT: A standard tour at the time consisted of 300 operational hours or thirty ops flown, whichever came first, but Roy exceeded both figures, ending up with thirty-five ops and 319 hours. Thus, neither the 300-hour nor thirty-op measuring sticks applied to him.

ROY: In anticipation of an early take-off, we arose at 0100 on the eleventh and set about getting our Mae Wests, etc., before heading to our kite.

MATT: Roy's Liberator, KG831 'B', took off in darkness at 0310. Jackson Grouse was Roy's skipper, and Bing Bingham was the second pilot. As second W/Op, Roy, when not relieving the first W/Op on radio duties, scanned the Bay of Bengal for the dinghy and the sky for enemy aircraft from his beam gun.

ROY: The first two hours were boring as we flew over the Bay of Bengal to the vicinity of BZ978's ditching off of Burma's west coast. Initially, the specialist gunners slept, except Jock Smith, who helped me drop flame floats for The Boong to calculate the wind drift. We carried twenty-six of them and twenty-four aluminium sea markers, some of which we hoped would be used should we spot the dinghy.

Before dawn, while approaching the Burma coast, the gunners got into their turrets, and I cocked each beam gun. We kept a good watch, now that we were in enemy airspace. The Boong's navigation was out, and we missed our target, Cheduba Island, but we quickly made up lost time and reached our search's starting point. I must add that very rarely was The Boong's navigation anything but perfect.

First we flew a creeping line search and then a square search. Staring at the sea for long periods was very tiring. At 0841 we spotted something that Jackson thought might be the dinghy, and I went into action furiously, going through the wireless procedure given at briefing. However, it turned out to be the ASR launch that was also searching for the dinghy.

Later by wireless I was given a position to investigate, the Oyster Island lighthouse (off the western coast of Burma and twenty-two miles from Japanese-held Akyab). I relayed this location to Jackson, who then headed there. We found nothing in that vicinity except partially submerged rocks.

At 1340, after again sighting the ASR launch, we finally set course for home. As soon as we were on our way everybody went to pieces. Long hours searching endless expanses of sea was exhausting. The Boong fell asleep over his navigation log, and I, too, conked out for a while. Even Jackson fell asleep. We landed back at Digri at 1725, having been airborne for fourteen hours and fifteen minutes. We were knackered from the long flight and the tedium of the assignment.

MATT: Roy and his crew had nothing positive to report.

Wednesday, 11 OCTOBER 1944 through Friday, 13 OCTOBER 1944
(Roy does not fly on these sorties)
Near BURMA – Air-Sea Rescue searches by 215 Squadron Liberators continue with individual flights by eight aircraft

Three other Liberators from 215 Squadron were sent out on individual ASR sorties that day, three flew ASR sorties on 12 October and two were despatched on 13 October, but there were no further sightings of the dinghy or any of the crew of BZ978 'W' after the evening of 9 October. The search was called off after the unproductive ASR sorties of 13 October.

When Rangoon Jail was liberated in early May 1945, it was learned that the three men in the dinghy had been captured. The rear gunner, Flight Sergeant Harry Richardson of the RCAF, had died on 28 October, having suffered from the ill effects of combat wounds, the ditching ordeal, his ultimate capture and his probable mistreatment as a PoW. Flight Sergeant L. Roper, the second pilot, and Sergeant S. Hill, the flight engineer, had survived. The fates of the three men were especially heartbreaking, because they were so close to being rescued, not that the injured Flight Sergeant Richardson would have survived.

The ASR flights offered solid experience for the participating 215 Squadron airmen, who soon would commence Liberator bombing ops.

Libs from 215 Squadron flew twenty-one sorties in search of BZ978 survivors. Including the aircraft from all participating squadrons, eighty-three ASR sorties were flown, adding up to 341 hours in the air.

Duties as assigned, leave in Calcutta and odds and sods

ROY: The day after our endurance search flight Squadron Leader Zoot Beadon said that our Officers' Mess needed smartening up, and he picked

The Boong and me to begin it. We washed down the Mess walls with a stirrup pump, followed by a wash of the ante room and part of the bar. I'd no idea repeatedly pushing down/pulling up a stirrup pump handle would be so hard!

When we were just settling down to our work in the Mess Jackson came in and said that the Court of Inquiry proceedings were on again, to our surprise, and that he and I had to continue our participation as members of the Court. In the unpleasant drive down to Midnapore we were coated by red dust.

An Anglo-Indian, a Major Egan, presided over the Court.

There were six witnesses to interview and take statements from, but we finished by 1730. Though the cause of death might have been suicide, we brought in a verdict of 'accidental death'. By the bruises on the dead man's nose and knee, it was evident that he'd fallen, and the position in which he was found supported an 'accidental death' ruling.

Nevertheless, we had to consider the fact that he had a black cloud over his head. He suffered from bad cases of VD and dengue fever, and his wife in England was living with another man. It was also said that his mother's nagging had brought about a nervous breakdown. His letters home were pitiful.

Yet he was a popular and well-mannered man. Ultimately, declaring his death 'accidental' truly seemed like the correct decision.

On the next day, Friday the thirteenth, The Boong and I were back decorating the Officers' Mess; I guess one could say that there was no rest for the wicked! We sprayed the ceiling, and by the time we'd finished we were in a helluva state. I was pleased to be on the ground, not flying, on this inauspicious date; undeniably superstitions were widespread on the squadron.

We moved quickly to take advantage of a three day pass in Calcutta, going by rail to experience some semblance of culture and civilization. Digri was far removed from the hustle and bustle of city life. Jackson and Pissy claimed they couldn't afford it, and they also said they had too much work to do, whatever that might have been. The Boong and I stayed at the Grand Hotel, which was a destination for officers on leave. It was a grand hotel then, and it is still grand.

I was fortunate to take such occasional weekend leaves over the course of my operational tour, and beyond.

Several of my friends were honorary members of various clubs in Calcutta, affording each the right to swim, with guests – including me. This we did a lot; it was very refreshing to be able to do so.

The Japanese had bombed Calcutta sporadically until 1944, and gladly I didn't arrive there until the threat had passed. Though damage was isolated, any bombing had caused absolute pandemonium among the population. This promptly led to every road out of Calcutta being blocked by the congestion of escaping hordes in an already overcrowded city. The population was very easily frightened.

Back to my Calcutta leave in October 1944, I left my shoes on a train platform, but Paddy found them before an Indian could conveniently walk away with them, or in them. That the shoes were still there was a major surprise.

I'd wanted to buy some presents for my parents, and the time had come to indulge in a little smart spending. I scouted the market and found a Miss Lanchard, who was a well-known dressmaker and jewellery expert. She selected two towels and some material for me to send back to Mother. From here I visited the officers' shop, where I bought a pair of boots, sheets, towels and stockings. Later in the day I bought a Kashmir woollen tablecloth.

On the ensuing day, among other things we had our photographs taken at Bourne and Shepherd, one of the oldest established photographic businesses in the world. I ordered a large photographic etching of myself and six smaller ones.

When the time came to return to Digri we shared our rail carriage with a middle-class Indian who was recovering from a bad case of malaria. That worried us.

Back at Digri at 1100 on the following day, the fifteenth, Jackson drove over in a *gharry* and said that we had to go to Midnapore again to sign the Court of Inquiry documents. There in Midnapore we were introduced to a couple of nurses, but that went nowhere. Major Egan took us over to lunch at his Officers' Mess, where we listened to his thrilling stories of tiger shooting.

Having again returned to Digri I went over to the Station Sick Quarter regarding an infected burn on my arm. I hadn't the foggiest idea of how I'd burned the arm, but it hurt. A red line running up my arm was a sign of blood poisoning, I was sure, and an armpit gland was swollen. I copped heaps from our squadron's Medical Officer, Dr Tom Steele-Perkins, for not presenting earlier. He gave me a poultice of magnesium sulphate and a sling to immobilise the arm.

My arm was much better one day later, but I still had to wear the sling for another day.

MATT: Not only could Roy garner sympathy from those of his comrades who didn't poke fun at him, but having his arm in a sling relieved him of some of the physical duties he'd have otherwise been required to carry out.

ROY: To celebrate Jackson's 20 October birthday, we had a terrific party after my day of whitewashing the Officers' Mess. We debagged – pulled down the pants of – Squadron Leader O'Connor, one of our pilots and flight commanders, but despite fighting back hard he lost in the end. So did I, because I was kicked in the nose; it was only a temporary pain.

There was often a big nightly party. We were miles from everybody in Digri, so we couldn't bother anyone. Non-operational life on the squadron as far as I was concerned was mostly one big holiday.

The Boong and I continued our Officers' Mess renovations on the twenty-first, but now we wore flying helmets and goggles, looking like asbestos technicians. It was more so for protection than to act silly.

Nothing much happened on 25, 26 and 27 October. The Boong and I both had heavy colds, which we put down to working on our assignment. The Boong went on sick parade, but despite all of our whitewashing I felt well enough to do a different kind of painting: 'painting the bar' – enjoying drinks – with Ronny Mercer and Bill Waddington.

Though not aircrew, Dr Tom Steele-Perkins was one of the gang from the moment we met him. Doc (his moniker) phoned me halfway through one morning and insisted that I come down to be examined again regarding a lung issue I'd previously reported. Why, he wondered, had I not followed up with him already. Good old Doc. I abided and was re-examined shortly thereafter. Doc said my lungs were clear, so the inhalations I'd been practicing since my previous medical visit with him must have done some good.

Our kite was declared unserviceable again, needing a new number two engine, so my crew was in store for more down time. Because Zoot Beadon was flying, Jackson filled the role of Flight Commander, while I worked on cleaning my guns. The barrels were gleaming by the time I finished.

From typical use an awful lot of grease, oil, smashed insects and crud had marred the airframe, and this impacted flying efficiency and resulted in increased petrol consumption. To improve matters slightly we washed the kite with petrol.

In the afternoon I went for a walk across an adjoining paddy field. As I was moving along a narrow earthen levee separating rice cultivation patches this beautiful snake appeared almost out of nowhere. I gasped in sheer horror, and seemingly at the same moment the snake gasped at me with a similar expression of absolute horror. I started to turn back and flee for my life, instinctively, and

Mr Snake did the same. Not all slithery snakes were poisonous, but I certainly didn't want to find out what species this beauty was!

Monday, 30 OCTOBER 1944
(Roy flies on this sortie, but it does not count as an op)
INDIA – Exercise GLAXO *(including practice bombing and later mock bombing, both in daylight)*

On 29 October six crews were briefed for a lengthy training flight set for 30 October. I'd be second W/Op flying aboard Jackson's Liberator, KG830 'A', with Bing as the second pilot.

MATT: The flight, Exercise GLAXO, was designed to replicate actual operational conditions as nearly as possible in preparation for 215 Squadron's first real Liberator combat op. The plan was to release practice bombs on two specific ranges in India, at Jessore and Amarda Road, followed by a simulated attack upon the main railway station at Madras. The Liberator airmen were told to expect interceptions from both RAF and US fighters. This aspect would be akin to being back at 22 APC for Roy, except that there were no cameras on his bomber's guns.

ROY: On the day of Exercise GLAXO for once I was early for breakfast, arriving at 0400. My crew and I collected our flying rations and headed for our assigned aircraft, Liberator 'A'. With heavy petrol loads, needed for the lengthy flight, all six participating Liberators were airborne in darkness, starting at 0558. The planned route, all within Indian airspace, was Digri-Krishnagar-Jessore-Amarda Road-Madras-Digri.

At Krishnagar, eighty-three miles north-east of Digri, we divided into two V formations of three Liberators each and headed south-east forty-five miles to Jessore's bombing range. The target, however, turned out to be flooded, so with each Liberator still retaining four bombs meant to have been released there we headed south-west 165 miles to the Amarda Road bombing range.

Liberator 'C', with engine trouble, returned to Digri carrying all of its bombs.

At Amarda Road Pissy unloaded four practice bombs in daylight from 7,500 feet, with one hitting bang-on the target and the others falling close by.

The bomb aimer in 'F' released his practice bombs when Pissy did.

MATT: The load from 'F' fell slightly to the right. The bombs on another aircraft hung up. Two other Libs had planned to drop when this one released its load. Thus, no bombs were toggled from three aircraft. The squadron's show of force at the bombing range was unimpressive.

Five Liberators continued on to Madras to mock bomb the rail station. Due to excessive petrol consumption aircraft 'H' dropped out of formation after the simulated bomb run and landed at nearby St. Thomas Mount. This Lib returned to Digri the following day.

British and American fighters made three separate interceptions along the Liberators' route. The assaults were pressed home aggressively, minus gunfire, as the fighter pilots honed their attack skills. The Liberator gunners practiced defensive techniques.

At Krishnagar between 0650 and 0719 at 5,000 feet and soon after sunrise, five Hurricanes made mock attacks mainly directed against the three Liberators of the first vic, including Roy's aircraft.

In the Amarda Road vicinity between 0810 and 0840 at 7,000 feet approximately twelve American Thunderbolts mock attacked in a spectacular show from all quarters.

Finally, over Madras between 1235 and 1250 at 10,000 feet RAF Thunderbolts pressed home attacks from all quarters, both above and below the Liberators.

For all involved the mock fighter attacks were chaotic but realistic training.

ROY: Liberator 'H' claimed that a Thunderbolt had clipped its wing, but if it really happened no noticeable damage resulted. No doubt, however, the fighters were close.

For four Liberators, mine included, the long trip home from Madras to Digri – 815 miles in a north-easterly direction – still loomed ahead of us that same day. On this remaining journey, mostly flown over the Bay of Bengal, the gunners got in some welcomed air-to-sea practice firing, but things got shaky when a beam gunner aboard 'F' nearly shot our tail off. I saw a line of splashes just under our tailplane, and it frightened the hell out of Joe Marsh, our tail gunner.

The last of our four Libs (minus the two that had exited the exercise early) landed at Digri at 1908, after sunset. From the time the first bomber took off until this final aircraft was safely on the ground at Digri that same day a whopping thirteen hours and ten minutes had elapsed.

Tuesday, 31 OCTOBER 1944
(Roy does not fly on this sortie)
BURMA – weather reconnaissance flight to Preparis Island – *ABORTED*

MATT: On October's final day a single Liberator, aircraft 'V', set out from Digri in the morning darkness on a weather reconnaissance sortie destined for Preparis Island, Burma, situated off the coast of mainland Burma ninety-five miles south-west of the mouths of the Irrawaddy River.

The weather was moderate on the outward flight with local storms being encountered.

Engine trouble forced the aircraft to turn back to Digri in daylight while still on the outward flight, resulting in a reduced flying time of nine hours, but it counted as an op. Although a belt of severe thunderstorms was confronted during the return, the Lib made a safe return to Digri.

No ships or other aircraft were sighted on the sortie.

Chapter 9

215 Squadron, India: NOVEMBER 1944 *(Part 1)*

At Digri, Liberator bombing ops begin, and training continues

ROY: On Wednesday, 1 November, I'd just started censoring letters when the phone rang at Flights. I was the only one there. 'Stand by' was the incoming message. A panic ensued. In preparation for what I assumed would be a command to fly I ordered gunners to clean their weapons, check their turrets and perform a hundred other tasks. Then the phone rang again. The message: 'Postponed'.

After lunch Jackson, with Smithy, our flight engineer, as second pilot, flew to Dhubalia to pick up some lads from the squadron. In straight-line flying distance, Dhubalia was sixty-three miles north of the Howrah Bridge in Calcutta and eighty-five miles north-east of Digri. It was a good opportunity for me to meaningfully practice on the wireless. Apart from the mid upper turret Perspex caving in, it was a quiet trip.

With stretches of fine weather and with most of its men still new to the complex Liberator, 215 Squadron in November continued to focus primarily upon training, but the squadron's first five Liberator bombing ops were flown this month. The war wasn't put on hold! Two operations were undertaken during the first week of November.

Thursday, 2 NOVEMBER-Friday, 3 NOVEMBER 1944
(Roy does not fly on this op)
Vinh, FRENCH INDO-CHINA – aerodrome and shipyards *(first bombing op by 215 Squadron Liberators, and a rare night bombing sortie)*

MATT: For 215 Squadron's first Liberator bombing sortie seasoned skippers (with Bingham as one of the second pilots) took their four Liberators to Vinh, French Indo-China. First, they flew from Digri to Chittagong, an Advance

Landing Ground (ALG) across the Bay of Bengal 290 miles closer to Vinh. At Chittagong the Liberators topped off their petrol tanks. Then, taking off after sunset on 2 November, the four Libs headed through a cloudless sky for Vinh, 930 miles away.

Three Liberators located and bombed Vinh aerodrome. The fourth, unable to clearly recognise this primary target due to ground haze, attacked Vinh shipyards, causing a fire still visible fifty miles away on the return journey. The anti-aircraft fire encountered was meagre and ineffective, and all four Libs returned safely to Digri after sunrise on 3 November via Chittagong's petrol stop.

French Indo-China was a long way to go to drop only 1,500 pounds of high explosive bombs per aircraft, but this op established 215 Squadron as an offensive Liberator force. Scores of impressionable young men stood taller with pride when the aircraft returned to Digri.

From 215 Squadron pilot Wally Frazer's book, *A TREPID AVIATOR*, came a comment indicating the squadron's excitement: 'Action at last! Not for me, the squadron. Just four crews, but 215's first ever bombing trip in Liberators.'

Saturday, 4 NOVEMBER 1944
(Roy's first 215 Squadron bombing op, but the second op of his tour)
Insein, BURMA (Rangoon area) – Insein locomotive workshops *(daylight bombing)*

On 3 November a Battle Order was posted for what would be Roy's first actual bombing op on the fourth. Six crews would make the flight, and, among other things, the load for each Liberator was also predetermined: four 1,000lb bombs. The target would be announced at the 1630 briefing on the third.

Roy was listed on the Battle Order as second W/Op aboard Liberator KG831 'B', skippered by Grouse and with Bingham as second pilot. Roy would mostly man a beam gun as second W/Op. His crew of eleven would comprise a pilot, second pilot, navigator, bomb aimer, flight engineer (also a beam gunner), first W/Op, second W/Op (also a beam gunner) and four specialist air gunners – one each in the nose, mid-upper, ball and tail turrets.

ROY: On Friday, 3 November, Jackson, as Officer Commanding 'A' Flight, raced around preparing for this op, so I was left alone in the office with phones pealing and blokes hungry for gen. I issued jungle kits, knives and torches to each participating crew, and I drew oxygen masks and leads for our crew to ensure that they could use oxygen as needed.

All went well on our 1000 air test.

Later we went down to KG831 'B' and cleaned the Perspex. I shined Jackson and Bing's windows and also The Boong's astrodome.

The briefing for the op was thorough preparation for what lay ahead on the fourth, but admittedly we were a little anxious when we saw the target, the Insein locomotive workshops on the north-western side of, gulp, Rangoon – Burma's meanest destination!

MATT: A pre-op briefing for all of the airmen scheduled on a 215 Squadron op, essential before every combat sortie, was similar to cinematic depictions of RAF briefings. The target location, concealed on a curtained blackboard at the front of the room, was carefully secured to avoid potentially life-threatening information leakage. After the crews had been seated, they all rose to attention when the squadron CO entered the room, before retaking their seats. The CO, standing beside the blackboard, drew the curtains aside to reveal a map with a length of string representing the proposed track from their aerodrome to the target.

At each of our briefings a murmur would go around the room as crews reacted to this news; sometimes their pre-briefing speculation would be confirmed, but often the true location would come as a complete surprise. Learning that the intended target was a location with a dangerous reputation, like any target in Rangoon, Burma, typically elicited some gasping. Whatever the reaction, it was then hushed as the CO gave details of general interest.

He was followed by the navigation officer, signals officer, armaments officer and finally the meteorological officer – the 'met man'. The vagaries in the weather and the limitations inherent in forecasting conditions far away over enemy territory made this man's job difficult; behind his back he was still typically mocked for his inability to be accurate even more frequently.

The pilots were briefed (with all crewmen still present), then the navigators, then the W/Ops and the air gunners.

From Wally Frazer's *A TREPID AVIATOR* came this mention of Wing Commander James Sindall's 3 November 1944 briefing address as 215 Squadron's CO:

> The WingCo started the meeting with a little speech. I guess it was intended as a pep talk, but it didn't come over like that because Sindall

is more a low-key type, wouldn't go in for razzmatazz stuff. Mostly he just wished us good luck.

"For those going on your first operational flight, just remember you are well-trained crews flying an excellent aircraft that is exceptionally well-armed. If you remain alert…keep your wits about you…you should have no problems whatsoever."

A further excerpt from *A TREPID AVIATOR* provided some additional information from the briefing:

Sq/Ldr Beadon announced he had a surprise. "For the first time," he said, masticating the words in his very English accent, "bombers of 231 Group are to receive fighter support. RAF pilots flying American P-47 Thunderbolts – and another squadron of P-38 Lightnings of the US Army Air Force – will meet you, escort you into Burma."

For this scheduled daylight bombing op the target was revealed to be the locomotive workshops at Insein, eight miles north-north-west of the Rangoon docks.

Also scheduled on the same op were eleven Liberators from 355 Squadron and ten from 356 Squadron, both based at nearby Salbani.

ROY: Some minutes before a target the lead navigator would determine the wind's influence upon bombing. Over the intercom he'd then tell his W/Op, who'd radio the rest of the formation so that each crew's navigator could make proper calculations to ensure accurate bombing. If we were dropping all at once the other bomb aimers would release their loads when the leader's bombs dropped.

MATT: As previously explained, an essential part of accurate navigating involved understanding and allowing for the effect of wind on the aircraft in flight and then making appropriate course corrections, if any. Wind affected aircraft performance, not just bomb accuracy. Thus, wind analysis was undertaken not just prior to 'bombs gone' but also along the flightpath to and from a target.

ROY: Take-offs for Insein commenced close to daybreak at 0635 on 4 November. One of 215 Squadron's six Liberators scheduled for the raid,

KG969 'U', was held back due to engine trouble, but five Libs soon formed up and headed for the target.

MATT: On the approach to Burma 215 Squadron followed 355 and 356 Squadrons. The escort – nineteen USAAF P-38s and twenty-four RAF P-47 fighters – protected the bombers.

The Insein locomotive workshops were easy to pinpoint in relation to the neighbouring Hlaing River and to the notorious Insein Prison, whose main buildings were shaped like spokes in a wheel. (Insein Prison shouldn't be confused with the similarly shaped Rangoon Jail complex situated to the south and close to the Rangoon waterfront.)

Though the southern half of the target was obscured by smoke following the attack by 355 Squadron, 215 Squadron's five aircraft were able to add to the destruction anyway. Unfortunately, the bombs of 356's ten Liberators fell eight miles north of the target due to a malfunction in the lead aircraft's bombing mechanism. The trailing 356 Squadron aircraft, in formation, had visually bombed on the leader, as instructed.

ROY: The flak seemed dense; the official records put it this way: 'Many bursts moderate to intense H. A. A. all around formation, accurate for height and direction.' 'H. A. A.' was heavy anti-aircraft fire. It wasn't fun to experience! For a moment after one burst right under our tail I feared that Jock Smith in the ball turret had bought it. Thankfully he was fine.

When the bomb doors were opened I had a bird's eye view of everything below. Here and back on the starboard beam gun following 'bombs gone' I witnessed about seven enemy fighters after us from all directions, most likely single-engine Japanese Army Air Force Ki-43 Oscars and Ki-44 Tojos. The P-38 Lightnings and P-47 Thunderbolts worked feverishly to keep these fighters away from us.

I saw an enemy aircraft shot down by one of our fighters and a destroyed Oscar, confirmed as having been downed by a gunner aboard our squadron's aircraft 'D'. Bits appeared to fly off of another Oscar attacking us head-on when Paddy McCartney in the nose turret had a go at it. We spied an odd, greenish burst from another enemy aircraft. Back at base we were told that the enemy fighters were trying to hit the leading Lib with phosphorous bombs. Fortunately, this tactic failed.

One fighter swung around towards our rear from a three o'clock position. I wasn't nervous; it seemed like a game at first, not a life-or-death encounter. I saw twinkling little lights coming from its wings as he swooped in, and I distinctly remember thinking, 'Gosh, he's trying to kill us!' I had to stop shooting because our tailplane quickly entered my line of fire, and I didn't wish to damage our own horizontal stabiliser!

MATT: All Liberators from Roy's squadron returned to Digri by 1625, still in daylight, although skipper Wally Frazer's EW224 'P', having suffered a flat port tyre, went off the runway despite an excellent effort to land. 'P', consequently, was written off. Thankfully, its crewmen were uninjured.

All 355 and 356 Squadron Liberators came home to nearby Salbani, and the US fighters returned to their respective airfields.

Roy's bomber suffered a hole in the tailplane, though it wasn't his own doing.

A post-op report stated that the five Liberators of 215 Squadron had flown for forty-eight hours and twenty-five minutes, which averaged out to nine hours and forty-one minutes per aircraft.

Back at Digri, after ops, activities continue

ROY: I had little to do on 5 November except to clean guns. Our photos taken in Calcutta at Bourne and Shepherd had arrived, and I thought they were pretty decent. I decided that I'd send the big etching one back home.

The write-up of our Insein raid in Calcutta's newspaper, *The Statesman*, was quite good, and worth cutting out and preserving as a reminder of a milestone in my life and in the squadron's history.

MATT: The wording of the newspaper story was positive:

> LIBERATORS RAID LOCO WORKSHOPS
> OUTSIDE RANGOON
>
> The big railway workshops at Insein, seven miles from Rangoon [really just over eight miles from the south-facing Rangoon docks] on the line to Prome, were attacked today by RAF Liberators escorted by fighters of the 3rd Tactical Air Force, Eastern Air Command.

This was the first time in this theatre that a Jap centre has been subjected to major attacks on two successive days: the previous day Superfortresses made an attack (see full story on page 5).

This time, Jap defending fighters were more in evidence, and several were shot down. F/Lt Harry Whitbourn of Alton, Hants, [a 30 Squadron P-47 fighter pilot whose name was spelled 'Whidborne' and 'Whichborne' in other sources] got one Tojo fighter with a burst in the cockpit. A U.S. pilot got another; a formation of Lightnings got two more certain kills and several probables.

Fighter pilots say the Liberators flew in formation over the target through heavy flak, and their bombing was good.

The Insein works are the only plant in Burma capable of handling heavy repairs to locomotives.

ROY: On 5 November a big party came over from 159 Squadron, but I didn't feel like joining in on the entertainment.

Several times Jackson and a skeleton crew, but without me, flew in KG831 'B' with other 215 Squadron Liberators on practice bombing and formation flying exercises. The squadron was honing its collective skills as a fighting unit. As second W/Op I really wasn't essential on these flights over territory free of Japanese fighters, so I remained in the Flight Commander's office. I was plenty busy answering questions and doing odd jobs, such as preparing my report on the day's training programme. Zoot had made me the Joe for these daily reports.

I received a letter from my old friend from Hong Kong, Audrey Nash, tearing a helluva strip off of me for various things. I knew I mustn't fall out with Audrey, whatever happened.

I also spent a lot of time censoring mail – an awful bore, but which had to be done quickly, along with the daily reports.

MATT: From the eighth to the twenty-first a further period of specialised training was carried out, with objectives of ever-improving formation flying abilities and also of finding the best lead crews for formation attacks. Lead crews received intensive instruction over local bombing ranges, and towards the end of the period the 'full wing formation attack' protocol, frequently employed on actual operational sorties, was rehearsed with 99 Squadron.

ROY: On Friday, 17 November, Jackson and our crew in KG831 'B', including me this time, joined five other Liberators on another practice formation bombing and cross-country flight, this one being of three-plus hours' duration. Our machine took off at 0900. As second W/Op, and mostly just manning a beam gun, there was little for me to do on a flight where no fighters would be making runs at us. And so, I dozed.

For the next few days there was little on the agenda except training and censoring. On one of these days when out shooting with The Boong, I accidentally hit him with pellets. Fortunately, he was too far away to have been injured, but boy, was he mad. And was my face red!

On Tuesday, 21 November, with official work successfully accomplished (report writing, censoring a little mail and taking 'B' up on a practice exercise), I went for a walk back to our billet with Bing and another pilot, Dizzy Neville. We discussed the news of the day and straight gossip, including the rumour that 215 Squadron's move to Dhubalia might be imminent.

On an air exercise around this time we brought along a young ground crewman to give him a view of our world, as seen from above. The poor lad, removed from terra firma, got terribly excited. His response to going airborne in our noisy bomber reminded me of myself in earlier times.

Two of our Liberator's turrets had become inoperable on this flight, a mechanical issue which had to be remedied immediately. Lives might depend upon guns functioning properly over enemy territory.

While airborne over the Bay of Bengal I fired off some practice bursts. This meant that back on the ground I had the added responsibility of cleaning the gun. It was well worth it, because shooting a .50-calibre weapon in a safe environment was fun – a highlight of my day.

After our flight the crew chief in charge of our Lib's maintenance promised to eliminate our turret gremlins.

Bing and I dispensed standard escape and evasion packages to all participating airmen prior to flights. These kits contained survival aids to be used, if necessary, after crashes or bale outs. We turned in our own unused jungle kits after our flights, and we also collected the unused kits of any men who'd returned after being airborne on other Liberators.

Snippets of life on an RAF Liberator squadron in India

I mix up the locations of some 215 Squadron recollections, from either Digri or the squadron's future base, Dhubalia, but the following anecdotes relate to my time on 215, and they paint a picture applicable to either base.

Every day my crew and other acquaintances used to go down to Flights, near the runway. There was always flying going on. Flights was a little office where the aircraft captain would get status reports about his kite. It was really for the skippers, but all of my crew would often accompany our skipper there, and visits there kept us together, without us even realizing their value in benefitting crew bonding.

Winter nights could be chilly and mornings, too, although we often wore shorts on winter mornings. Ten o'clock on a typical winter's morning would be hot enough to remove one's shirt, and we were rich shades of walnut due to the climate. Winter was a beautiful time in our part of India with fabulous weather – usually dry, and with comfortable temperatures. But in the summer heat and in the monsoon season discomfort was frequently unavoidable.

Between the *bashas* and the Officers' Mess were roads, sometimes of dirt, sometimes all-weather. The road distance from our hut to the Mess was about 125 yards. Night-time navigation was by means of the Mess facility's illumination, or from 'the light of the silvery moon' (to quote from a popular song's lyrics). Most didn't bother to carry a torch.

Feral dogs called pye-dogs were around the camp. We encountered these ownerless wild dogs everywhere at Digri due to unrestricted breeding and the availability of food scraps. At night, in approaching the Mess, we'd first see one pair of eyes gleaming in the darkness, then more. They'd keep pace with us, but those 'in the know', like Doc, said they'd never heard of a dog attacking a human. Nor had I, but I didn't want to be the first. The silence of the dogs made matters worse. I'd stamp my foot and growl at them if they got too close, and they'd move off a bit. Lots of pye-dogs, maybe ten or more, congregated around the kitchen door and at the rubbish bins.

On occasion, pye-dog hunts were organised, but ridding the base of these animals was impractical.

Speaking of wild animals, one late night the CO announced that he was turning in after a card game in the Officers' Mess, and he bid a goodnight to all. By this point everybody was pretty drunk. Eventually, the Mess phone rang, and one player got up to answer it. In a panic the caller, identifying himself as the CO, said, 'Get over quickly! A leopard's eating a dog on my verandah!' The sceptical reply went something like this: 'Yeah, sir, good joke. Go to bed. See you in the morning.' More phone rings followed, eventually even threats, but in the end the phone was left off the hook.

The next morning blood and bits of flesh and bone were found all over the CO's verandah, and the CO was mad! I only heard about this. Certainly, a large cat fancying the CO as a meal would have had little trouble, because the walls were only about eight feet high.

That incident caused a bit of anxiety in the camp. After that, everyone wore his revolver. Normally, an airman would only carry his revolver on ops, but now, moving about the camp, the gun was worn for possible protection.

Perhaps four nights after the incident I was the last in our billet to head to dinner. It was pitch dark and quiet when I set off for the Mess. About halfway there, when under this large leafy tree, I heard a rustling above me. Taking out my revolver, I swore that this leopard would pay dearly if it came for me. More rustling followed, so I flashed the torch around the low-hanging branches looking for the reflections off of a leopard's eyes. Not seeing them, I took off.

Bursting into the Mess I shouted that the leopard was in a tree up the road, whereupon a crowd of half-smashed officers grabbed their guns and torches and raced for the tree. Somebody pointed out that with all our noise, the cat would now be 100 miles away, but I pointed out that if it was the same cat as the other night the CO's shouting had not fazed the creature at all.

Then somebody asked, 'Is this your leopard, Chico?' A cow was munching upon leaves in a nearby tree! I protested that it wasn't the leopard I'd seen, but I realized I'd only spotted this cow. I felt such humiliation, though I never came clean and admitted the truth!

Everyone wanted to get back to the bar, so nobody argued. In pitch darkness, already fuelled up with alcohol and with more Mess drinks beckoning criticism was almost nonexistent. The evidence did point to an aggressive, violent creature. Fortunately, it was never seen again.

There were also monkeys in the trees about the camp. Worth mentioning was another monkey-related incident involving myself. One day an officer from a neighbouring *basha* returned to his billet for something he'd forgotten. My crew's officers and I had taken a *gharry* to Flights from the Mess, leaving our *basha* deserted. As the airman departed his adjoining *basha* he heard loud chattering in the tree above him. He stared up at a huge monkey glaring at him, shaking branches in anger and acting as though it would come down after him. Heading back into his *basha*, he shut the flimsy door and waited nervously for the animal to lose interest.

After some time the chap came out when all seemed quiet and decided to leave, but the creature was still in the immediate vicinity. In reaction, the monkey again screeched and shook branches and leaves, once more appearing to be on the verge of attacking.

Having retrieved a rifle from my room next door, the airman again attempted to leave. This time the monkey, lower down in the tree, acted even more threateningly. Without aiming, the chap fired the gun at it and raced inside his *basha*. He heard the monkey hit the ground and assumed it was coming at him in the room, but there was silence.

He waited and waited. Finally, he poked his nose outside and found a dead monkey lying on the ground.

This is where it got serious, because it was a major offence to harm what Hindus considered sacred, yet here the airman was with the dead one that he'd shot and then dragged into a neighbouring *basha*. My *basha*. I got involved when he came to me and said, 'Chico, help me! I'm in big trouble. I've killed a sacred monkey!'

MATT: The Hindu legend of the sacred monkey traced back more than twenty centuries to an epic about Hanuman, the god of monkeys. In a battle of good versus evil it was said that Hanuman leapt from the coast of India to rescue his king's abducted queen from the island of Lankah (present-day Sri Lanka). Setting the island kingdom ablaze with his tail, Hanuman distracted the queen's captors and freed her. Hindus worshipped monkeys as a symbol of strength because of Hanuman's fabled brave deeds.

ROY: I asked the shooter, 'Where's the body?'

His reply was, 'I dragged it into your room.'

'Into MY room?' I replied, aghast at the thought of being blamed for its death.

We couldn't bury it outside the *basha* in daylight, so we waited until dark. Then, taking an arm each, we dragged it out from my billet and buried it in the scrub. Others knew what we were doing, and we endured remarks like, 'Can I have your big knife when you're taken away?' Was I glad when we successfully buried it. To my knowledge the Indian bearers never found out. We cleaned up the evidence – and it was almost as if we were tidying up after murdering a human.

One day at Flights when a fellow flung his jacket over his shoulder something hit the ground. It was a large scorpion, which scuttled around with its tail curved over its back. The venomous arachnid was killed. I wouldn't have liked being stung!

In the sky overhead there were always kitehawks – we called them shitehawks ('shite' being vulgar slang) – circling round looking for carrion. And there were also vultures. Both types of birds were sometimes seen on the ground consuming dead animals. I'd see a dead cow surrounded by vultures, and as I passed by, disturbing the birds, they lumbered along for a slow, cumbersome take-off. Occasionally, one would even appear from inside the carcass of a dead beast. Natural recycling, it was!

I recall another incident that was unpleasant for the victims but amusing and safe in comparison to the monkey escapade. Most crewmen entered a Liberator through open bomb doors. One had to bend down to clear the side before stepping up onto the girder that traversed the bomb bay lengthwise. Those at positions in the front of the aircraft – such as the pilots and the navigator – moved forward. To reach the ball turret, the beam guns, the rear turret and an area where aircrew sometimes mingled, an airman would move sternward.

There wasn't a proper toilet onboard, just the portable Elsan toilet – mainly used when sitting was necessary. One typically peed on the bomb doors, and in flight the urine would disappear through the area where the doors closed. Then the urine was blown away, harmlessly, in the slipstream. Normally. However, while in flight one day two or three of the crew, sitting back in the communal area, were sprinkled with 'water' until somebody realised what it was. Roars followed!

Chapter 10

215 Squadron, India: NOVEMBER 1944 *(Part 2)*

Some reflections on prepping for take-off, conditions aboard a Liberator, taking off, navigating and petrol issues

On the morning of a sortie we'd go straight to the aircraft by *gharry*. All the crew members would have had with them their necessary maps, or radio frequencies in my case – all the things we'd need to carry out our respective duties. Since we sometimes had to go great distances to reach our targets, occasionally our sorties would involve flying during both daylight and darkness.

Conditions inside the fuselage on the ground were fine in the cool of the early morning, but if we took off later in the day aboard a metal aircraft that had been standing in the sun for hours, the air inside was brutally hot, like, say, 65° Celsius (149° Fahrenheit). If the bomb doors had been in the closed position and then were opened to allow crew access, a monstrous mass of heat from within the fuselage enveloped anyone nearby. By the time the Lib reached 1,000 feet the temperature would typically be cooler.

Since we'd be going up in cooler conditions we had to have flying suits for warmth at the higher altitudes. To climb inside a Liberator and then to wait for take-off could be terribly uncomfortable. I've often wondered how tank crews endured the heat in the desert with the lid closed.

The Liberators taking part in the op would taxi towards the end of the runway and wait for a green flare signalling the OK to commence taking off in sequence. A Lib's pilot would run up the engines with the brakes fully depressed as a final check and then release the brakes to initiate the take-off roll. The Lib would thunder down the strip, with its crew inevitably praying that their aircraft would lift off and climb skyward.

Often trees beyond the runway were cleared by just feet. Kites did crash and blow up, and there were stories of Liberators returning with branches caught in their wheel housings during take-offs.

MATT: Sometimes bombers flew in formation, while on other occasions, such as at night or in poor weather, independent flight by individual aircraft was called for, to avoid the possibility of aerial collisions. Navigation accuracy was greatly enhanced by radio aids and by sun or star fixes. If possible.

ROY: For our longest ops, as appropriate, each Lib carried a large removable overflow bladder situated at the forward end of the bomb bay, in order to supplement the wing tank fuel load. A Liberator went into combat not exceeding the maximum take-off weight. Naturally, the fuel load limited the weight of bombs carried; a greater bombload meant that more destruction could be meted out, and sticking it to the enemy was our purpose. Of course, we needed enough fuel to get to and from a target with a little to spare for emergencies and atmospheric challenges.

Other recollections of life on a bomber squadron in India

At 1100 daily we eagerly greeted the *char wallah* (tea man) at Flights as he made his rounds. He'd have a pole across his shoulders with a brass canister at each end, one holding tea and the other a small charcoal fire, and we'd take our mugs of tea outside. The boiled water was safe to drink. We consumed this hot tea in often sweltering conditions, but it seemed to cool us down somehow. Additionally, it had the psychological value of focusing our thoughts on returning home in the future, when we could really enjoy our tea in peace.

The leopard and the large monkey incidents, previously mentioned, hit home because of the way my particular *bashas* were constructed at different postings, with walls made of thatch. These walls only went up maybe eight feet, and then there was open space to allow air flow. The door was thatched as well, meaning that scary animals like leopards and angry monkeys theoretically had a way in to grab human prey, yet such incursions were unknown to me. The roofs of all *bashas* were thatched, and it wasn't unheard of that snakes, even a cobra in one instance, made their ways into this thatch. I never heard of a man being bitten.

There was an incident when one fellow who used to sleep on his verandah woke one night to feel a hand coming under his pillow looking for his wallet. He grabbed at the hand but lost his grip on it, as it had been greased. After that the near-victim and his neighbours each slept with a revolver under his pillow. Days later the fellow again felt the hand pulling out the mosquito net. He quietly gripped his revolver, waited and then yelled and leaped out of bed with his gun. But he forgot about the mosquito net! He fell onto the verandah firing off a shot as he fell, but the wannabe thief got away; mosquito nets could be a hindrance at times.

RAF *gharries* would pick us up from various locations, including the railway station and, for me, a neighbouring squadron's Officers' Mess. The chaps coming back would sometimes be nearly paralytic from excessive drinking. The *gharry* would race down these dirt roads, and the occupants, swaying furiously from side to side, would sometimes be singing at the tops of their voices while hanging precariously onto whatever they could.

It's said that drunks can get away with things that would kill a sober person, and I was witness to one such incident. This chap, laughing and shouting as we raced along, was sitting at the back of the *gharry*. Suddenly, the *gharry* swerved, and he vanished over the back and into the darkness. The driver was alerted by a lot of shouting, but because of the noise and because the driver was probably a bit under the influence himself, it was some time before we got him to retrace his steps. We all expected a dead body, or a badly damaged one at least, but no, here came the 'victim' running along the track to meet us and killing himself laughing! With a happy ending it turned out to be great fun

Letters, our means of communicating with those who were far away, were terribly important to everybody. I wrote letters at the drop of a hat, all conforming to the rules of censorship, and it was marvellous to get a stack of letters when the mail came in. My parents were great at keeping me 'in the know' about people and places from my earlier life. In addition to sending me such details (and their heartfelt words) they were also diligent about sending food parcels, and news cuttings of our bombing missions. Some of my old Hong Kong friends, especially Audrey Nash and Enid Watson, and lots of other old Form 5 classmates from school there sent me correspondence. Even girls that I'd met in England – not girlfriends in the accepted sense, but just girls I'd met – sent letters.

Incoming mail kept me in touch with the rest of the world. In a faraway and exotic environment where I was isolated from real culture as I knew it, I was so grateful to receive this mail. I'm still grateful for their efforts.

Sunday, 26 NOVEMBER 1944
(Roy's third op)
Pyinmana, BURMA – railway station and sidings *(daylight bombing)*

MATT: From 21 to 25 November essential Liberator maintenance was prioritised following a period of recent concentrated flying. Three further ops were made during the month's last week. Roy was on two of them.

Twenty-two days after returning from his baptism of fire, literally, on an actual bombing sortie Roy saw his name again on a Battle Order – posted on 25 November – in advance of an op the next day. Once more Roy's crew, skippered by Grouse and with Bingham as the second pilot, would take Lib KG831 'B' into battle, one of twelve 215 Squadron bombers on the raid. The Battle Order also revealed that Liberator bombloads would vary slightly; four aircraft would release 5,000 pounds of explosives, four would toggle 4,500 pounds and four more would drop 4,000 pounds.

Reflecting upon his emotions as an inexperienced combat flyer then learning that a second bombing op loomed, Roy recalled that his anxiety was well under control. Far more telling of his state of mind was his strong memory of being imbued with a sense of purpose, determination and satisfaction; Roy knew that he was again being entrusted with the duties required of Liberator airmen.

ROY: On the previous day I'd checked the intercoms at the beam gun positions of 'B' and found that the starboard side electronics seemed damaged. The problem needed to be rectified quickly, as communication in the air could be the difference between life and death. I spent the morning of the twenty-fifth getting headsets for everyone in the crew, among other tasks.

Again, my intercom connection acted up. We weren't scrubbed from the op, though, and, to my delight, as soon as we took KG831 'B' on an air test the result was *theek hai* (Hindi for 'it's okay') and remained so for the rest of the test and for the op, too.

After tiffin (our midday meal) on 25 November and knowing Jackson's crew was on the Battle Order for the op we saw that all of KG831's turrets again performed beautifully, and we checked to ensure that the kite had been prepped with a full ammo supply.

The 1900 briefing on the twenty-fifth lasted only an hour.

MATT: It was learned at the briefing that in addition to 215's contingent of twelve Liberators being sent out to bomb the railway station and sidings at Pyinmana, Burma, a dozen Libs from 99 Squadron were also headed to Pyinmana.

Roy's squadron would bomb in formation.

ROY: I had the notion that the op would be easy, but this was impossible to know in advance. As I was new to aerial warfare against the Japanese, I had no basis for believing this; even seasoned veterans couldn't predict their futures with any certainty.

Bing and I distributed jungle kits at the briefing, and of course I retained one for my own potential use. I also took possession of a blood chit and money when these were handed out. I then went to bed in advance of a big day coming up.

MATT: A blood chit contained a British Union Jack flag and statements in several languages explaining that the Allied airmen's goal was only to drive the Japanese away as quickly as possible, not to harm the Burmese – his friends – and that the airman's government would reward whomever aided the downed flyer once the Japanese were driven away. The coins that were distributed to the airmen went into a money belt worn by each man. A money belt was a canvas strap about four inches wide divided into pockets and filled with silver rupees to be used for bribing the native Burmese into assisting an airman to escape should the flyer come down behind enemy lines.

ROY: Our twelve Libs safely took to the sky in daylight starting at 0816 on the morning of Sunday, 26 November. We'd bomb in four vics of three aircraft each in line astern formation. 'B' led the second vic of the formation with the CO, Wing Commander James Sindall, at the front in Liberator KG830 'A'.

MATT: Despite good weather 215 Squadron's attacking force missed a key identification point and the formation was a shambles. Some bombs fell west of the sidings, outside the target area, but many bursts were observed on the tracks and among station buildings. Squadron Leader O'Connor in KG970 'V' pranged the target well, down the centre of the railway yard.

ROY: One of the bombs from our vic blew up a truck with a terrific flash of red flame about fifty yards wide followed by much black smoke.

Wing Commander James Sindall, 215 Squadron's CO, rides Liberator KG830 'A' towards Pyinmana, Burma, on 26 November 1944 – Roy's third op. Conditions encountered are shown. Roy flew two ops and one long exercise on KG830. Sindall, the artist, left off some aircraft features, including the nose turret. The unit's unique rudder markings are absent; possibly the directive to paint stripes had not yet been received. (*Squadron Leader Tim Sindall*)

MATT: No enemy fighter opposition was encountered.

All twelve of 215 Squadron's Libs returned to Digri, with the last touchdown coming at 1719. The total time in flight for the bombers was 103 hours and twenty minutes, so each aircraft's average time aloft was eight hours and thirty-seven minutes.

99 Squadron's twelve Libs, on that unit's first Liberator op after converting from Wellingtons, also pranged the railway station and safely returned to their Indian base. It was reported by 99 Squadron that approximately 130 railway carriages, called 'rolling stock', were visible at the time of the attack.

The raid was later assessed as being a very effective operation.

A brief mention of the op was printed in the newspaper:

HEAVY BOMBERS
RAID PYINMANA

EAST AFRICANS PUSHING
ON KALEWA

KANDY, Nov 27 – Heavy bombers of Eastern Air Command yesterday attacked the station and sidings at Pyinmana, on the Rangoon-Mandalay railway, says today's SE Asia Command communiqué.

Roy's brush with death or serious injury

ROY: There was a fair bit to do on the morning of Monday, 27 November, the day after the op. I had to collect jungle kits handed out at the briefing before the op. I'm happy to say that none had been needed. Then there was my beam gun to clean. I surprisingly found that Smithy Smith had already cleaned my gun, but he'd left me his own beam gun to properly clean!

Around this time there was a flying incident where the potential for my death or maiming seemed as strong as from enemy action. On this day, date unknown, Jackson was screening a pilot. I was sitting and working at my Liberator wireless desk when Jackson called to me to look out the little window above my desk at something he could see in the sea.

I stood up and leaned over my metal desk in order to look downwards. After only a few seconds I became aware of the mid-upper gun turret starting to press into my back. At first I didn't pay much attention to it, because I was focused upon what I was supposed to see in the water, but then I became aware of mounting pressure. While the aircraft was flying the constant engine vibrations caused the turret to rotate gradually, and what was now pressing on my back was the metal ammunition box for the turret.

I couldn't move when I went to slide away across the desk, because the turret pressure was preventing it. I yelled and did everything I could think of to extricate myself from this trouble spot. It was very serious. The turret's movement caused by the judder of the Lib was slowly but surely crushing my spine.

The key to my fate lay with what the mid-upper gunner might do next. Should he turn his turret my way, my spine would undoubtedly fracture in the action. Just when I thought I was about to pass out he turned his turret the other way, and I fell on the floor.

Though it was a painful ordeal I avoided injury. I was very careful after that.

Tuesday, 28 NOVEMBER 1944
(Roy's fourth op)
Mandalay, BURMA – marshalling yards *(daylight bombing)*

I was listed on a Battle Order for the squadron's next op posted on 27 November, one day prior to the sortie. Warrant Officer Jack Hadaway would be my skipper, and again I'd be aboard KG831 'B'. Jackson, in the second pilot's seat to Jack's right, would act as screen pilot to ensure that Jack passed muster as a Liberator captain. The Boong and Pissy were pissed off (living up to the nickname of the latter) that they weren't on the Battle Order. Flying as second W/Op, I'd once again man a beam gun.

Nine Libs from our squadron would be sent out.

The briefing was at 1900 on the twenty-seventh. Knowing that I'd be a beam gunner, I worked on prepping those two guns and their ammo through the afternoon of the twenty-seventh, but I only checked the intercom performance at each crewmate's aircraft position on the way to the target the next day.

I sat at the briefing hoping that Wing Commander Sindall would reveal what I considered a good target. Wow! Was I surprised to learn that it would be a hotspot – Mandalay marshalling yards; Mandalay was said to be the toughest target after Rangoon. As with our last op twelve Libs from 99 Squadron would attack the same target, but 99's aiming point would differ slightly from 215 Squadron's.

The morning of the op on 28 November brought clear and cool conditions. Even at Digri's latitude at this time of year there could be relatively chilly temperatures on the ground in the morning, and it was even colder at altitude. Because we typically flew high to and from the target, I had a helluva pile of stuff to take along on the op, including a roll neck pullover. Additionally, my usual gear included knives, a parachute and its harness and an uninflated Mae West life preserver around my neck.

'B' took off in daylight at 0731, four minutes after the first of 215 Squadron's Libs departed Digri. The initial two hours of flight were routine – and boring. We climbed over Burma's Chin Hills, which are 10,000 feet high, and our Liberators looked wizard in formation in the clear bright sky. On oxygen above 10,000 feet I knew I wouldn't get the headache experienced on my first bombing op back on 4 November.

Our nine Libs neared Mandalay at 1100 in three vics of three aircraft each; the line astern configuration with one vic after another was the standard daytime bombing formation. In the excellent visibility I saw the enemy's usual smoke release, designed to obscure the target, when we were still ten miles away.

I perceived our squadron's bombing as being similar to its Pyinmana raid of two days earlier, in that we again blew up the station buildings but only put two sticks of bombs down the railway lines.

MATT: At least that's what Roy thought. One official summary later put it this way: 'A good concentration of bursts were [sic] obtained on the yard, in the vicinity of the station buildings, and amongst rolling stock, debris from which was seen in the air.'

Furthermore, the post-sortie report was quite specific about the accuracy:

KG831 'B':	Bursts seen down centre of sidings [Roy's Liberator];
Aircraft 'C':	Bursts seen believed just east of station buildings*;
KH214 'D':	Bursts seen believed east centre of yard, near station buildings;
Aircraft 'F':	Bursts seen east centre of yard. Rolling stock seen 'going up' from one stick down centre of yard*;
KH274 'H':	Bursts seen across sidings, near overbridge [This 'overbridge' was a structure above and over the northern end of the tracks.];
KH284 'P':	Bursts seen across main sidings and engine shed sidings;
EW284 'Q':	Bursts seen across centre of sidings and railway station. Two bombs believed to overshoot;
KG846 'R':	Bursts seen, extending down lines near station platform;
KG970 'V':	Bursts seen in western position of yard amongst rolling stock.

*The serial numbers and/or letter codes of the Liberators identified as 'C' and 'F' in the 215 Squadron ORB aren't certain. The official records contain conflicting information for the full identities of these two aircraft.

Post-sortie analysis of photos taken from Roy's aircraft determined that about three quarters of their bombs burst in the target area. Perfection was next to impossible to attain, even in the excellent flying weather of 28 November 1944 when no fighter opposition was encountered; 215 Squadron airmen saw only one fighter, which chose not to attack. It was certainly felt that 215 could improve its performance, but seventy-five per cent of bombs falling on the target seemed pretty decent.

ROY: We experienced meagre anti-aircraft fire over the target, but just beyond the target the ack-ack quickly became more accurate. Although the initial bursts were 1,000 feet below us, they soon came up to our height. I saw one heavy burst near KH284 'P', but the aircraft seemed alright at the time. In fact, only one Liberator suffered Category I damage – aircraft 'F', which reported slight shrapnel damage to bomb bay hydraulics; I picked up a message coming home reporting F's ack-ack damage. Its pilot made a fine landing despite having no brakes because F's hydraulics had been shot away.

MATT: The last of 215 Squadron's nine aircraft landed at 1458, long before sunset. Each Lib was airborne an average of seven hours and eighteen minutes.

The twelve Liberators of 99 Squadron, having all returned safely to Dhubalia, their home base, reported a heavy pall of smoke rising to 7,000 feet, visible up to fifty miles away. Their intelligence people assessed the results as being very successful.

Roy kept a news cutting that reported on this op:

MANDALAY RAILYARD
BLASTED

DAYLIGHT RAID BY
LIBERATORS

Japanese-used rolling stock concentrated in Mandalay railway yards, isolated by the destruction of bridges on Central Burma railway lines, were hit by RAF Liberators of Strategic Air Force, Eastern Air Command [the Strategic Air Force included the combined Liberator forces of the RAF and the US], in a daylight raid on Tuesday.

Crews found plenty of tracks and carriages waiting to be bombed and straddled the sidings with high explosives. Buildings in the station area blew up, and from one part of the yard there shot flames and a huge column of brown smoke, over 6,000 ft* high and visible 50 miles away.

"We caught plenty of rolling stock in the yards. I saw five or six trains and there were scattered trucks as well," said one tail gunner, Sgt Raymond Brown, of London.

"It was a fine sight to see one stick of bombs falling along a line of tracks. I don't know who dropped that stick but it must have sent the tracks up in the air," said Flt-Sgt B.A. Byers of Bournemouth, wireless operator in a Liberator piloted by Warrant Officer W.T. Tindall, of Slough (Bucks).

*7,000 feet per the 99 Squadron ORB.

Post-sortie snapshots taken at Digri

ROY: On Tuesday, 28 November 1944 I was photographed playing darts with two fellow Australians by a visiting Australian public relations officer for printing in newspapers back home. He also snapped a photo of eleven men, including me, at the bar in the 215 Squadron Officers' Mess.

Because 215 Squadron aircrew personnel included so many men from British Commonwealth countries, not just England, a notice over that bar read 'AUSTRALIAN SPOKEN, CANADIAN UNDERSTOOD, ENGLISH INTERPRETER AVAILABLE'. In fact, the English officers started a 'Free English' movement as a lark. They wore 'Free English' flashes on their shoulders when in the Officers' Mess.

MATT: Propped up on the bar was that sign, seen in one of the 28 November photos. In the image Roy and ten of his mates, some with tankards, were obviously enjoying themselves. The group consisted of one officer from Calcutta, four from Australia, one from Fiji (with Australian roots), one Canadian, one South African, two from Wales (including Taffy Humphreys, the NCO barman) and one from the UK (who was a leader of the 'Free English' movement). Participating in style with the officers, Taffy was a member of the 'Free Welsh' movement.

Among those in the photo was Roy's then-skipper, Jackson Grouse, who was approaching the end of his 215 Squadron tour of ops.

Roy's parents back in Australia were thrilled to see the photo in the newspaper. Pictures, it's said, are sometimes 'worth a thousand words', and the images taken on 28 November strongly hinted at the camaraderie among the men.

Also at Digri, post-sortie

ROY: On Wednesday, 29 November – the day following the Mandalay op – I still faced a chore: cleaning my beam gun.

MATT: The weapons were potential lifesavers in a scrap with the enemy, and the importance of keeping a gun in great working order was drilled into Roy during gunnery training. Though cleaning a .50-calibre Browning consumed a little bit of time, it was well understood that it was a necessary responsibility. The end result was of undeniable benefit not only to Roy but also to his crewmates and even beyond that to all 215 Squadron airmen.

ROY: Regarding Brownings, I also had a positive chat with Bill Wright, our mid-upper turret gunner. We thought alike. Some air gunners didn't quite comprehend the big picture, but Bill did.

Walking into the Officers' Mess late for lunch on 29 November, I got a helluva shock. Seated with the CO were two wing commanders (one an air gunner), an air vice-marshal and three squadron leaders. I had a long talk with the Public Relations Officers.

Thursday, 30 NOVEMBER-Friday, 1 DECEMBER 1944
(Roy does not fly on this op)
Three FRENCH INDO-CHINA targets – shipyards at Vinh, military camp at Vinh Yen and Gialam aerodrome in Hanoi *(night bombing)*

MATT: On 30 November-1 December four crews, not including Roy's (and not Roy individually, either), again put 215 Squadron's stamp on faraway French Indo-China in a night-time attack. Starting from Jessore, not Digri, again they used an ALG across the Bay of Bengal to reduce the distance flown to the target when fully fuelled and bombed up. Their Liberators carried more than triple the payload dropped by four aircraft on the 2-3 November French Indo-China raid.

A detailed briefing was held at Chittagong (the ALG) on the thirtieth.

Two Libs bombed Vinh shipyards, just over 1,100 miles away from Jessore. A third Lib attacked a Japanese camp at Vinh Yen, about 1,060 miles from Jessore. Releasing its load on an estimated position due to ground haze and low clouds, and unable to see the camp, this crew feared that its Liberator's bombs undershot west of the camp. The fourth aircraft opted to abandon Vinh Yen, instead hoping for better conditions over Hanoi's Gialam airfield, the secondary target twenty-five miles to the south-east. Haze and drifting low clouds were a major hindrance there as well, and though the runway was targeted through gaps in the clouds, the bomb bursts couldn't be pinpointed.

After refuelling at Chittagong 215 Squadron's four Liberators safely returned the nearly 290 miles to Digri.

Hardly a legendary raid, it and the early November Vinh-area bombing emphatically reminded the enemy that to the Allies the 'Far East' had, in essence, become more like the 'Not as Far East'.

Chapter 11

215 Squadron, India: DECEMBER 1944 *(Part 1)*

Friday, 1 DECEMBER 1944
(Roy's fifth op)
Mergui, BURMA – jetties, docks and adjacent stores areas *(secondary target in Mergui),* after an unfruitful search for the primary target *(a naval convoy near Mergui) (daytime bombing)*

Roy joined a crew as part of a four-Lib assignment on 1 December destined for the Mergui, Burma, area.

ROY: On November's final day at Flights a posted Battle Order notified all that Jackson would be on the 1 December op, but for his second consecutive sortie he'd fly as second pilot, this time aboard EW285 'C', known as *Clarence.* Again, he'd screen official skipper Jack Hadaway. I chased Jackson up and tried to be added to the crew for this op, but the crew list, I was told, was set, so I couldn't go. This really browned me off, and I showed my displeasure, but my antics initially came to nothing. Still, I was responsible for preparing and distributing jungle kits, one for each of the forty-four men on the Battle Order.

As for me flying on the op, I didn't take no for a final answer, and eventually I convinced Zoot to let me join the crew of EW285 'C'. Only three of my regular crewmates would join me on 'C': Jackson, Jack Hadaway and Jock Smith. I would be flying as second W/Op.

I whizzed down to 'C', soon to take me for a ride, and I ensured that the guns were harmonised and checked. The briefing at 1700 this same day excited me; I knew that the op would be a humdinger. It was learned at the briefing that our target would be either Japanese shipping near Mergui (lower Burma) or else, failing to find any shipping, the jetties, docks and adjacent stores areas of Mergui itself.

It would be at least a fifteen-hour trip, and it didn't sound at all healthy. The wisecracks zinged in my direction were along the lines of, 'Go in your oldest clothes, and I'll have what you leave behind.' Such talk was typical, but it was all in jest among my uniquely close-knit brothers in arms.

With our squadron's four participating Libs scheduled to begin taking off at one minute after midnight on 1 December, supper was two hours earlier. All aircraft departed Digri safely and proceeded towards the target independently.

As usual the first five hours aloft were boring as hell. In good weather we flew across the Indian Ocean and down to Preparis Island, situated between the northern tip of the Andaman Islands and the mouths of the Irrawaddy River on mainland Burma. From there we set course to the south-east across the Gulf of Martaban towards Mergui and Burma's southernmost expanse. By skirting the Burmese mainland we avoided flying over enemy territory for many hours, both when heading to the target and in returning; when clear of the Indian coast water was below us almost all of the time.

Being dark for the first few hours of flight, it was impossible to read, and on the flight deck there was no room to settle down to sleep comfortably. Just before dawn I went back to my beam gun and tested it, with fine results.

Once we reached the general area assigned to us we wandered about in search of Japanese warships, but despite our diligence not one was found. We spotted small native coastal vessels, which I wanted to attack from close range, but Jackson and Hadaway wouldn't take *Clarence* down to the deck for a squirt or two; instead, we had a secondary target to attack, so we climbed to 6,000 feet and beelined for Mergui town.

Just before the flak started I took a photo of the aerodrome with a hand-held camera provided for intelligence gathering. What little ack-ack did come our way seemed frighteningly accurate – more so than I'd previously witnessed. The official records called it 'meagre to moderate' light anti-aircraft fire, but to me the potential seemed plenty deadlier than was implied by these words!

We weaved about the airspace over Mergui before prepping for the drop as the third of the four Libs to attack. With 'C' in a shallow dive in the early morning light our bomb aimer, Warrant Officer J.M. Clifford, toggled our load, striking a red-roofed building, followed by a huge burst of flames seen ascending skyward. The building was a petrol and ammo dump with Japs living on top. Boy, did we prang it! Smoke was still visible twenty miles away on the return journey.

MATT: Roy's aircraft and the three other 215 Squadron Libs bombed at different times and heights. KG846 'R', the first Liberator over Mergui, released 1,800 pounds of explosives at 0705 from 3,500 feet. Next came EW176 'G' (which dropped 2,100 pounds of bombs at 0734 from only 1,800 feet), then Roy's Lib (which also dropped 2,100 pounds of high explosives, toggled at 0806 from 5,000 feet) and, finally, KH274 'H' (which, like 'R', only released 1,800 pounds of bombs, at 0859 from 5,500 feet).

(The serial number for 'H' was mistyped as 'KH214' in the official pre- and post-op records.)

ROY: While heading back to India in the full light of day one of our engines went on us. We thought the intense vibration, which led to the engine's shutdown and its prop's feathering, was associated with a damaged rudder control, but we held our own on three engines and returned safely. The other three 215 Squadron Liberators also safely reached Digri.

MATT: The last of 215's Libs landed at 1539. The four bombers each averaged fifteen hours and twenty minutes in the air.

US 7th Bomb Group B-24s, also actively on the prowl in the area on this day, were tasked with specifically searching for a large Imperial Japanese Navy vessel reportedly off the coast near Mergui. Despite a dedicated search they, too, found no obvious large vessels, spotting nothing more than a few small coastal ships and fishing boats. One American bombardier said, 'We sighted the Japanese Navy, and they threw down their paddles and swam like hell.'

The Americans also returned home safely.

Saturday, 2 DECEMBER 1944
(Roy does not fly on this sortie)
Bay of Bengal, near BURMA – Air-Sea Rescue search *(daylight)*

Skipper Wally Frazer led his ten crewmates on a one-Lib ASR search for survivors of a missing American B-29 Superfortress, 42-24452, of the 45th Bomb Squadron, 40th Bomb Group, that had gone down while returning from a Bangkok, Thailand, raid.

Sadly, there were no sightings. The eleven-man Superfortress crew was never found.

Back at Digri

ROY: I started 2 December, the day after the Mergui op, very tired, but I still had duties to attend to, including gun maintenance. I'd found that the crew that had borrowed our regular kite, KG831 'B', for the 30 November-1 December trip to French Indo-China had left it in good trim after the op. However, I had to chase up the rear gunner to properly clean his guns.

An Australian war correspondent visited the Officers' Mess on 3 December. Dressed in tweeds he seemed a fine type and was full of honesty. We all enjoyed his company, and the Australians were especially pleased to hear about home.

Zoot tore a strip off of us for being late getting down to Flights on 4 December. Those being chewed out disliked being treated in this manner, and at the time Zoot's barking reminded us of an angry headmaster unreasonably scolding schoolkids. On further reflection I realised that 215 Squadron, like any unit, functioned best when everybody meshed together and owned up to his responsibilities. Those who were supposed to be down at Flights at a set time but weren't were, indeed, at fault. Zoot treated us that way in order to knock some sense into us. In retrospect I came to admire the man even more for doing what he undoubtedly knew wouldn't win a popularity contest.

Later in the day I returned to another of my responsibilities as a 215 Squadron officer – the censoring of outgoing mail. There wasn't much volume of correspondence to wear out my eyes this time.

MATT: A Battle Order for a bombing op to Hanoi, French Indo-China, staging out of an ALG (presumably Chittagong again), was posted on 3 December. A preliminary briefing was held at 1430 on the third, and a final briefing was planned for the morning of 4 December at the ALG. However, due to unsuitable weather conditions this four-Liberator sortie was cancelled. Roy and his crew had not been earmarked for the op.

Tuesday, 5 DECEMBER 1944
(Roy's sixth op)
Imphal, INDIA – Exercise EARTHQUAKE II *(daylight bombing)*

ROY: My crew and I were notified on the afternoon of the fourth that we'd be heading out on an exercise on the following day, but the briefing wouldn't be until the morning of the flight. I knew from the Battle Order, posted on

Monday, to start preparing for action and to take it easy on alcohol intake, as did the listed crews of twelve other Liberators. Included was one crew from a backup Liberator on reserve to replace, if necessary, a Lib experiencing problems before, during or soon after take-off.

MATT: Per the Battle Order Roy's eleven-man crew would be flying aboard their trusted regular Liberator, KG831 'B', skippered by Grouse, their usual captain. W.G. Abbott (Bopp the W/Op), their normal first W/Op, was away from Digri, so Roy would slip into Abbott's role. Replacing Roy as the second W/Op and manning the starboard beam gun as needed/if needed would be Flight Sergeant Byers. 'B' would be carrying twelve 500lb bombs.

ROY: The specific details of this flight would be laid out at the briefing on Tuesday morning, but the participants were informed on Monday that this flight wouldn't be a true bombing operation against the enemy. Instead, it would be a sophisticated training flight to Imphal, near the India-Burma border.

MATT: Being in an active war zone, where Japanese aircraft could conceivably make an appearance, it counted as an op, not just as another training flight. Imphal is legendary in British military lore as one of the sites (Kohima being the other) where British and Commonwealth forces had persevered when besieged by the Japanese earlier in 1944, and where parachute-dropped resupply by air forged a new chapter in modern warfare.

ROY: Airmen from the thirteen Liberator crews listed in the Battle Order were also told on Monday that the exercise would entail up to seven and a half hours of flying. When I heard this, although it wouldn't be an attack against the enemy, I nevertheless felt that a drink or two could benefit me, so, joined by a mate, I indulged, but in moderation.

The briefing for Exercise EARTHQUAKE II was held at 0830 on 5 December. Twelve 215 Squadron Libs would head to a point ten miles north-east of Imphal, roughly three and a half hours from Digri, in an experimental bombing attack upon an 800x200-yard area on two small hills set up to mimic a front-line Japanese position. Our Libs would be separated into bombing formations. The object was to discover, in cooperation with the British Army, the effect of close pattern bombing upon a given area characterised by various types of defensive positions protected by earthworks. A stretch of ground had been prepared, and at our briefing each formation was assigned a separate and precise aiming point.

MATT: Although Grouse was listed on the Battle Order as Roy's skipper, in command on the actual op would be Bingham, normally their second pilot, to gain further valuable experience prior to taking over the captaincy when Grouse finished his tour of ops. Grouse would be alongside Bingham on the flight deck in the second pilot's seat.

ROY: Twelve Liberators took off into a bright daylight sky, starting at 1055; the reserve crew and Lib weren't needed.

As first W/Op I spent almost the entire time on the wireless set, which functioned smoothly from the start. For the attack upon my formation's specific target I went back to peer downward through the open bomb bay doors and watched as our bombs were released. They looked good going down. Bombs from other Libs were also reported to have fallen satisfactorily, with one exception – the screwed-on tail unit from a solitary bomb released from KG830 'A', the lead aircraft skippered by Wing Commander Sindall, detached from its bomb and hit our kite on the way down. It didn't appear to have done any damage, but, hell, it scared us!

MATT: The area was well-covered by bursts, and army officers observing the experiment expressed satisfaction with the results.

No enemy aircraft were seen – a pleasant realisation, no doubt.

The exercise ended safely for all twelve 215 Squadron Liberators; the last Lib touched down at Digri at 1822, after sunset. Each aircraft averaged seven hours and fifteen minutes aloft.

Twelve Libs from 99 Squadron at Dhubalia and American Libs from the 7th Bomb Group also safely participated in Exercise EARTHQUAKE II.

ROY: Bing did very well in taking on the mantle of aircraft captaincy; Jackson's help wasn't required.

Back at Digri

To our great disappointment Pissy, our much-admired bomb aimer, was posted to No. 6 Refresher Flying Unit (6 RFU) at Kolar, the home of 1673 HCU. We'd miss his old face like mad. In the evening of 5 December, after returning from Exercise

EARTHQUAKE II, Keith Palmer and Ray South, both warrant officers, and some other NCOs were invited to the Officers' Mess bar to both celebrate Pissy's time with us and to lament his departure. We even got old Zoot to stand on his head while drinking a beer! It was a good send-off for our cherished friend.

Bill Wright tried to get me to clean Smithy's beam gun on the following day, the sixth, but I wouldn't play.

Before dinner that evening Jackson brought our new bomb aimer, 'Nick' Nicholas, to the Officers' Mess to say hullo. Nick was RAF and seemed a nice guy – and on the quiet side. I don't think that he'd done any ops yet. We had a few drinks with him as a goodwill gesture. The consensus among us was that Nick would do us proud. He did, as we were to find out.

Thursday, 7 DECEMBER 1944
A toilet block burns and

Friday, 8 DECEMBER 1944
(Roy does not fly on this op)
THAILAND –Thailand-Burma Railway locomotives and rolling stock between Ban Wang Yai and Kanchanaburi, plus the railway station at Kanchanaburi and a nearby stores area *(daylight bombing and strafing)*

It was announced on 7 December, the third anniversary of the Japanese attack on Pearl Harbor, that an op was on for the next day, with a 1900 briefing scheduled for the seventh. However, my crew wasn't on the posted Battle Order, and this made me mad as hell. Zoot seemed to be going on more than his share of ops, meaning that it would take longer for my crewmates and me to complete our individual 215 Squadron tours. And as learned at the briefing this op would be long, at over thirteen hours, adding a nice chunk of time to the tally of op hours flown for any airman involved.

Our kite, KG831 'B', was being taken by Warrant Officer Tindall, so I cleaned some of the aircraft's guns in readiness for his crew.

Something disgusting, and frightening, really, prompted me to ask to be appointed Officer in Charge of toilet blocks around this time in early December. Cockroaches and spiders were constantly emerging from the toilet hole beside us; I hated this like you wouldn't believe. Our enemies weren't just the Japanese! My wish was granted, and at 1100 on that Thursday I did the trick that would make me famous, or perhaps I should say infamous – I burned down our toilet block! Consequently, I'd forever be associated with 215 Squadron latrines.

I sent a sergeant down to the Motor Transport Section for some petrol to burn out the cockroaches, spiders and other creepy crawlies. He was told that they couldn't spare the petrol but had suggested that we use 100 octane fuel instead, which he'd collected from the Aircraft Section. The lads in the Motor Transport Section told him that it would be safe if done quickly, before the fumes had accumulated. At my youthful age it never occurred to me that the Motor Transport boys would play such a dangerous trick on us. So, I said to the sergeant, 'I'll pour, and you throw down the match quickly when I tell you.'

I poured as quickly as I could, the match was thrown and...

BOOM!

I flew back, hit my head on the wall behind me and collapsed semiconsciously on the floor. When I collected my wits I saw the sergeant lying motionless on the floor and the roof blazing. I raced over to him and found that he was OK, and we got the natives going with a bucket brigade.

It was useless. The palm leaf roof was beyond saving.

I decided that I'd better tell Wing Commander Sindall, so I wobbled over to the Officers' Mess, where everybody was having a pre-meal drink. They all burst out laughing when I appeared, which I couldn't quite understand.

The CO asked, 'What the hell have you been doing? Look in the mirror over there.' My reflection revealed scorched hair, burnt eyebrows and black marks on my face and clothes. I tried to explain it all, but the tale only set everybody laughing again.

There was now no roof on our officers' toilet block, and I had to endure the complaints that the officers using the latrine would all get sunburned bums! A couple of drinks eased my embarrassment, though.

MATT: Despite Roy being the brunt of the jokes the comic relief would have done a world of good for men stuck out in the middle of nowhere in the boondocks of Bengal, India, for an indeterminate stretch of time, and with little opportunity for distraction from the very serious business of waging war against a hated enemy.

ROY: Ah yes, the war and 215 Squadron's contributions to bringing it to a victorious conclusion for the Allies! Back to my story of flying and fighting, which was why we were in India in the first place.

Having been shut out of the op of 8 December, my crew missed a terrific one: bombing the Thailand-Burma Railway – the vital Japanese supply route located far to our south-east. It might seem odd that we actually wanted to go on the op, but that's the way most of us were wired.

MATT: Here's what Roy missed.

Nine 215 Squadron Libs took off in daylight from Digri starting at 1002. In the last ninety minutes of daylight in good weather Libs from the squadron attacked locomotives and their trains along a stretch of the notorious Thailand-Burma Railway, built by Allied PoWs and native Asian labourers under brutal conditions. The squadron's assigned segment of the railway in Thailand stretched from Ban Wang Yai to Kanchanaburi. The secondary target, also attacked, was specifically the railway station at Kanchanaburi and a nearby stores area.

Between 1622 and 1744 the nine Libs attacked from low altitudes. Three of the Liberators struck the secondary target. Two of these three also joined in attacking locomotives and rolling stock along their prioritised stretch of railway.

Great damage was reported due to the bombing and to the strafing by Liberator gunners. At Kanchanaburi a large fire started by the bombing was seen from forty miles away on the return flight until the hills obscured the view.

The opposition from Japanese anti-aircraft fire, including rifles, was considerable; two unspecified 215 Squadron aircraft were holed by bullets.

If there were injuries suffered on the 8 December op, they were unreported in the 215 Squadron ORB, and certainly no airmen were killed.

Per the ORB one attacking 215 Squadron Liberator opted for a Chittagong landing to refuel, while the other eight squadron aircraft headed directly home. All nine Libs, averaging thirteen hours and forty-four minutes of flight time per aircraft, returned safely to Digri, with the final participant noted as having landed at 2336.

Roy's compadres at 99 Squadron sent out twelve Libs to attack rolling stock, installations and sidings along a different stretch of the Thailand-Burma Railway than that assigned to 215 Squadron. B-24s of the American 7th Bomb Group's 9th, 436th, 492nd and 493rd Bomb Squadrons also attacked Thailand-Burma Railway targets on this day. Like 215 Squadron, neither 99 Squadron nor the Americans suffered any deaths.

Sunday, 10 DECEMBER 1944
(Roy's seventh op)
THAILAND – Thailand-Burma Railway locomotives and rail wagons at three sites: Milestones 174, 175, and 176¾ *(daylight bombing and strafing)*

ROY: On 9 December, my crew learned that we'd be on an op again, set for the following day.

MATT: They would fly aboard the reliable KG831 'B'. The Battle Order presented this welcome news to Roy and his crew, with Grouse named as skipper and Bingham as second pilot. Roy would be mostly manning a beam gun back in his assigned role of second W/Op. 'B' would be loaded with six 500lb and four 100lb high explosive bombs (3,400 pounds – same as one other aircraft, but seven other Lib would carry less bombs). Overall, the nine 215 Squadron Liberators were scheduled to carry bombloads ranging from 2,600 pounds to 3,400 pounds.

ROY: In discussing the beam guns with Bing it was decided that I should fire both guns as needed; this was thrilling to me. Jackson, however, reversed the decision. Our flight engineer, Smithy Smith, would still be responsible for the port gun, while I'd still only be on the starboard Browning. I wondered why some people couldn't leave well enough alone, but Jackson, as the Liberator captain, had the final word. It made sense, but I wouldn't admit it at the time.

Before our midday meal I cleaned and harmonised both beam guns ahead of our op.

MATT: The airmen listed on the Battle Order learned target and other specifics at the 1900 briefing that evening. Nine 215 Squadron Liberators were detailed to repeat the operation of two days earlier, the object being to cause further disruption of the Thailand-Burma Railway in Thailand. The Libs of 215 would wreak their low-level bombing and strafing destruction along the same stretch of railway between Ban Wang Yai and Kanchanaburi that was previously attacked by the squadron on 8 December.

They would be one of two RAF Liberator units on the raid, the other being 99 Squadron, which would put up eleven or twelve bombers – the records conflict – to attack separate targets of opportunity along the same railway. The RAF would be joined by US 7th Bomb Group B-24s seeking their own Thailand-Burma Railway targets.

In good weather 215 Squadron's take-offs commenced at 0832 in daylight on 10 December. Grouse hit the Burma coast at 1500, and aircraft 'B' eventually arrived at its designated stretch of rail line to begin its beat-up.

ROY: It didn't take long to find a train, at Milestone 174. This first one, which we came upon at 1534, was carrying timber to repair the line. We bombed it in two passes, each time in a forty-degree dive from about 1,800 feet. I got a wizard burst of gunfire in, and so did Joe from the rear turret. As we pulled away at 1538 after our second pass one railway wagon was in flames, and steam spewing from the locomotive was clear-cut proof that we'd damaged it.

I made repeated calls to Jackson about an ack-ack gun blazing away at us from a nearby compound, but the intercom intermittently cut out every time I tried to speak on it, so I had to stop. The enemy forces, fortunately, were lousy shots, as we were flying so low – well within range of the guns.

MATT: At Milestone 175 Roy's bomber attacked another train laden with timber, again in two passes during which bombs were released from about 1,800 feet. The first Milestone 175 attack was at 1543 in a shallow dive, while the second pass at 1556 was made in a steeper forty-degree dive. As with the train at Milestone 174, guns aboard 'B' strafed this second train thoroughly, and much steam was seen to be escaping from the locomotive as the Liberator departed – resulting, they believed, from both the bombing and the strafing.

They still had bombs remaining aboard. At Milestone 176¾, KG831 came upon five diesel locomotives, including one in a shed, plus numerous railway wagons camouflaged with nets strung between the trees. 'B' attacked in two passes, at 1600 and 1604. On each pass Roy's Lib bombed in a shallow twenty-degree dive from 1,800 feet. Although it was difficult to ascertain all of the bombing results, it was obvious that 'B' had meted out some serious damage. In addition, Roy and his fellow gunners on 'B' strafed the diesel locomotive in the shed, causing smoke to rise from the shed's roof, and they also strafed the camouflaged railway cars, obtaining strikes but not causing a fire.

ROY: After leaving the railway line for the return to base we found that one of our wing petrol tanks had been holed, and we were losing fuel. The self-sealing membrane surrounding the tank closed up and stopped the petrol leak, but still we'd lost vital fuel. Everybody was very pleased – make that relieved – when calculations showed that we could safely reach Chittagong in Allied territory on the east side of the Bay of Bengal.

A bullet had also passed through the aircraft just behind where I'd been standing during part of the attack. On this op I fortunately wasn't in the wrong place at the wrong time; although KG831 was hit, things could have been far worse.

Our wireless went out on the way back from the target spoiling the trip from a W/Op's point of view.

MATT: At Chittagong, after assessing the battle damage to their Liberator, Roy's crew opted to take on some more petrol and to return to Digri to complete the sortie that same day.

By the time the last 215 Squadron Liberator landed back at Digri at 2312, each of the nine participating aircraft from the squadron, including Roy's, had averaged fourteen hours and seventeen minutes in flight.

The damage to 'B' was severe enough that it had to leave 215 Squadron for repair. It later joined 356 Squadron and flew as their aircraft 'C' until downed by flak off of Moulmein, Burma, on 27 May 1945.

ROY: The plight of the CO's Liberator, KH314 'L', involved the loss of a life. Japanese defensive fire resulted in Category II damage to the aircraft, and at Kanchanaburi, Thailand, the rear gunner, Sergeant George Day, died after being hit in the head by shrapnel from a small-calibre shell fired from the ground. The Lib made a safe landing back at Digri.

KG970 'V', skippered by Flight Sergeant T.C. Brooks, also suffered Category II damage, and its flight engineer, Flight Sergeant Cyril Geeson, was hit in the leg by gunfire. He recovered but never flew another op with 215 Squadron.

MATT: (On 26 July 1945, while attached to the Air Fighting Training Unit at RAF Amarda Rd, an airfield where Roy's crew had taken a course the previous year, Geeson died when his Liberator, EW247, collided with another Lib, EW225, during formation flying training in poor weather.)

Certainly, Japanese opposition on 10 December was heavier than two days earlier, with defensive gunfire being experienced on the tenth at many points along the routes taken by the attacking Liberators. Yet the op of 10 December was deemed a success despite the death of Sergeant Day, Flight Sergeant Geeson's injury and extensive damage to Roy's Liberator.

From 215 Squadron's ORB came this assessment of the harm inflicted by the squadron's nine Liberators and also by the enemy on 10 December:

> …still more congestion was found on the railway, and 13 different objectives were subjected to 31 separate bombing and straffing [sic] attacks. At least 5 locomotives received heavy damage, and 3 Diesel-Truck Locomotives were well shot up, in addition. Four trains were set alight, and one of these was seen to explode violently almost an hour after the original attack. KANCHANABURI RAILWAY STATION

> and Stores Area was again attacked by 2 aircraft, bursts being seen amongst rolling stock on the tracks, and in the stores area, with a direct hit on one building. The opposition was even heavier on this occasion, machine gun fire being experienced at many points along the railway. 3 a/c [aircraft] were hit, two receiving heavy damage. F/Sgt Geeson, Flight Engineer of a/c 'V', was wounded in the leg at M/S 179 [Milestone 179], and at KANCHANABURI, Sgt Day, Rear Gunner of a/c 'L', was killed by shrapnel from a small-calibre shell, fired from the ground.

The Libs of 99 Squadron sent out on 10 December hunted along the same forty-mile stretch of railway in Thailand that they'd searched two days earlier. Thanbyuzayat, Burma, at the north-western terminus of the Thailand-Burma Railway, was the target for US 7th Bomb Group B-24s from the 9th and 493rd Bomb Squadrons, while the American 7th Bomb Group's 436th and 492nd Bomb Squadrons attacked Phadaw, Burma, railway facilities fifty-one miles down the Thailand-Burma Railway line from Thanbyuzayat. However, due to poor visibility and despite dedicated practice the 9th and 492nd Bomb Squadrons misidentified their targets and instead bombed Anankwin, Burma, another legitimate railway-related locale.

As on 8 December, no Allied aircraft were lost, a fact that nobody ignored. Recognising that each RAF and US Liberator returned to its home base, even those that were damaged (like Roy's KG831), was one way of putting a positive – a realistically positive – spin upon what happened on 10 December, yet there was also solid reason to mourn, because of one death and one battle injury.

Following the liberation of Allied PoWs mistreated in the construction and maintenance of the Thailand-Burma Railway, 215 Squadron's CO during its Liberator period, Wing Commander James Sindall, received a letter from Ken Porter, a PoW from New Zealand who'd witnessed Liberator bombing attacks from below. Ken wrote:

> Naturally we were all scared when bombs began to fall and some blokes' nerves were in a bad state already, but I personally, and some of our mates, welcomed the sight of those big birds floating over seemingly all powerful and indestructible, as this was the first real sign to us that the Allies were now on the offensive and the end was in sight.

> Perhaps just as well we never knew you were flying down from India but imagined you were using captured bases around Rangoon or thereabouts, a few hundred miles away. When I lay on my back in a shallow monsoon rain outside our hut by the Kwai bridge, the adrenaline surged, and I thought, now these bastards are getting some of their rain back.
>
> The great thing was that you appeared just when morale was at an all-time low and gave us a much-needed boost, so I feel we are indebted to you.

From a short newspaper cutting came this coverage of the 10 December 1944 raid:

> A Press Note says: Flying at fighter-bomber altitude, B-24s of the Eastern Air Command in daylight on Sunday strafed and bombed the Burma-Siam Railway, the vital 300-mile supply line linking Bangkok and Moulmein in South Burma. Two locomotives and many rolling stock were damaged while considerable damage was done to tracks over a seventy-mile stretch between Bang Kasl and Ban Kao, both in Thailand.
>
> It is thought that a bottleneck may have been created on this important route, which carries a considerable part of the Japanese supplies from Bangkok over the Burma-Thailand border to Rangoon and the Burma fighting fronts.

Onward, further into DECEMBER 1944

The personnel of 215 Squadron grieved over the death of George Day and the injury to George Geeson on 10 December, but they also understood that unpleasant human losses and injuries were likely to befall them; flying could be tense and sometimes deadly to the attacking force.

All things considered, however, the squadron's airmen emerged from their initial period of Liberator flying in good order. In fact, many rated 215's results to date as triumphant. The odds had been in their favour, and they'd continue to approach their roles with a no-nonsense understanding of their responsibilities and the need to ever-improve. The members of 215 Squadron would savour their lighter moments, too; a balance was essential for sanity and positive health.

ROY: I heard on Tuesday, 12 December that fellow Aussie Norman Harrison, a Liberator skipper on 99 Squadron, had 'gone for Burton' – died – on a 3 December 1944 raid. His Lib, EW286, collided with another 99 Squadron bomber, KG973, over the Andaman Sea off the southern Burma coast on the way to bomb the Hnong Pladuk, Thailand, railway station.

MATT: At the time, twelve Libs from 99 Squadron were in the process of tightening their ranks after a sea crossing in very loose formation before heading inland towards the target. All twenty-two men aboard the Liberators were killed. Even though, in this case, the victims were from another Liberator squadron, learning of such losses would have been sobering for everyone on 215 Squadron, because they certainly realised the thin line between living and dying.

ROY: Another acquaintance, 355 Squadron's Flying Officer Jimmy Ingham had also been in a tight spot, but, thankfully, he came home.

MATT: Ingham, a second pilot, survived an ordeal where a crewmate, an air gunner, died. On a cross-country exercise over India on the night of 5-6 December 1944 Ingham's Liberator, KH164, suffered engine trouble and couldn't maintain altitude. All twelve crewmen aboard the Lib successfully parachuted out after the 2230 bale out signal had been given, but one, Sergeant Kenneth Hackers, died in a fall upon releasing himself from his parachute harness while dangling from a tree. The other crew members, widely scattered, landed in wild, hilly tree covered country. Reunited, they reached 355 Squadron in a few days after travelling by elephant, bullock cart, lorry and train.

Wednesday, 13 DECEMBER 1944
(Roy does not fly on this op)
Twenty-one miles west of Bangkok, THAILAND – Nakhon Chaisi River railway bridge busting *(daylight bombing)*

The Battle Order for an upcoming op scheduled for 13 December included Bill Wright from Roy's regular crew as a gunner but not Roy or the remainder of his crew. It wasn't unusual for an air gunner from one crew – in this case Wright from Roy's crew – to fill in for an air gunner from another crew who was not flying the op, sometimes due to illness or injury, or, among other reasons, because the regular air gunner was away on leave. Wright took the opportunity to join another crew on 13 December, when, once again, his regular crew (including Roy) was left out of the action.

ROY: I tried every way to get added to the operation, but none of the regular W/Ops or second W/Ops from the eight crews chosen already for the raid were away from Digri, out sick or injured or had cancelled out of the op for another reason. I wouldn't be going.

I was late arising on the morning of the op, so I missed the *gharries* taking men down to the aircraft. Wanting to see the take-offs, I began walking. It was my good fortune that Dr Tom Steele-Perkins, our Medical Officer, picked me up halfway there, also affording me the opportunity to watch the start of the op from the vantage point of Flying Control.

MATT: The briefing for the op had been at 1900 on 12 December. The bombloads for the eight Mk VI Liberators would only average just over 2,200 pounds per aircraft.

Take-offs commenced in daylight at 0932 the following morning. The op was a formation bombing attack on a railway bridge, No. 286, across the Nakhon Chaisi River located in Thailand halfway between Bangkok and the eastern terminus of the Thailand-Burma Railway.

One aircraft turned back early, at 1140, with engine trouble and landed in daylight at Digri with its full bombload aboard, but the seven other 215 Squadron Liberators forged onward to Thailand and bombed the bridge in misty conditions.

No major bridge damage was observed.

Although one single-engine fighter was spotted no enemy aircraft attacked.

The Libs that bombed the bridge returned to Digri for safe night-time landings by 2326. No airmen were killed or injured on the op.

The elapsed time from the first take-off to the last landing was thirteen hours and fifty-four minutes.

And so, 215 Squadron's third successive op to a railway target or railway targets in faraway Thailand was in the books. Each of those ops involved a round trip of over 2,000 miles. Certainly, Roy would have loved to have been part of all three flights, but he was only able to be on the sortie of 10 December. He still had a long way to go to complete his tour of operational flying.

DECEMBER continues to roll along at Digri

ROY: Around this time I received a letter from a woman I knew back in England who was in a bad emotional way after being attacked by a fellow while walking. She asked me to come back to England to help her recover and insisted that her influential father would arrange for my transfer. I had to explain to the poor girl that I was in a war, that I was a member of a Liberator crew and that it wouldn't be right to abandon my position and go back. I knew that she'd been bashed up quite badly, and it really hurt me to say no. (I still feel the same today whenever the memories arise.)

The Maintenance Unit delivered our new aircraft, serial number KH324, to replace KG831, which had been damaged on the Thailand-Burma Railway op of 10 December.

MATT: When the squadron handed over KG831 – a 'B'-coded aircraft – for repair, that same ID letter was quickly reassigned to KH324. Grouse's crew then still 'owned' aircraft 'B', although its serial number identity had changed.

ROY: On the fourteenth we took our new 'B'-coded Liberator on a training flight. The Libs of 215 now also carried unique squadron identification markings: twin horizontal rudder stripes.

Officers' Mess work occupied my time all day on 14 December. Zoot wanted the task finished by the next night, but only with a concerted effort could this goal be reached. When Ned Kelly came over for arvo tea – that's Aussie slang for afternoon tea – we had a general gripe session, especially in regard to one of the navigators.

On the following day only a few Mess bearers were present. Several of our personal bearers assisted these sweepers and *pani wallahs* (water bearers) in cleaning up. All of the personal bearers were wanted in the Mess, but with one of them leading a strike they refused to do the Mess cleanup. We did OK without them. By lunchtime most of the cleanup had been accomplished, and only the floor was left to be washed and scrubbed. Zoot was very pleased, and so he should have been.

Chapter 12

215 Squadron, India: DECEMBER 1944 *(Part 2)*

Saturday, 16 DECEMBER 1944
(Roy does not fly on this sortie)
INDIA – Exercise GUINNESS *(flown mostly in daylight)*

Exercise GUINNESS, a group training flight involving twelve 215 Squadron Libs, was set for the sixteenth, but neither myself nor my crewmates were called upon to participate. The briefing was at 1700 on 15 December.

MATT: Take-offs began in daylight at 0833 on the sixteenth. The purpose of the flight, all within Indian airspace, was to practice long distance daytime formation flying, long-range fuel management and cross-country navigation. As one of the four Liberator units on this exercise, 215 Squadron joined forces with 99, 355 and 356 Squadrons; each RAF squadron put up twelve aircraft. Forty-eight Liberators set out from three Indian airfields: Digri (215), Dhubalia (99) and Salbani (355 and 356).

The route flown by the 215 Squadron Libs was from Digri to Nagpur, then onward to Poona, Bombay and Bhopal before returning to Digri. The participating Liberators made simulated bombing attacks on the railway stations at Nagpur, Poona and Bombay, and practice bombs (only two 11½ pounders per each 215 Squadron Liberator) were dropped on Bhopal's bombing range. One wonders what the citizens below thought as they saw so many Libs lining up to overfly them.

The 215 Squadron Battle Order for this sortie listed the amount of petrol, 2,984 gallons, carried by each of its Liberators – indicative of a long flight – but times aloft (for individual aircraft or for the interval from the first take-off to the last landing) weren't then noted in surviving 215 Squadron records. However, the surviving logbook of 215 W/Op Jack Johnson, who flew that day, indicates that his Liberator's flight was exactly thirteen hours in length. The existing logbooks of four other airmen on the exercise that day (three from

355 Squadron and one from 356 Squadron) reveal flight times varying from thirteen hours to thirteen hours and fifty-five minutes. Clearly, the exercise required extensive time in the air.

The long exercise went well. Because it was not near enemy territory the hours flown didn't contribute to the completion of a participating airman's tour of ops. The training, however, had a healthy purpose, and though a fair amount of it could be seen as being tedious it made its participants better at their craft. And it was flying, which the air force men tended to just plain love – if the aircraft, the weather and the Japanese cooperated, that is.

Based on logbooks and knowing that all twelve of 215 Squadron's participating Liberators returned to Digri, it's safe to assume that each returning aircraft landed in the dark after being airborne for thirteen to fourteen hours. Other than two of the forty-eight Liberators, all bombers returned safely to their home airfields. The two exceptions were 99 Squadron's KG881 and KG972, each of which was abandoned in flight by its crew due to fuel starvation.

Only one airman, 99 Squadron's Sergeant Morris Taylor, was injured out of all who flew on Exercise GUINNESS; Taylor, the flight engineer aboard KG881, was hurt after baling out.

Meanwhile, on the ground with 215 Squadron at Digri

ROY: Shag Shaw and I had the idea of going down to Midnapore to try to get WAAFs (members of the British Women's Auxiliary Air Force) to come over for a party. Zoot, who thought our plan was excellent, offered the suggestion that nursing sisters might be keen on a fun-filled distraction in a land where such opportunities were far too few. Apparently, the CO didn't hold my latrine pyrotechnics of 7 December against me, as I was named Officer in Charge of the ladies' lavatories for the upcoming visit.

On Saturday, 16 December, Shag, Ned Kelly and I, not involved with Exercise GUINNESS, made a stab at rounding up interest among the ladies. We first took a *gharry* to Midnapore to try and organise some WAAFs and nursing sisters, and then we continued down to Kharagpur to interest even more girls in joining us for the party.

We only succeeded in getting four girls, but Zoot, also ground-bound and not on the exercise, had already arranged for ten to come from Midnapore in his *gharry*. The boys who'd participated on the day's Exercise GUINNESS were back home in the evening, and while there was no Guinness Stout to drink, any liquid refreshment, especially of the alcohol variety, was much desired.

I really liked one particular girl at the party, but while I was away Warrant Officer Curly O'Connor moved in on her. He told me to go away, but I reminded him he couldn't pull rank on me in the Officers' Mess, so he left. (I don't know if what I said to him was true, though as a flying officer – two ranks above O'Connor's NCO rating – I did outrank O'Connor, and it worked).

At midnight we took the visiting girls back to Midnapore and then Kharagpur, another few miles to the south, and I turned in at 0500. It had been a wizard night.

Bing and Zoot got into a scrap that night, though over what I haven't the foggiest notion.

MATT: Learning that one's second pilot had been in a spat with the Flight Commander wasn't the most reassuring thing for Roy to awaken to. Details were kept close to the vest, so concerned fellow airmen could just hope that it was nothing more than a noisy exchange between dedicated professionals with maybe too much alcohol in them and that no long-term negative consequences would result.

Monday, 18 DECEMBER 1944

(Roy flies on this sortie, but it does not count as an op)

INDIA – Exercise GUINNESS, Round Two *(flown mostly in daylight)*

Roy and his crew learned in the Battle Order posted on 17 December that they'd be in on Exercise GUINNESS, Round Two – the next day's near-repetition of 16 December's exercise. Again, four Lib squadrons would join forces on the eighteenth for a combined group navigation, formation flying and bombing exercise, but forty, not forty-eight aircraft, would participate this time. The 1700 briefing on the seventeenth was followed by take-offs by eleven 215 Squadron bombers the next morning starting in daylight at 0830. Aboard Roy's Lib, their new 'B', KH324, Bingham did most of the piloting from his position in the left-hand seat while being groomed by Grouse (flying as second pilot) to replace him as aircraft captain very soon; the end of Grouse's tour of ops loomed.

ROY: Bopp the W/Op started on the wireless, but I – the second W/Op – took over at 1100 and came off at 1700. The audio reception was scratchy, which made for more attentive listening when we worked the wireless equipment.

At Poona The Boong acted as our Fighter Control when Hurricanes made mock attacks.

MATT: Roy affirmed that the fighter affiliation training was always fun, even if being thrown around the sky stressed both the men's psyches and the physical parameters of the Liberator. The thrills were a shot of adrenalin to most airmen, who knew that they were far from enemy territory. Thus, the fear of being blown out of the sky or injured by incoming Japanese firepower and the worry of falling into enemy hands were absent.

ROY: At Bhopal's bombing range the efforts of the Libs brought forth good results in the simulated formation attack – except for our aircraft, that is; a mechanical glitch led to the bombs hanging up. Our new kite otherwise served us well; we approved of a few new gadgets.

My time aloft aboard KH324 'B' for Round Two amounted to eleven hours and fifty minutes.

MATT: The logbook of 355 Squadron navigator Roy Hill, whose Liberator took off from Salbani airfield less than thirteen miles south of Digri, revealed a flight time of twelve hours and thirty minutes.

Because 215 Squadron's ORB stated that the exercise was repeated 'exactly as on the 16th, December, 1944', presumably Roy's Liberator touched down at Digri in the dark; there were no times given in the ORB.

Only one of the forty participating aircraft, from 356 Squadron, failed to complete the full exercise, landing safely at Nagpur, India, on the return flight instead of at Salbani.

A squadron relocation is imminent and a latrine burns

As Christmas approached a directive reached 215 Squadron: to relocate from Digri to Dhubalia, but with minimal impact upon flying assignments. A move to Dhubalia – the rumour for the past month – became a reality in December, to nobody's surprise. As previously stated, Dhubalia, an existing aerodrome, was located sixty-three miles north of the Howrah Bridge in Calcutta and eighty-five miles north-east of Digri, both in straight-line distances.

The other Liberator unit sharing Digri with 215 in the latter days of 1944, 159 Squadron, had moved from Digri to Dhubalia in early March of that year but only remained there for about five weeks. Although there were numerous problems at then-underprepared Dhubalia, it was one issue above all others that forced a return to Digri after little more than a month. In their condition Dhubalia's taxiways and hardstands were unable to take the weight of fully bombed-up Liberators. A move by 159 Squadron back to Digri was deemed essential.

Eight months later it was 215 Squadron's turn to play musical chairs. Some improvements had been made at Dhubalia since 159 Squadron's departure, and it was already the home of another RAF Liberator unit, 99 Squadron, which had settled there in September 1944. Like 215 Squadron, 99 had converted from twin-engine Wellingtons to four-engine Liberators in 1944, and 99 had begun flying Liberators on bombing ops from Dhubalia on 26 November, before 215's move there.

However, there was still an issue with the Dhubalia concrete's ability to bear the weight of 99 Squadron's Liberators – the very issue that had led 159 Squadron to abandon the airfield back in March 1944 – as noted in 99's October 1944 ORB:

> The hard standings and taxi tracks in the 'A' Flight area gradually broke up and eventually became u/s [were deemed unusable or unserviceable]. 'A' Flight was therefore moved to the other side of the runway.

The first phase of 215 Squadron's move, an Advance Party, arrived at Dhubalia from Digri on 19 December to immediately begin preparing the new headquarters and the technical and domestic sites for the squadron's use after Christmas. Their task was made more difficult by the lack of essential furniture and suitable accommodations.

Like 99's ORB, the 215 Squadron ORB in December 1944, prior to the unit's relocation, also noted the issue of inferior hard surface construction at Dhubalia:

> Some anxiety was felt as to the safety of the southern dispersal site to be occupied by 'A' Flight, pending construction of new hard-standings suitable for heavy aircraft.

Many problems encountered at Dhubalia by the Advance Party were eventually dealt with. It was understood that given time Dhubalia would come to be accepted as 215 Squadron's home. It had to be, as there would be no return to Digri.

The Advance Party's work was well-choreographed by 215 Squadron's leaders; those men not participating in the initial move activities still waged war against the Japanese from Digri.

ROY: On the evening of the twentieth the Digri Officers' Mess had some senior visitors, including the top RAF man in India, Air Marshal Sir Guy Garrod, South East Asia Command's Air Commander-in-Chief. Digri was rarely visited by the high and mighty, as it was off the beaten path and hardly a garden spot!

Also that evening a session over in the Sergeants' Mess finished with their latrine going up in flames.

MATT: Had Roy started a new trend? No. He was told that there was already a tradition of setting latrines alight, and it was recognised that he wasn't the leader of the pack when it came to torching latrines. Take for example a prank gone awry on 159 Squadron early in 1944 before Roy was even in India. It resulted in a latrine bonfire, which infused merriment into the normally drab existence of life in rural Bengal, India. While dancing around the burning latrine that night young men spontaneously broke out into the bawdy song, 'PLEASE DON'T BURN OUR SHITHOUSE DOWN', singing:

Please don't burn our shithouse down
Mother is willing to play
Father's been run out of town
And Nell's in the family way.

My brother dear has gonorrhea
Don't make us shit in the rain
Little Bill has diarrhea
And he wants to go there again.

Please don't burn our shithouse down
For times is fucking hard
And if you burn the damn thing down
We'll have to shit in the yard.

— Anonymous writer

The date of a similar occurrence at nearby Salbani is uncertain, but it equates to one of the monsoon seasons. The following recollection came from 356 Squadron ground crew member Frank Tinsdale per the 355/356 Squadrons Association history, *SIGNED WITH THEIR HONOUR*. Because 356 Squadron had been at Salbani since just prior to the 1944 monsoon, the year of this incident was either 1944 or 1945:

> One night, having had their monthly beer ration, they were singing one of their favourite songs – title [sic] 'Please don't burn our shithouse down'. One of their number, Paddy Corcoran, vanished. Across a monsoon ditch behind their hut stood the latrines – a double row of open cubicles under a thatched roof. As they finished the last chorus of their song, they noticed a glow coming from the latrines. Paddy returned with a big grin on his face.
>
> Trooping outside they watched his handiwork as the thatch over the latrines blazed fiercely; being late summer the thatch was bone dry. They were still standing outside, singing the song over and over again when the station fire brigade arrived. The brigade could not get their Jeep across the monsoon ditch and stood there helpless. The Group Captain in charge of the Wing arrived in his Jeep – he was livid! Deciding he could not put them all on a court martial, he left instruction that no rebuilding would take place until after the monsoon was over. For three months they had to squat in torrential downpours cursing Paddy and his unbalanced sense of humour!

ROY: Regarding the torching of 215 Squadron latrines, a guard was actually mounted at the entrance on either Christmas Eve or New Year's Eve 1944 to prevent another latrine fire. What happened, however, was that someone approached the guard and said hello. Once inside the latrine the mystery individual tucked a long piece of furry string up into the roof, tied a piece of paper to the other end of the dangling string and then walked out after lighting the paper. The flame then crept up the string to the roof, and to the guard's astonishment the roof caught fire. By that point it was really getting out of hand.

I was very annoyed decades later to hear some actor recount this story on the BBC and claim that he started it all. Not that I'm proud of 215 Squadron's legacy of burning shithouses, rather the reverse, but that actor was a bloody liar.

Thursday, 21 DECEMBER 1944
(Roy's eighth op)
Taungup, BURMA – storage dump, Area '3' ***(daylight bombing)***

MATT: Still based at Digri 215 Squadron had an op coming up on the twenty-first, announced a day earlier on the posted Battle Order. On that document Roy found his crew, including himself as second W/Op, assigned to Liberator KH324 'B' with Grouse as skipper and Bingham as second pilot. The briefing for the op would be held at 1900 on the twentieth.

ROY: In advance of the op I had guns to clean as usual. I was pleased to discover that ammo had previously been loaded onto KH324. Our ammo was always rationed; my .50-calibre beam gun, for example, was only allotted 300 rounds for this op. We'd be carrying a load of 8,000 pounds of bombs like all the Liberators on the sortie, consisting of four 1,000lb and four 500lb high explosive bombs and also 2,000 pounds of incendiary clusters.

MATT: The amount of machine gun ammo allotted to each Liberator prior to an op took into consideration weight, the distance to the target, the type of op (low-altitude strafing called for more ammo if the distance to the target allowed), the types of machine guns on the participating Liberators (mostly .50 calibre but an ever lessening number of .303 calibre guns in the rear turrets) and the decreased enemy fighter threat.

Revealed at the briefing 215 Squadron would put up twelve Libs for a daylight attack upon a Japanese supply dump at Taungup, close to Ramree Island in the Akyab district on the west coast of Burma. The squadron would be joined by RAF Liberators from 99, 355 and 356 Squadrons and B-24s from the US 7th Bomb Group. With several dump areas in Taungup the aiming points varied. Specifically, the plan was for 215 Squadron's bombs to single out the dump identified as Area '3'. It would be a big show, indicative of the growing might of the Allied juggernaut.

ROY: The twenty-first started early for those of us on the op. Breakfast at 0300 was followed by the first 215 Squadron aircraft departure at 0533. 'B' took off at 0545, and with sunrise coming just after 0700 the initial stretch of our flight was in darkness. I snoozed for the first one and a half hours; Bopp the W/Op handled the radio equipment on the way out.

My mate, Dizzy Neville, was flying as skipper Steve Brodie's second pilot, but their Lib, EW176 'G', reached the rendezvous point early and failed to join up in formation with the other 215 Squadron aircraft as designed. Instead, Brodie went in with another squadron assigned to bomb a dump neighbouring ours. That move was hardly ideal, although 'G' broke away upon arrival and bombed Area '3', as ordered, at 0927 from 6,500 feet in the same minute that 215 Squadron arrived; despite the missed rendezvous the Brodie crew's bombs were still 'gifted' to the Japanese at Area '3'!

MATT: The other eleven 215 Squadron Libs, including Roy's 'B', had formed up, line astern, into three vics of three aircraft, and with the final duo bringing up the rear. Inland from the coast by about six miles 215's target was readily identified by key geographic landmarks: telltale roads, Taungup *Chaung* – the waterway that divided the town and flowed into the Bay of Bengal – and the bridges over the *chaung* (stream).

In good weather conditions 215 Squadron's formation bombed between 0927 and 0930 from altitudes of 7,000 and 7,500 feet.

ROY: From my perspective the bombing seemed wizard, but because of the column of smoke and dust rising from the dump it was hard to see the extent of the damage.

Skipper Shag Shaw's KG969 'U' was hit by incendiaries dropped by KH352 'M', the Lib skippered by our CO. Suffering damage, 'U' had to opt for an 1120 emergency landing at Cox's Bazar on three motors (number three engine was shut down), a propeller that couldn't be feathered, no hydraulics, no intercom and a damaged nose wheel.

MATT: Everyone aboard KG969 survived, although the damage to the Liberator was rated as Category III with the airframe 'reduced to spares', meaning that it would be cannibalised for spare parts to repair other machines.

Located north-west of Taungup on the eastern coast of the Bay of Bengal just over 300 miles from Digri, Cox's Bazar was the Allied aerodrome nearest to Taungup.

The last of the eleven Liberators returning to Digri was safely on the ground in daylight at 1317. From first take-off to this final landing and not counting 'U' at Cox's Bazar the op's length spanned seven hours and forty-four minutes – it was a relatively short one.

No enemy anti-aircraft fire from the ground or from airborne fighters was encountered.

Twelve Liberators from 99 Squadron, twelve from 355 Squadron, twelve from 356 Squadron and B-24s from the US 7th Bomb Group also bombed the Taungup area dump without loss or injury.

ROY: After the post-op analysis of bomb-strike photos had been made, an angry group captain told us that 215 Squadron had completely missed its assigned supply dump target, Area '3', and that instead the main concentration of bombs had fallen on Area '4'. Our designated target, admittedly, was difficult to find.

MATT: Certainly, however, 215 Squadron, bombing in formation, clobbered a Taungup supply dump. Also one of the 215 Squadron crews saw flashes on the ground suggestive of ammunition exploding. Still, the photos didn't lie, and 215's bomb aimers could and would improve.

The next phase of the squadron's relocation from Digri involved a second Advance Party of only thirteen men who travelled to Dhubalia by road on 22 December.

Saturday, 23 DECEMBER 1944
(Roy's ninth op)
Taungup, BURMA – storage dump, Area '7' *(daylight bombing)*

On that same day, Friday, 22 December, as soon as Roy and his crewmates arrived at Flights (still at Digri) they saw their names on the Battle Order for a raid the next day. Grouse, on the final scheduled op of his 215 Squadron tour, would again take the second pilot's seat, as he did back on the eighteenth, giving Bingham another valuable spell as aircraft captain. This would continue the process of grooming Bingham to succeed Grouse as skipper. Roy would embrace his usual role of second W/Op.

ROY: According to the posted Battle Order my crew was assigned KG830 'A'. This was because our usual Liberator, KH324 'B', was in for a routine inspection.

MATT: The Battle Order called for twelve 215 Squadron aircraft in all. Bombload totals were impressive: Nine Libs would carry 8,000 pounds of high explosives each, while three, including Roy's aircraft 'A', would carry 6,000 pounds of incendiaries but no conventional bombs.

ROY: On Friday, 22 December, I cleaned guns on 'A' in preparation for the next day's op that was announced in the posted Battle Order.

At our 1900 briefing that evening we learned that this would be a repeat of the 21 December combined daylight mission against the Taungup, Burma, supply dump. Our squadron's specific target this time was Area '7'. Once again, the participants would be the American 7th Bomb Group and four RAF Liberator units (twelve aircraft from each unit): 99, 215, 355 and 356 Squadrons.

As on the twenty-first, 215 Squadron's Liberators were airborne early on Saturday morning, the twenty-third; the first of our Libs took off from Digri in darkness at 0514. My crew's KG830 was on its way at 0535. In good weather with excellent visibility the squadron formed up over Chittagong, India, roughly 285 miles north-west of the target, but 215 made a poor job of organising into three boxes of four aircraft each. We still needed to polish our skills in forming up, obviously, but we also accomplished the task with plenty of mileage to spare and made a good run towards the target. The clear weather was a boon to navigation, as the town of Taungup was easily identified.

At 0928 and 0929 215 Squadron's formation hit our specific primary target, Area '7', in a cloudless sky at 6,000 and 7,000 feet and in level flight. Area '7' measured approximately 700x700 yards.

MATT: No fighter opposition was encountered, a clear sign once again that the Japanese just couldn't muster an airborne defensive presence. While the 215 Squadron airmen knew that the enemy could still pack a punch, the fact that enemy fighters were rarely encountered was reassuring. There was no anti-aircraft fire, either, and nobody from 215 would have complained about this.

ROY: The overall Taungup target was well-covered with high explosive bursts and incendiary-started fires from all participating squadrons, causing several secondary explosions after bombing and with smoke and dust rising to a height of 2,000 to 3,000 feet.

MATT: All participating Liberators, including 215 Squadron's aircraft, safely returned home that day. Back at Digri the last of the squadron's contributing Libs touched down in daylight at 1326 to complete another relatively short and successful foray into enemy airspace; the twelve Libs averaged seven hours and forty-eight minutes in the air per aircraft.

Summing up the general feeling about fighting the Japanese in the tropics versus facing enemy foes in the European theatre (and likely referring to Mediterranean and North African aerial warfare, too) Wing Commander Lucian Ercolani, then-CO of 99 Squadron, stated:

> There was an entirely different atmosphere flying in the Far East compared to the European show. The risk from enemy action was considerably less in the Far East, but, really, the anxiety and fear was probably worse...[We had a] real fear of the Japanese and of coming down amongst them.

Neither Roy, his crewmates, nor any single member of the Allied air forces in the Far East likely disagreed.

ROY: On the way home I reflected upon the man who was poised to be my future Liberator captain; I hoped that Bing would live up to Jackson's record. I was lucky to have had Jackson as my skipper. Not only was he my friend, but when coming home from an op, over the Indian Ocean, he'd let me fly.

I was a frustrated non-pilot, having been turned down for this training early in my RAAF career due to imperfect eyes. Jackson, however, used to humour me and allow me to fly. It was quite safe, and in any case Bing and Jackson were close by, if needed. On ops we always flew back over the Indian Ocean to avoid flying over enemy-held land as much as possible. The airspace was sort of clear sailing for a Lib – when the weather cooperated, that is. With the pilots already being exhausted from hours of shepherding us to that point on the op it was a perfect time for me to take the controls. If I wasn't exactly on course, The Boong's head would appear in the astro hatch, noticeable a few feet in front of the cockpit window, and he'd put his hands together as if praying because he was worried with me at the controls.

To a non-pilot like me it was challenging, early on, to keep all three h's in order: horizon, heading and height. For example, I'd fly one wing a bit low, but on course and at the desired altitude, or both wings would be straight with the

Lib on the correct heading, but I'd be losing height. The Liberator certainly didn't fly itself, and I owe a huge debt of gratitude to my Lib skippers, who sometimes had to manhandle the beast. Over the course of hours this could be wearying, to say the least.

Roy's tenure at Digri ends and Christmas 1944 arrives

Back at Digri Flight Lieutenant Hkun U Sao, the Gunnery Leader of royal blood from the Shan States in Burma, had a verbal scrap with the 215 Squadron Adjutant. I didn't like the Adjutant much, either. I had no clue as to their issue.

MATT: Sao was the Oxford University-educated son of the *Sawbwa*, or hereditary ruler, of the Tawngpeng region of Burma. A native Burmese airman flying and fighting for the RAF was rare.

ROY: Like everyone else I was aware of the impending move to Dhubalia, and I knew that it would soon be time for me to join the main party making the transfer by rail, scheduled to depart Digri on Wednesday, 27 December. Ahead of this date I did most of my packing early, so that I'd have more free time for our limited Christmas celebration at Digri; further festivities were planned for a week later at Dhubalia.

MATT: And then Christmas 1944 was upon them. The celebration had to be shoehorned in between serious wartime business, but it was an especially important time of year for men far from home in what many considered a godforsaken locale. The third annual 215 Squadron Christmas concert was held on successive days, the twenty-fourth and the twenty-fifth. Once again it was a smashing success.

Despite the stress of the Dhubalia relocation looming over the 215 Squadron's members, morale was high, and the overwhelming majority would have looked forward to 1945, and the defeat of the Japanese, with unwavering enthusiasm and confidence.

ROY: I went over to the 159 Squadron Officers' Mess to bring an Aussie mate, Les Marsh, back to our Mess for some seasonal good cheer. Les flew, like me, as a W/Op/AG. The 159 Squadron Officers' Mess, I thought, seemed funereal, but I imagine I just stepped in at the wrong moment, and that for most of

Christmas Day it would be as raucous as 215's Officers' Mess. Or maybe the dour air of the place was due, in part, to the fact that I was from the other camp and not part of their club! No bother, really, as my visit was brief, by design.

The bar in our Mess, on the other side of the aerodrome, opened at 1100 for the official reception of Senior NCOs. In this air force Christmas tradition the privileges of rank were essentially reversed, and the NCOs were feted by the officers. On this one day only! And it was a roaring session. We, the officers, kept putting people up on chairs and either cheering them or booing them, according to their popularity. One bloke who'd caused trouble in Keith Palmer's crew came around and apologised to everybody. Somebody else brought a cow into the Officers' Mess, and the poor thing, crazy with fright, ran around butting everybody. As with so many antics where there could very easily have been dire consequences, nobody was hurt, and it was a riot well worth the aggravation!

From 1300 until 1500 we waited on the airmen in the Sergeants' Mess. It was also a wizard show enjoyed by all.

I joined three of my fellow RAAF officers for two hours, from 1600 to 1800, in the billet of one of them, the same Keith Palmer mentioned above, to drink Richmond beer brewed in Melbourne and to reminisce about our homes and families. Joining Keith and me were Bopp the W/Op and Ray South. I really appreciated our gathering – alcohol made me pretty 'happy' – but The Boong was in a horrible state.

Later, after the drinking had slackened off, we played craps back in the Officers' Mess. I lost fifteen rupees. The action was spirited, but Dr Tom Steele-Perkins kept uttering nonsense and making costly mistakes. The CO repeatedly told him to sit down, but Doc's reply would be, 'I won't!'

On the following day, Tuesday, 26 December, I felt OK, but The Boong was still in a bad way with a hangover. Apparently, he'd uttered regrettable things, such as telling the CO where he could put his squadron! Old Doc told us that he'd had a scrap with Wing Commander Sindall, but though I'd witnessed Doc's antics at the craps game I doubted that it had escalated. However, the CO was boiling mad about something, so maybe there was truth to there being bad blood between Doc and Wing Commander Sindall.

With the main move to Dhubalia scheduled for the twenty-seventh, I went ahead and packed up the squadron's flying rations on Tuesday, the day before. Later, Jackson came in and told me that he'd been put in charge of flying rations, a job that entailed far more than just packing them up for the move.

Someone had to be in charge, but it wasn't an assignment I'd have wanted. Better Jackson than me!

The evening was spent across at 159 Squadron saying adios. The spirit of the place was livelier and warmer than during my last brief visit. Les Marsh was there. They asked me to remember them to Bernie Bailey and others at Dhubalia.

Packing our gear continued to occupy my time early on Moving Day, Wednesday, 27 December. That morning I couldn't rouse The Boong, so I got cheesed off and left him to continue his recovery from too much 'celebrating'.

215 Squadron moves to Dhubalia

MATT: At 1930 a large rail party of 215 Squadron men departed from nearby Chandrakona Road railway station, bound for Dhubalia. The lot consisted of forty-five commissioned officers, forty-five warrant officers (non-commissioned), 160 flight sergeants and sergeants, 290 British other ranks (corporals, leading aircraftmen and aircraftmen), nine Indian other ranks and 128 Indian followers (both enrolled and unenrolled).

Although the distance wasn't great the rail journey was tedious and indirect, taking twenty-four hours to travel south to Kharagpur, then east to Calcutta and finally north to Dhubalia. The main rail party arrived at Dhubalia at 1910 on the twenty-eighth, and within an hour the unloading of personnel, equipment and stores had been completed. The men were all given a hot meal and sleeping accommodations.

That same morning and into the afternoon the transfer in flight of sixteen Liberators and one Harvard from Digri to Dhubalia was accomplished. Each Liberator carried a crew of four, plus passengers; in all, five Senior NCOs and ninety-seven corporals and aircraftmen were whisked off to Dhubalia as passengers. No doubt it was a thrill for many of these men who'd never previously flown. Grouse (skipper), Bingham (second pilot), Smithy Smith (flight engineer) and Bopp the W/Op (wireless operator) were the four from Roy's crew who transported their Lib, KH324 'B', and passengers to their new station.

ROY: There was a spot of panic in the Dhubalia circuit with multiple Liberators all trying to get in first, but ultimately all seventeen aircraft, including a lone single-engine Harvard, landed safely.

The aircraft dispersals at Dhubalia, where our Libs were parked, were terrible. We knew they'd been condemned more than once, and the taxi tracks were worse, yet here we were at our new home with the directive not to look backwards, but to move ahead. Change for the better would come our way, although this move to Dhubalia from a much more comfortable Digri tried our patience at times.

MATT: Another party left Digri by road on the morning of the twenty-eighth, arriving at Dhubalia late that evening.

The final phase of 215 Squadron's move to Dhubalia entailed two further parties departing from Chandrakona Road railway station on 28 December: a Motor Transport and equipment train of forty-five wagons that exited the station at 0540, and then a second equipment train setting off at 1930 the same evening. The first train reached its destination, Dhubalia railway station, at 0830 the following day, with unloading being completed within ninety minutes. The second train arrived at Dhubalia on the twenty-ninth at 2110, but unloading was postponed until first light on 30 December.

Despite the anticipation of resuming old friendships with the men of 99 Squadron, there were many regrets among 215 Squadron's personnel at leaving Digri, where they'd become well-establish and had received essential cooperation from 159 Squadron. However, being again based on the same aerodrome as another Liberator squadron took away some of the pain of departing Digri.

And so the transfer from Digri to Dhubalia was completed. Members of 215 Squadron would have recognised the complexity of the task and relished the accomplishment in relocating an entire heavy bomber squadron from one airfield to another. Yet, there was much work still to perform to make Dhubalia a comfortably functioning base of operations.

ROY: The Boong, Dizzy Neville, Ned Kelly, Jackson and I were together in the same billet, a good setup protected by a big tree. The Officers' Mess, however, was far from satisfactory. For example, the Mess wasn't yet prepared to serve us food. We had to shower under taps outside of the kitchen, as ablutions were inadequate. Easing our dissatisfaction, though, 175 Wing and 99 Squadron officers invited us over to their separate Messes, where we were terrifically received. Ned, Jackson and I ate at Wing, and it was the first time I'd ever felt welcomed in a strange Mess.

From there we three went over to 99 Squadron's Officers' Mess, and the welcome seemed even better, if that was possible. The bar was open to us for the rest of the evening. Their CO, Wing Commander Lucien Ercolani, introduced us to everybody we didn't know, and we were quite pleased to be reacquainted with old mates, including Bernie Bailey and Mickey Bryant. We finished early, by design.

Upon arising the morning after reaching Dhubalia we headed over to the Sergeants' Mess for something to eat. They managed to supply us with eggs and bread in sandwich form. While standing outside as I raised the sandwich towards my mouth, it suddenly wasn't there anymore. A kitehawk had literally taken it from my hands in one swoop! Unbelievable!

The day before some bamboo poles had been cut, and we tied them to the legs of our *charpoys* for hanging our mosquito nets. At the same time we found a six-foot snakeskin in the roofing material, and we didn't want to meet its owner!

Disarray, naturally, still abounded. Ned, The Boong and I rigged up a boiler for our billet by burning out two old pitch drums in a nearby gully. Then we got two guys from the Indian Central Public Works Department to dig us a fire pit and to construct a brick base over the pit, upon which would stand the drums.

The end of 1944 was spent in servicing aircraft and continuing the preparation for operations.

Chapter 13

215 Squadron, India: JANUARY 1945 *(Part 1)*

215 Squadron's January 1945 summary

MATT: At last, with the physical move now a thing of the past time was found on 1 January to organise another Christmas tradition – a holiday meal. Palates were put to the test sampling an assortment of foods, and it should be of no surprise that where there was delicious food, there was accompanying good cheer, especially as such food was hard to come by. Liquor added to the satisfaction of the occasion.

As new arrivals on an RAF station that wasn't up to par yet Roy and the other 215 Squadron members were presented with many challenges to overcome in order to make their facilities functional and comfortable. The shortage of necessary furniture was frustrating, but they knew that they weren't unique in facing such annoyances; RAF squadrons frequently relocated. One plan of action, now seen as discriminatory, was the way to solve one problem. By depriving 275 Wing's enrolled followers – native Indians – of their *charpoys*, it was just possible to provide all white British and Commonwealth personnel a bed.

A further summary of how 215 Squadron's men improved conditions came from their ORB:

> Our various Messes were equipped with the bare minimum of furniture, and for many days amateur carpentry was going on in all parts of the camp. Ammunition boxes were found to be easily adapted into useful writing desks, tables, seats and so forth. RS [Rupees] 34,000 of furniture was on order to remedy these deficiencies, and was not expected for some weeks. Many of the billets were already fitted for electric light, but the remainder could not be wired owing to a shortage of switches, joint-boxes, and other necessary gear.

Towards mid-January Liberator bombing priorities shifted for several weeks from the usual strategic role to one in direct support of Allied ground forces pushing the Japanese southward through Burma. Starting on 13 January and continuing until late February the focus of 215 Squadron's Libs switched from disrupting Japanese airfields and lines of communication (such as the Thailand-Burma Railway) to supporting British General Sir William Slim's 14th Army.

Monday, 1 JANUARY 1945
(Roy does not fly on this op)
215 Squadron's first op flown from Dhubalia, and tragedy: BURMA – rail targets near Thanbyuzayat and along the north-westernmost forty miles of the Thailand-Burma Railway *(daylight bombing and strafing)*

ROY: Up until 8 January my crew wasn't called upon for ops in 1945; instead we honed our skills during Liberator training, such as through local flying around the Dhubalia district and on a trip south-eastward to Cox's Bazar on the coast of the upper Bay of Bengal.

MATT: As Roy's crew willfully undertook this additional training 215 Squadron's assault against the Japanese continued without pause. A Battle Order was posted for an op scheduled for 1 January 1945. No rest for the weary! Most men likely felt confident that this would be the last New Year's Day during wartime.

Since Roy's crew wasn't earmarked for this op they were better able to enjoy the New Year's festivities than those who would be flying the op.

The important briefing for this op was held at 1500 on Sunday, 31 December. Six of 215 Squadron's Liberators were detailed for a daylight bombing and strafing attack designed to disrupt enemy lines of communication near Thanbyuzayat, Burma, and along the north-westernmost forty miles of the Thailand-Burma Railway in Burma. The goal would be to damage and destroy locomotives, rolling stock, railway facilities and railway bridges. Thanbyuzayat was where the notorious Thailand-Burma Railway joined the existing north-south Ye-to-Moulmein stretch of railway line.

On this occasion, New Year's Day, it would be another long one for six crews.

The daytime take-offs from Dhubalia for the raid were from 1000 to 1007. Unescorted, presumably avoiding radar detection by flying low over the water (where no enemy shipping was encountered) and with no aerial interceptors spotted, the six aircraft made their way across the Bay of Bengal, down the Burmese coast, around the Irrawaddy River delta and eastward towards their target zone.

ROY: The op proceeded routinely in good weather with few clouds until 1620, when Zoot Beadon's aircraft, KH274 'H', was hit in the tail by intense light anti-aircraft fire at Milestone 37 of the Thailand-Burma Railway near Shitpyit, Burma. The rear gunner, Sergeant Arthur Harding, was killed outright, and his turret was set on fire. At an altitude of 1,500 feet Pilot Officer J. Johnstone, Zoot's bomb aimer, safely jettisoned the bombload. Zoot then headed for home.

MATT: After initially exhausting the contents of fire extinguishers, crewmates dumped bottles of tea and drinking water on the fire in the rear of 'H' and even beat at the flames and embers with their clothing. Despite extensive damage to KH274's tail and rear control surfaces Beadon brought the Lib back, over 1,000 miles, to Dhubalia for a successful wheels-down landing in the 2315 darkness. Warrant Officer A.C. Combes, Beadon's second pilot, suffered superficial burns on both hands in his heroic effort to save the plane, but he could do nothing for the unfortunate Sergeant Harding. Combes, admitted to the Station Sick Quarters, made a routine, uneventful recovery.

ROY: Some of the boys went down to have a look at KH274 despite being warned not to go; 'You don't want to see it,' was the advice. Needless to say, seeing the damage to Zoot's aircraft was sobering.

MATT: With the damage classed as Category III, KH274 was reduced to spares, never to fly again.

Between 1624 and 1700 the five Libs that were able to press home their individual attacks struck a variety of railway targets, all in level flight from altitudes ranging from 1,500 to 4,200 feet. The five returned to Dhubalia (before 'H' hobbled back), landing in darkness between 2230 and 2302. For each of these five the time aloft averaged twelve hours and forty minutes.

The squadron's efforts were part of a large Liberator force sent out that day to southern Burma and, for some aircraft, even further east to within twenty-one miles of Bangkok, Thailand. Wreaking their havoc along stretches of railway between Moulmein, Burma, and a rail bridge on the Nakhon Chaisi River in Thailand were RAF Liberators from 99 Squadron (twelve aircraft), 159 Squadron (sixteen Libs), 355 Squadron (twelve aircraft) and 356 Squadron (eight bombers), as well as US B-24s from the 7th Bomb Group. Motor transport vehicles and coastal shipping in the Andaman Sea close to shore off of southern Burma also received attention, but in one attack upon seaborne vessels a 99 Squadron Liberator, KH360 'G', ditched in the sea, downed by enemy fire. Three crewmen emerged alive from PoW incarceration in Rangoon Jail, but the remainder of the eleven-man crew, including the skipper, Flight Lieutenant H.C.L. White, died on 1 January 1945.

Of the Liberators sent out from India, from all squadrons, only KH360 was destroyed. One Lib from 99 Squadron, having been hit by flak, landed at Cox's Bazar, and one 355 Squadron aircraft put down at Chittagong to refuel. All other bombers safely returned directly to their bases.

Wednesday, 3 JANUARY 1945
(Roy does not fly on this op)
Another tragedy: BURMA – bridge and rail targets between a point ten miles north of Thanbyuzayat and along the north-westernmost forty miles of the Thailand-Burma Railway *(daylight bombing and strafing)*

In the dry season the pace of operational flying was relentless, but again Roy's crew wasn't listed on the Battle Order for a 3 January op. In the 1500 briefing on 2 January details were provided.

This time seven 215 Squadron Libs took off from 0700 to 0721.

ROY: Tragedy struck 215 for the second op in a row.

MATT: In needing to press home attacks and with hills and thick vegetation (ideal for concealment) bordering sections of 215 Squadron's assigned sector of the Thailand-Burma Railway line, it was inevitable that Libs would be within range of potent enemy fire.

ROY: The op, consequently, proved fatal for the crew of Liberator KH214 'D', skippered by Steve Brodie, one of six Canadians in the crew of eleven. There was no chance of survival when they were shot down.

MATT: They died attacking a bridge upon which a locomotive sat, maybe as a decoy. As they flew up the valley at the low altitude of 400 feet near Shitpyit,

Burma, prior to 'bombs gone' ack-ack from guns on the hills adjoining the valley opened up. Hit in number four engine and the starboard wing at approximately 1335, KH214 'D' burst into flames. In a matter of seconds the wing folded up, the aircraft plummeted to the ground near Milestone 37 and the doomed Lib exploded upon impact. Nobody was seen to have baled out. Ultimately, none of the crew survived. Among the casualties was the Burmese air gunner, Flight Lieutenant Hkun U Sao, who'd sparred with the 215 Squadron Adjutant just prior to the move to Dhubalia.

Liberator KH258 'O', after having suffered combat damage to engine numbers three and four in the same locale where 'D' crashed, jettisoned its bombs and safely beelined to Cox's Bazar for an emergency landing. Its uninjured crew were returned to Dhubalia by aircraft on 4 January, the following day.

After attacking Thailand-Burma Railway bridges at Milestones 8, 32½ and 42 and the railway junction at Milestone 1½ on 3 January, the five other surviving 215 Squadron Libs returned to Dhubalia without incident on that same day.

ROY: Following the op, the Officers' Mess back at Dhubalia went into a sort of mourning for the eleven airmen on the Brodie crew who died and particularly for the seven officers, five of whom were Canadians. With a heavy Canadian presence on the squadron, the loss of six Royal Canadian Air Force compatriots (and the loss of the five non-Canadians, too) was deeply felt by 215 Squadron's Canadians.

MATT: US 7th Bomb Group B-24s had also attacked the Thailand-Burma Railway that day without loss. Over at 99 Squadron nine RAF Liberators had safely bombed and strafed locomotives and rolling stock along the Ye-to-Moulmein, Burma, stretch of railway line. With the exception of KH214 'D' all Liberators and their crews sent out from India on the 3 January 1945 op survived.

Monday, 8 JANUARY 1945
(Roy's tenth op – his first flown from Dhubalia)
A shocking incident: Thailand-Burma Railway, BURMA – Milestone 54, road and rail cutting *(daylight bombing)*

Planned ops on 6 and 7 January had been cancelled due to inclement weather. On the eighth, finally an op was flown, and Roy's crew was involved. The op's Battle Order, posted on 7 January, alerted ten chosen Liberator crews, including Roy's. He'd be the second W/Op on Lib KH324 'B', captained by Bingham and with Flight Sergeant Raby in the second pilot's seat. No longer would Grouse be flying, as he was 'tour-ex', having finished his required operational flights upon completion of the 23 December 1944 op. After taking some leave he departed 215 Squadron in February 1945 to return to Australia.

The bombload would be identical for all aircraft: 5,000 pounds (ten 500lb bombs per Liberator).

At the 1600 briefing on the seventh the 215 Squadron participants were informed of the unique target: a road and railway cutting at Milestone 54 of the Thailand-Burma Railway in Burma – fifty-four miles from the north-west terminus of the railway at Thanbyuzayat, Burma. The plan was to bomb the cutting in order to cause a landslide that would block the tracks.

So, again 215 would be sent far afield to the Thailand-Burma Railway.

Off they went in the early morning of the eighth. 'B' was the first airborne B-24 at 0700, followed by seven more Libs. Two aircraft aborted with engine trouble before take-offs commenced.

The force progressed smoothly towards the target until EW176 'G' suffered a complete, though temporary, loss of engine power roughly thirty-seven miles down the railway line from Thanbyuzayat upon approaching Shitpyit village, Burma – the same area where the Brodie crew had gone down five days earlier. EW176's multiple engine failure, which occurred prior to reaching the target, led the ball turret gunner, Flight Sergeant Hubert 'Wilbur' Reekes, to mistakenly bale out over enemy territory. It was a horror story, of sorts.

ROY: After a cock-up in the second pilot's seat caused the four engines to cut out the Liberator rapidly fell out of its box of attacking aircraft. There was panic on the flight deck. The bombload was immediately jettisoned live at 1253, and Dizzy Neville, the skipper, issued an alert to the crew: 'Stand by to bale out.' In response some of the crew crouched around the escape hatch opened on the floor of the rear fuselage; they were primed to jump.

There are two stories about what happened next. In one, Reekes, having exited his turret, heard the words 'bale out', and, following what he thought was a common-sense command, he dropped through the hatch. The second story, as told by 215 Squadron pilot Wally Frazer in his book, *A TREPID AVIATOR*, probably reflects the truth – that the W/Op, who was on the intercom with the skipper, raised his thumb to indicate that the problem had been solved. Then in a shocking moment of poor communication Reekes misinterpreted the hand gesture as the signal to jump and propelled himself backwards out the hatch.

Regardless, it was hard to imagine how Reekes felt when he saw his kite pick up speed, four propellers turning, and fly away. And he was all alone.

He was seen to land amongst the trees near the railway. The word was that he was treated badly by his captors.

MATT: Following the Reekes bale out, the release of the aircraft's bombload, the successful restart of the engines and the recovery of flight, EW176 turned back towards Dhubalia, no longer a participant in the plan to cause a landslide.

Though captured along the Thailand-Burma Railway Reekes didn't join the ranks of PoW labourers. Instead, in a move that may have saved his life, his captors fortuitously delivered him northward to Rangoon Jail, notorious in its own right but generally safer than any of the Thailand-Burma Railway camps. His recounting of the Liberator incident to his fellow Rangoon Jail prisoners was worked for laughs – a fond memory, decades later, for his ex-PoW mates.

On 3 May 1945 Reekes emerged in Rangoon from PoW incarceration. He wasn't punished by his superiors for his errant jump.

The incident of 8 January would have been anguishing to all on 215 Squadron, as many would have thought it unlikely that he'd ever be seen again.

His ordeal, described in a 1945 report entitled 'BRITISH PW LIBERATED FROM RANGOON CENTRAL JAIL', is worth repeating:

> A ball gunner, in a Liberator with all four engines cut on 8th January 1945, mistook instructions and baled out. As he was going down he saw the aircraft holding its course with all four engines running again.
>
> The gunner landed safely in the jungle south-east of ANANQUIN [sic; 'Anankwin' (sometimes 'Anakwin') is the common spelling] and started walking in a north-easterly direction, sleeping out at night and continuing the next day and the following night. On the third day, having used some of his emergency rations, he found himself on a track which appeared to lead to a village, so he decided to ask for help.
>
> The villagers appeared quite friendly and hid him in a cave because they said there were Japanese in the vicinity. During the same afternoon the village headman took him to his own house under an armed guard and cared for him until the arrival of the Japanese to whom he was handed over.

The Japanese officer in charge of the party warned him that he was now a Prisoner of War and that if he behaved correctly he would be well treated.

Late the same night they arrived at ANANQUIN [sic], some 12 miles distant. P.W. was given bed and blankets in the barracks and the following morning he was taken to THANBYUZAYAT and in the afternoon left in a truck for MOULMEIN.

Throughout this journey the treatment received by P.W. was strictly correct and fair.

At MOULMEIN P.W. was kept at the Missionary School which was being used as a barracks and during the night he was beaten up and kicked by an individual whom he thought to be the Orderly Sergeant.

The next morning an Officer produced a questionnaire which took all day and part of the next day to answer. The questions were mainly about aircraft on which the Japanese appeared to have a good deal of correct information. P.W. managed to convince them that he was unable to answer some of the technical questions as he was only an air gunner. In addition, there were a number of general questions about the conditions in service and civilian life in INDIA and about the prisoner's family.

The next afternoon he was taken across the airfield which had been heavily blitzed and he noticed that the hangars and run-ways were considerably damaged and were partly overgrown with grass. On the far side of the field he was again interrogated in a small building on exactly the same lines as before. After this he returned to Military Police H.Q. and left the following evening by train for RANGOON.

Interrogator's Note:

The above report is of particular interest as although P.W. landed in the neighbourhood of ANANQUIN [sic] [he was something like nine miles from Anankwin] he was not taken eastwards down the railway as might have been expected but was returned to MOULMEIN. Having arrived at MOULMEIN, instead of being placed in MOULMEIN JAIL, the Japanese took the trouble of sending him North to RANGOON. It is possible that the explanation for this is that the Japanese insist [sic; it should be 'insisted'] on all Air Force personnel being interrogated at the J.A.F. H.Q., which in this particular case was situated at JUDSON COLLEGE, RANGOON.

In Reekes' own words, from a snippet of his 4 December 2001 letter to Matt Poole:

> When I was in the jail [Rangoon Jail] the Japs seemed to be less cruel, as if they knew that the end was near. I landed in the southern part of Burma where the natives where [sic] Karens, many of them Christians, so I wasn't treated badly, so, all in all, I was very lucky, ending up with only a few jungle sores. When travelling on a train full of Japs, a Beaufighter attacked us, but none of the cannon shells got me. That, among other things, gave me my philosophy of life, "Better to be lucky than smart."

His story is remarkable...and it could have been Roy's ordeal. 'There but for the grace of God go I', Roy might have thought to himself.

To return to the details of 8 January 1945, the seven remaining 215 Squadron Libs bombed the cutting in formation from 1248 to 1250 at altitudes ranging from 6,000 to 8,000 feet. On 'M', leading the entire formation, all bombs initially hung up but were finally released fifteen seconds beyond the aiming point. Roy's aircraft, 'B', was in a three-aircraft vic trailing the front grouping of bombers; Roy's particular formation had been reduced from a box of four Libs by the happenings aboard 'G'.

Significant cumulus buildup was encountered on the flight along the railway line towards the cutting, but the target, clear of clouds though less than fifty yards wide, came into view sooner than expected. It was feared that 215 Squadron's attack resulted in little damage along the railway, and certainly no landslide blocked the rails. The scheme was creative, with great potential, but the end result did prove to be highly disappointing.

All eight Liberators safely returned to Dhubalia, landing in darkness between 1847 and 1932. Roy's aircraft was the second down, at 1900, after a flight time of twelve hours exactly, while the hexed 'G' was fifth, at 1915.

ROY: There was considerable controversy about our load for this trip: a mixture of normal and delayed-action bombs. As planned, the latter, when they eventually exploded, would impact the timetable for reopening the line by causing a further cascade of rocks onto the tracks and by killing those trying to remove the debris and repair the track.

One of our members pointed out that the Japanese would surely use PoWs to do the repair work, and that the cutting was close to a PoW camp. He refused to go on the mission, as he said that his brother, believed to be a PoW on this railway, might become a casualty of his own air force, either as a result of the initial bomb explosions, the hoped-for landslide or the detonation of delayed-action bombs.

The op went ahead without him.

MATT: Also on 8 January, as part of a large Allied effort, eleven 355 Squadron Libs and eleven from 356 Squadron attacked targets near Milestone 41 of the Thailand-Burma Railway, thirteen miles north-west of 215's target. One 355 Squadron Lib and one from 356 Squadron bombed Anankwin, Burma, an additional thirteen miles to the north-west. Sixteen Libs from 159 Squadron bombed the railway workshops at Moulmein, Burma. US B-24s deploying Azon (meaning 'azimuth only'; it was a cunning new 'smart' weapon) bombs and also US Liberators utilising conventional bombs very successfully knocked down three Thailand-Burma Railway bridges in Burma, while additional American B-24s attacked bridges on the Ye-to-Moulmein stretch of railway line in Burma.

In addition to the successful return of 215 Squadron's eight Liberators all other bombers safely reached their home bases.

After 215 Squadron's Libs failed to cause the desired landslide at Milestone 54 the op was repeated the following day by fifteen aircraft from 99 Squadron. Their bombs caused severe track damage but again failed to cause a landslide.

Thursday, 11 JANUARY 1945
(Roy does not fly on this op)
Bangkok-to-Chiengmai stretch of railway, THAILAND – bridge busting *(daylight bombing and strafing)*

On 11 January, before Roy's crew's next op, six 215 Squadron Libs were called upon to make low level attacks on bridges 26, 36, 37, 42 and another at Milestone 187½, all on Thailand's Bangkok-to-Chiengmai railway line. Details were spelled out in the 1500 briefing on 10 January.

Significant damage resulted from the attack by the bombers. With only one unspecified Liberator having suffered minor anti-aircraft damage in the bomb bay and port flap, the op was deemed quite the success.

Wing Commander James Sindall made the following remarks in the official 215 Squadron records:

> Two bridges (Nos. 26 & 42) were put out by bursts in spite of the difficulties of aiming bombs so as to embed themselves in the bridge supports. Many additional hits were scored but the bombs ricochetted [sic] away before exploding.

One Liberator, low on petrol, opted for a Cox's Bazar landing and returned to Dhubalia on 12 January after an overnight stay. All five other 215 Squadron Libs returned to Dhubalia on the same day as their take-offs.

The 215 Squadron aircraft were only a subset of the total Liberator force unleashed upon various targets on 11 January, including railway bridges on the Bangkok-to-Chiengmai, Thailand, line. The force included RAF and American Liberator units. In addition to the safe return of 215 Squadron's Liberators, each unit's aircraft made their ways to Allied control for safe landings, even despite combat damage in some instances.

Saturday, 13 JANUARY 1945
(Roy's eleventh op)
Mandalay, BURMA – Area '2', concentration of troops and supplies *(daylight bombing)*

The RAF and US Liberators were on a roll now in the heart of a stretch of great flying weather, and 215 Squadron was ever-improving as a fighting unit. Morale, surprisingly high despite the ongoing disruptions caused by the relocation to Dhubalia, seemed invigorated in early 1945 for anyone Roy knew.

Roy's crew got the nod for an op to be flown on 13 January. Starting on this sortie he'd be first W/Op, not second W/Op. His crew would fly the 13 January op aboard Liberator KH324 'B', commanded by Bingham and with Flight Sergeant Raby as second pilot.

At the 1500 briefing on the twelfth, ten Liberator crews learned that the daylight destination would be Mandalay, as requested by the British 14th Army. This sortie would mark the first of many ops through 25 February where the squadron would take a tactical role in directly supporting British Army combat activities.

13 January would also mark the first of nine consecutive 215 Squadron ops in which Roy participated.

Those present at the briefing were told that the combined Liberator operations on 13 January, involving numerous RAF and US squadrons, would constitute the greatest aerial bombardment of the Burma war – and, no doubt, hearing this would have made the men perk up with pride.

Specifically, 215 Squadron's bombs would be deposited upon a section of Mandalay identified on their target maps as Area '2', a concentration of Japanese troops and supplies in the area of the Mandalay Police Training School, the Courts of Justice and the football ground, just south-east of the moat enclosing Fort Dufferin. Seven 215 Squadron Liberators would each carry 10,000 pounds of bombs, while three Libs, including 'B', would drop 6,000 pounds of incendiary clusters, not high explosive bombs like the other seven aircraft.

Roy's squadron only managed to put up eight of the ten assigned Libs on the thirteenth. The eight bombers took off between 1010 and 1021; Roy's Lib was airborne at 1010. Leaving two machines behind at Dhubalia due to mechanical issues – each carrying 10,000 pounds of bombs – was something everyone hoped wouldn't reoccur, though sometimes it was better to be safe than sorry, even if the two crews, denied an op – and an historic one, at that – were frustrated and annoyed.

Also joining in on the action from Dhubalia were fifteen Libs from 215's sister unit on the station, 99 Squadron. Approaching from the west, the 99 Squadron bombers struck their own separate Mandalay target, located close to 215's, from 1313 to 1314, starting four minutes prior to 215 Squadron's first bomb release.

In addition to 99 and 215 Squadrons, 355 Squadron sent out twelve Liberators to target military camps located in Area '1', while twelve Libs from 356 Squadron, 355's neighbour at Salbani aerodrome, focused upon Area '3' on the Mandalay target map. Flying its only bombing op (before subsequently becoming a Special Duties unit delivering supplies and agents by parachute behind enemy lines), the newly-formed 358 Squadron, then at Digri, contributed seven Liberators to the attack on Mandalay that day.

US Liberators keyed in upon Sagaing, the town across the Irrawaddy River from Mandalay several miles to the south-west. While some of these bombers specifically went after Japanese troop concentrations in Sagaing, other US 7th

Bomb Group B-24s dropped more general strings of fragmentation bombs and incendiaries in and around the town.

By the time 215 Squadron was over its specific objective in generally good weather, having approached from the west, smoke drifting down from the areas already attacked by 99 Squadron partially obscured Area '2'. The eight 215 Squadron Liberators bombed in formation from 1317 to 1318½ at an average altitude of 9,000 feet. At 1317 from 9,500 feet Roy's bomb aimer, Nick Nicholas, toggled KH324's load of incendiaries upon the target.

Had 215's bomb aimers not intently studied ground details the accuracy of their aiming would have suffered because of the dust and smoke sweeping across the target. Yet despite the drifting smoke from previous bomb hits 215 Squadron obtained a good concentration of bursts squarely on Area '2'.

Over the general Mandalay area large fires and black smoke were witnessed rising to 5,000 feet, some fires having resulted from 215's own incendiaries and high explosives. Dense smoke and fires in Sagaing were obvious evidence of the punishment meted out by US B-24s. As reported by aircrews after the raid, smoke was visible for an average distance of seventy-five miles.

Ack-ack was mostly directed at other squadrons, not at 215. What little anti-aircraft fire 215 Squadron encountered was meagre and only fairly accurate, by and large. Yet it only took one shell to knock a Liberator out of the sky. In fact, 215 Squadron's EW285 'C' at 1318 was shaken up by a near miss from an exploding heavy anti-aircraft shell, and splinters were found to have penetrated number four engine's cowling. Except for that superficial damage 215's Liberators suffered no known harm, although two US B-24s were more seriously hit from below.

The problem of ack-ack, first from Sagaing and then from Mandalay, was dealt with by arranging for two squadrons of P-47 Thunderbolt fighters to strafe the gun positions before and during the Liberator bomb runs. No doubt the Liberator boys were grateful for these daring fighter jocks.

All Liberators from the various squadrons made it home that day. One of the American bombers, with its hydraulics shot out, successfully deployed parachutes from the waist gun windows upon landing to help brake the aircraft.

The eight Libs from 215 Squadron landed safely back at Dhubalia within a brief period from 1644 to 1700; Roy's bomber was the second of the returnees, at 1645, after a time aloft of six hours and thirty-five minutes.

Following the op it was estimated that Japanese casualties from the attacks in the Mandalay and Sagaing areas were as many as 1,000 dead.

ROY: It was a fairly easy and relatively short raid, though I can't say that I was overly satisfied afterwards, despite the air armada's record size and my enthusiasm at the briefing. During my previous ops the squadron had never attacked a town, so it felt a little disconcerting to think more than usual about innocent people being on the receiving end of our bombs.

MATT: (Later, in relation to his nineteenth op to Madaya, Burma, flown on 5 February 1945, Roy commented even further on the plight of innocent victims.)

With bold headlines, the Melbourne, Australia, newspaper, *The Sun*, ran a written account trumpeting the prowess of the attacking bombers on the mighty raid upon Mandalay and nearby Sagaing. Roy's parents clipped and saved the cutting:

Million-Lb. Raid
On Mandalay

From the Special Correspondent of Australian Associated Press at a [sic] R.A.F. Heavy Bomber Base, Somewhere in Bengal

Mandalay was attacked on Saturday by the greatest concentration of heavy bombers ever assembled in that area.

Liberator squadrons of the R.A.F. Strategic Air Force combined with U.S. bombers and nearly 1,000,000 lb. of high explosive and incendiary bombs were unloaded on the city in a few minutes.

The chief targets were that part of the town where the Japanese were believed to be concentrating ready for withdrawal, and the Sagaing ferry, eight miles to the west, where great stocks of equipment and transport had banked up for transport to the south bank of the Irrawaddy.

Crews said they had left the areas in ruins, with smoke rising to 7000ft. [5,000 feet, per 215 Squadron's ORB] where oil stocks had been hit.

Bombers avoided the Fort Duffering [Fort Dufferin] area, containing the old palace, administrative buildings and what is believed to be a prisoner-of-war camp.

Pilot-Officer H.J. Gibbs [99 Squadron], Leslie-rd. [sic], Essendon, Victoria, whose crew included Flying-Officer E.R. Loton, of Vancluse, Sydney, and B.J. Bailey, of Barnard gve. [sic], Kew, Victoria, said he counted 15 fires as they left the target area.

Anti-aircraft fire had not worried him, because by the time he passed over, American Thunderbolt fighters had searched out the Japanese gun positions and shot them up.

Back after his 1100-miles [sic] round trip, Warrant-Officer N. Biccard [99 Squadron], of Carpenter-st. [sic], Middle Brighton, Victoria, found that he could not lower his undercarriage.

After an hour added to the seven he and his crew had already spent aloft, the main wheels were wound down by hand, but the nose wheel defied all efforts.

Guns and ammunition were flung overboard, and Biccard, having ordered his crew to the rear of the plane to keep the tail down, landed perfectly without the nosewheel.

The fuselage scraped the runway so gently that no damage was done.

Even seasoned pilots applauded this effort by one of the "black troops," as Australians are called on this mixed station, where a sign in the mess reads, "Australian spoken, Canadian understood, English interpreter available."

Captains of bombers operating in the big raid included Warrant-Officer J. McCredie of Cotham-rd. [sic], Kew [99 Squadron], and Warrant-Officer J. Hathaway [215 Squadron's Jack Hadaway, not Hathaway] of McArthur-rd. [sic], East Ivanhoe.

Another contemporary newspaper report of the Mandalay raid referred to Roy Andrews as the 'evacuee from Hong Kong', but it didn't name him; an excerpt from this report stated that 'Those who took part in the raid were British, Australian, South Africans, Fijis and an evacuee from Hong Kong.'

A succinct post-op assessment of 215 Squadron's efforts on the Mandalay raid written by Wing Commander Sindall spoke volumes in just eight words: 'Planning and tactics satisfactory. A very successful op.'

Tuesday, 16 JANUARY 1945
(Roy's twelfth op)
Zayatkwin, BURMA – airfield *(daylight bombing)*

A Battle Order posted on 15 January for the squadron's next outing the following day listed Roy as first W/Op aboard KH324 'B', while the Bingham/ Raby brain trust on the flight deck would be the pilots once more, with Bingham as the captain.

At the 1500 briefing on the fifteenth the Bingham crew learned that nine 215 Squadron Liberators would join a force of twelve 99 Squadron aircraft in an effort to crater the runway of Zayatkwin airfield, located twenty-five miles north-east of Rangoon. Additionally, the plan was to stir up a little dust elsewhere on the aerodrome with time-delayed explosions. The bombing of Zayatkwin plus other attacks that day against Mingaladon, twenty miles to the south-west of Zayatkwin, would launch an Allied offensive against the main Japanese airfields in central and southern Burma.

Each of 215 Squadron's participating Libs would carry 6,500 pounds of high explosives, including one 500lb bomb with a time delay. On Roy's Lib and four others that time delay would be six hours, only half the detonation lag time of the single 500 pounder being carried by each of 215's four other Libs.

Nine 215 Squadron Liberators were airborne on the sixteenth between 0911 and 0923; 'B' was the eighth to take off, at 0920. At 1307 over Flatt Island off the western coast of Burma (south of the larger Cheduba Island) the twenty-one Libs of 99 and 215 Squadrons rendezvoused with twenty-four P-38 Lightning fighters and the same number of P-47 Thunderbolts and set course for Zayatkwin. With the Lightnings flying high cover escort and the Thunderbolts as close escort, the Liberators were well-prepared for a scrap with the Japanese Army Air Force. In the past, an aerial encounter had been the usual result of Allied incursion into enemy airspace in the Rangoon area, but there was no such opposition on this day.

The 215 Squadron ORB surmised why this was so: 'Possibly the Japanese realised that any attempt at interference with so formidable a formation was likely to be unprofitable.' Perhaps the enemy aerial adversaries who could have defended their interests simply chose to fight another day.

Leading 215's three vics towards Zayatkwin was 99 Squadron.

While the weather en route to Zayatkwin was good for a long stretch, over the lower Irrawaddy River valley a serious buildup of clouds impeded both target identification and bombing. Thus, it was difficult for some aircraft to pinpoint their bursts, even with bomb-strike cameras, but nevertheless sticks of explosives were seen to straddle the runway and taxi tracks nearby. Other bursts extended across the runway.

ROY: An airfield is always a challenging target, but the consensus was that our attacking formation's bombs resulted in a lot of, how shall I put it, 'cleaning up' before Zayatkwin airfield was of much use once again.

MATT: Roy's squadron had bombed in level flight between 1320 and 1328 from an average altitude of 9,150 feet. KH324 'B' released its bombs at 1328 from 8,700 feet. KH362 'O' of 215 Squadron had released its bombload live in wooded country six to ten miles north of the target prior to reaching Zayatkwin, due to an electrical failure.

Not only did the attacking 215 Squadron airmen meet no fighter opposition, but they also experienced no anti-aircraft fire. It was highly unusual but also highly relieving.

Only one of 99 Squadron's Libs, but none of 215's aircraft, chose to abort its attack on Zayatkwin because of obscuring clouds. Instead, this Liberator bombed the secondary target at Prome, Burma, on the Irrawaddy River.

Twelve 355 Squadron Liberators also attacked Zayatkwin that day, though their efforts were independent of the dual assault by 99 and 215 Squadrons.

Fourteen 356 Squadron Liberators and numerous B-24s from the US 7th Bomb Group pressed forward in attacking Mingaladon airfield, the main aerodrome serving Rangoon.

It can be said that the overall attacking force of RAF and American Liberators flexed their collective muscles and made an enemy combatant or two soil his pants that day.

Functioning as planned, 215 Squadron's nine Liberators safely returned to Dhubalia, landing between 1810 and 1828. After eight hours and fifty minutes aloft Roy and his crewmates aboard 'B' were on the ground at 1810, one of three returnees to land during that minute.

There were no Liberator losses or crew injuries among any of the RAF and US bombers out on the prowl that day.

The 215 Squadron ORB's post-op Sortie Report for the 16 January mission recorded these words: 'Great satisfaction was expressed by all crews with the fighter escort.'

Roy kept a newspaper account of the op:

RAF AND US PLANES CAUSE MUCH DAMAGE WITH 1,000-LB. BOMBS

EASTERN AIR COMMAND HQ, January 17.—A heavy and concentrated attack on two of the principal Japanese airfields at Zayatkwin and Mingaladon, near Rangoon, was made on Tuesday by RAF Liberators and USAAF B-24s of Strategic Air Force. They met no opposition from enemy fighters.

As the bombers swept over the airfields in the early afternoon and rained 1,000-lb. bombs on runways, dispersal areas, and buildings, fighters overhead waited for any possible interference. Only in one case was there any report of a fighter taking off from a strip, and it made no effort to intercept. Anti-aircraft fire was not heavy.

An hour or two after the bombers had gone RAF photographic reconnaissance pilots flew over the airfields and found scenes of feverish activity. Dozens of trucks and other vehicles had been brought up in an effort to repair the extensive damage. At Mingaladon, for example, they were faced with the filling of about 40 bomb craters on the runways alone, and at Zayatkwin at least 12 craters were seen on the runways.

The lack of fighter opposition in an attack fraught with so much danger to the whole Japanese air defence system of South Burma and Rangoon particularly surprised many of the RAF flyers who had taken part in similar attacks.

On his 35th trip over Burma and Siam since joining his present squadron 15 months ago was F/O M.T. Simpson, of Amble, Northumberland; he had also done five night attacks on Rangoon.

"On those raids" he said, "our aircraft used often to be engaged by night-fighters and there was plenty of ack-ack. But today we were around the target for 20 minutes, in broad daylight, to make sure of the exact aiming-point because of clouds. Nothing disturbed us.

"Not a single enemy aircraft was sighted although we flew within 10 miles of four or five other airfields which make up the South Burma defence ring just north of Rangoon."

Chapter 14

215 Squadron, India: JANUARY 1945 *(Part 2)*

Thursday, 18 JANUARY 1945
(Roy's thirteenth op)
Meiktila, BURMA – main airfield *(daylight bombing)*

ROY: On 18 January I was quickly back on ops.

MATT: A fresh Battle Order posted on the seventeenth, the day after Roy's previous op, listed twelve crews assigned to a sortie to be flown the following day. Included again was Bingham's crew – with Roy – but this time aboard Liberator KH320 'D', not their usual KH324 'B'. KH320, a new Mk. VI Liberator on the squadron, was assigned the fuselage 'D' code following the loss of the previous 'D' Lib, KH214, on 3 January. Bingham's second pilot again would be Flight Sergeant Raby, while Roy would be in his now-familiar position as first W/Op.

The loads for the twelve aircraft were to be heavy. Each of eleven Libs would carry four 1,000lb and seven 500lb high explosive bombs, plus one long delay 500 pounder not set to explode for six to twelve hours. The twelfth Liberator, KH322 'V', would also carry the same weight in bombs (8,000 pounds), but its extra 500 pounder would detonate upon impact.

The briefing at 1500 on the seventeenth informed the twelve Liberator crews that the assault upon Japanese airfields, begun on the sixteenth, would continue, this time with a concentration by several RAF and US Liberator units upon the Meiktila-area landing grounds of central Burma. (A newspaper account, copied below, referred to US B-25s also being a part of the force, but these medium bombers weren't mentioned in Liberator ORB documents.) Specifically, 215 Squadron would be targeting the main airfield at Meiktila, located seventy-five miles south of Mandalay.

Joining 215 Squadron in this daytime assault would be the same number of Libs from 99 Squadron.

All twenty-four aircraft became airborne, starting with 215's take-offs between 0941 and 0954 and followed by 99 Squadron's participating Libs. Roy's 'D' was ninth out of Dhubalia at 0951. The Liberators from Dhubalia flew to the target in separate squadron-based formations, led by 215 Squadron.

A fighter escort of twelve P-38s and twenty P-47s (only P-47s were mentioned in the newspaper account transcribed below) rendezvoused with the bombers at Chittagong. The Liberator airmen loved having the fighter boys watching out for them again, as had been the case on the previous op of 16 January.

The flight onward to the target was uneventful, with fair weather prevailing over most of the route but some clouds over the hills. Atmospheric conditions at Meiktila were quite good. The 215 Squadron Liberators, first over the main airfield, approached from the north and bombed between 1258½ and 1308 from an average altitude of nearly 9,100 feet. Roy's Lib 'D' toggled its bombs at 8,700 feet.

Only eleven of 215 Squadron's aircraft released bombs on Meiktila. When the formation had turned before reaching the target area EW285 'C' was forced far out in the manoeuvre. Being unable to turn sharply enough to get back onto the primary target, it instead opted for nearby Thedaw airfield, a satellite landing ground near Meiktila's main aerodrome. Bombs released there from 9,000 feet at 1259 hit a taxi track and dispersal road forty to fifty yards west of the runway; having damaged an airfield, the men aboard 'C' knew that it wasn't a wasted trip.

Following 215 Squadron over Meiktila by roughly seven minutes were their friends from 99 Squadron, whose Libs bombed Meiktila airfield in formation between 1311 and 1313 from an average height of about 11,500 feet.

The bombs of the two Liberator squadrons fell across both of Meiktila's runways, rendering the airfield unserviceable.

Twenty-three Liberators packed a hefty wallop in beating up Meiktila airfield. There couldn't have been an airman aloft who didn't feel a sense of accomplishment over both the efforts expended and the results achieved.

Although no Japanese fighter opposition was encountered, on the bomb run moderate heavy anti-aircraft fire from positions north-east of Meiktila town was experienced, being accurate for height and direction at first but becoming less accurate for direction later. One Lib reported that a sighting burst was fired by a heavy ack-ack weapon ahead of the formation on 215 Squadron's run-in. This was done as a guide to enemy gunners in concentrating their aim, but the Liberators came through the bomb run in fine fashion. Though KH322 'V' was holed in twenty to thirty places by shrapnel, there were no casualties aboard and no worrisome damage to the aircraft.

The crew aboard 'V' dodged a bullet. Or, putting it in a more accurate way, they dodged a worse anti-aircraft shell detonation.

A sizeable force of B-24s from the US 7th Bomb Group targeted Thedaw, the same landing ground where 215 Squadron's 'C' had released its load.

Eleven 355 Squadron aircraft attacked another aerodrome in the Meiktila airfield group, Kyaunggon, though a twelfth Liberator, suffering a temporary bomb hang-up, jettisoned its bombs over a different satellite airfield. Twelve 356 Squadron aircraft successfully bombed Kangaung, yet another of the airfields in the area.

Among all of the Allied Liberator participants no bombers were lost and no crewmen were seriously injured on the raids; all aircraft made their ways home, and, as always, that would have been a relief to hear.

The twelve B-24s from 215 Squadron safely landed at Dhubalia between 1608 and 1632; Roy's KH320 'D' was the tenth one to return, at 1622. The average flight time for each of the 215 Squadron bombers was six hours and twenty-nine minutes, two less minutes than Roy's own aircraft spent airborne on the op.

The newspaper coverage of the op reported the following:

300 TONS ON BURMA
AIRFIELDS

HQ, EASTERN AIR COMMAND – More than 300 tons of high explosive bombs were dropped by Allied aircraft of Eastern Air Command on Thursday on six airfields in the Meiktila and Heho defence ring, 75 miles south of Mandalay. RAF Liberators and USAAF B-24s of Strategic Air Force, U.S. B-25s [their participation is uncertain] and Air Commando P-47s [P-38s also took part in the action] formed a force of more than 150 aircraft which were making the most concentrated attack yet against these groups of airfields. Heavy anti-aircraft fire was encountered, but not one Japanese fighter offered opposition. One Allied fighter [a P-38] is missing.

The RAF heavies attacked Meiktila, Kyaunggon, north of Meiktila, and Kangaung, west of Meiktila.

Devastation at Kangaung was particularly severe. Reconnaissance photographs taken soon after the attack revealed 50 direct hits on the strips and considerable damage in dispersals and among buildings. One enemy aircraft was destroyed by a direct bomb hit. The runways at Meiktila were thoroughly cratered and at Thédaw, north of Meiktila, which was the target of the USAAF 7th Bombardment Group, at least 20 craters were counted with a large concentration around the centre.

One RAF squadron taking part in the attack was the Madras Presidency Squadron [99 Squadron] which, two and a quarter years ago, flying Wellingtons, bombed Meiktila as its first target in the Burma war.

Wing-Comm L.B. Ercolani, DSO, who led the squadron, described the ground defences as the heaviest he had experienced in that area. "One member of my crew," he said, "counted 30 ack-ack bursts near my aircraft as we passed over Meiktila airfield. As we went in we could see other squadrons bombing adjoining airfields.

"Over Meiktila the clouds parted just as we got within a mile or two of the airfield and we could see smoke rising from the bombing by another squadron a few minutes earlier."

B-24s of the 7th Bombardment Group… [The last sentence is cut off.]

Sunday, 21 JANUARY 1945
(Roy's fourteenth op)
Ramree Island, BURMA – Mount Peter *(daylight bombing, as part of Operation MATADOR)*

The afternoon briefing before 215 Squadron's next op – Roy's fourth in nine days – was held at 1500 on 20 January. Aboard Liberator KH398 'H' this time, Roy's crew would again be commanded by Bingham, assisted by Flight Sergeant Raby in the second pilot's seat. Roy would continue in his role as first W/Op. It was planned that the squadron would put up twelve Liberators in support of Operation MATADOR, the amphibious landings on the north side of Ramree Island on the Burmese coast, in which the Allied navy, army and air forces would jointly participate. Also in support of this amphibious assault, sixteen 99 Squadron Liberators, plus US 7th Bomb Group B-24s, were earmarked to attack separate Ramree Island targets, and 355 (twelve

Above left: Roy poses for a formal portrait in his RAAF uniform. His flight lieutenant's rank – his final rank – is marked by ribbons on the sleeves of his uniform. (*Greg Andrews*)

Above right: Roy Andrews's Royal Australian Air Force induction photo taken either on 21 September 1942 (when he signed his 'Oath or Affirmation' papers) or else on 6 November 1942 (when his full-time RAAF service commenced). (*National Archives of Australia*)

Below: Three Royal Australian Air Force officers play darts in the 215 Squadron Officers' Mess at Digri on 28 November 1944. Left to right: Stanley Clarke (pilot), Roy and Alan Stephens (navigator, bomb aimer). (*SEA0024, Australian War Memorial*)

Above: In the 215 Squadron Officers' Mess a sign reading 'AUSTRALIAN SPOKEN, CANADIAN UNDERSTOOD, ENGLISH INTERPRETER AVAILABLE' was photographed on 28 November 1944. 3rd from the left: Australian pilot Ted Coulin, with whom Roy later flew on the Communication Flight at 231 Group Headquarters. Far right: Roy's first skipper, Reg 'Jackson' Grouse, RAAF. Front row, far right: Roy, smoking a pipe and with a tankard in his left hand (*Crop of SEA0025, Australian War Memorial*)

Opposite above: A 99 Squadron bomb-strike photo (pilot and Liberator unknown) from 13 January 1945 shows billowing smoke and dust rising after a tactical attack upon Mandalay, Burma. Note the water-filled moat which surrounds Fort Dufferin. Roy (aboard Liberator KH324) and 215 Squadron also attacked Mandalay on this date; it was Roy's eleventh op. (*James Payne*)

Opposite below: On 13 January 1945 215 Squadron Liberator KH362, letter code 'O', takes off from Dhubalia at 1021 to begin its op to Mandalay, Burma. This was Roy's eleventh op and his initial sortie flying as his crew's permanent 1st W/Op. (*SEA0108, Australian War Memorial*)

Above: An 8 January 1945 photo recce image of the Anankwin, Burma rail bridges on the Thailand-Burma Railway. The lower bridge is the main steel-and-concrete one, while the upper bridge is a wooden bypass. Possibly the main bridge was breached before this photo was taken. At lower left are zigzag slit trenches and camp buildings. (*Matt Poole, via US National Archives and Records Administration*)

Opposite above: Photo recce imagery taken on 8 January 1945, the same day as Roy's tenth op to attack the Thailand-Burma Railway in Burma. The bridge in the photo crosses the Winyaw River at Shitpyit, Burma. The damage seen in the photo is from an earlier raid. (*Matt Poole, via US National Archives and Records Administration*)

Opposite below: An undated aerial photo of Zayatkwin, Burma, aerodrome, located twenty-five miles north-east of Rangoon, is seen here. On 16 January 1945 Roy bombed Zayatkwin on his twelfth op, aboard KH324. Note the numerous taxiways to remote aircraft revetments. (*Edward M. Young*)

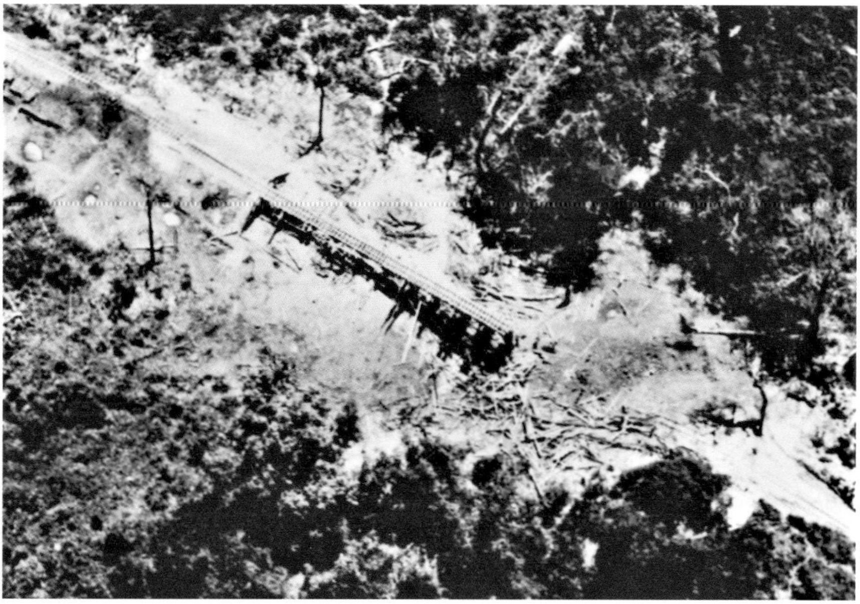

Above: A Thailand-Burma Railway bridge destroyed in an unspecified Liberator bombing attack. (*Edward M. Young*)

Below: Two Canadian Liberator pilots enjoy one another's company. Left: 215 Squadron's Eddie Gilbert, who died in a 13 March 1945 non-combat flying accident. Right: 159 Squadron's Johnny Poag. Possibly the photo was taken at Digri, where 159 and 215 were based until 215's move to Dhubalia in late 1944. (*Wally Frazer*)

Above: In a 1945 photo the shadow of a Liberator is seen as bombs fall from low level towards a wooden bridge. Timber for the bridge's construction is visible on the left. (*Crop of C 5203, Imperial War Museum*)

Below: Illustrating a typical Thailand-Burma Railway station is this 30 November 1944 photo recce image of Thailand's Tha Mayo railway station, now underwater. The box highlights a likely smoke plume from a locomotive at the front of the train. (*Matt Poole, via US National Archives and Records Administration*)

Above left: Unable to reach Cox's Bazar, India, 159 Squadron Liberator BZ978, seen here, ditched in the Bay of Bengal on 6 October 1944. Numerous Air-Sea Rescue missions were flown in search of survivors, including one by Roy on 11 October – his first op – aboard KG831. Of the men photographed, only RAAF W/Op/AG Errol Ford, in the middle, was aboard the doomed BZ978; he was declared missing and has no known grave. (*Matt Poole*)

Above right: Two 215 Squadron airmen pose in front of the nose art of KH320 'D'. Roy flew his thirteenth op aboard KH320 on 18 January 1945. (*Tony O'Toole*)

Below: On 10 April 1945 a violent storm caused tremendous damage to both 99 and 215 Squadron facilities at Dhubalia. This photo shows one example of the destruction and also the resilient spirit of the victims. (*Simon Jervis*)

Above: Seen in this 29 March 1945 bomb-strike photo from a 99 Squadron Liberator are smoke and dust plumes resulting from the attack on the Rangoon, Burma, target. On this date Roy flew his thirty-third op, also to this target, aboard skipper Bill Waddington's KH372. (*James Payne*)

Below: 215 Squadron's KH214 'D' was shot down at low level while attacking a Thailand-Burma Railway target in Burma on 3 January 1945, killing the crew of eleven. At an unknown date when the Liberator was photographed the twin horizontal lines identifying it as a 215 Squadron aircraft had not been painted on the rudders. (*Pavel Turk*)

Above: A close-up of devastation resulting from the 3 February 1945 bombing of railway yards at Jumbhorn, Thailand. This was Roy's eighteenth op. (*SUK13886, Australian War Memorial*)

Below: An unidentified RAF Liberator flies at a low level over Kaungmudaw Pagoda, Burma, on 22 February 1945. Bomb blasts adjacent to the pagoda were used by the propaganda machine to tout the prowess of the Liberator bomb aimers in purposely avoiding the sacred structure. 215 Squadron, but not Roy, participated on this op. (*Crop of CI 1904, Imperial War Museum*)

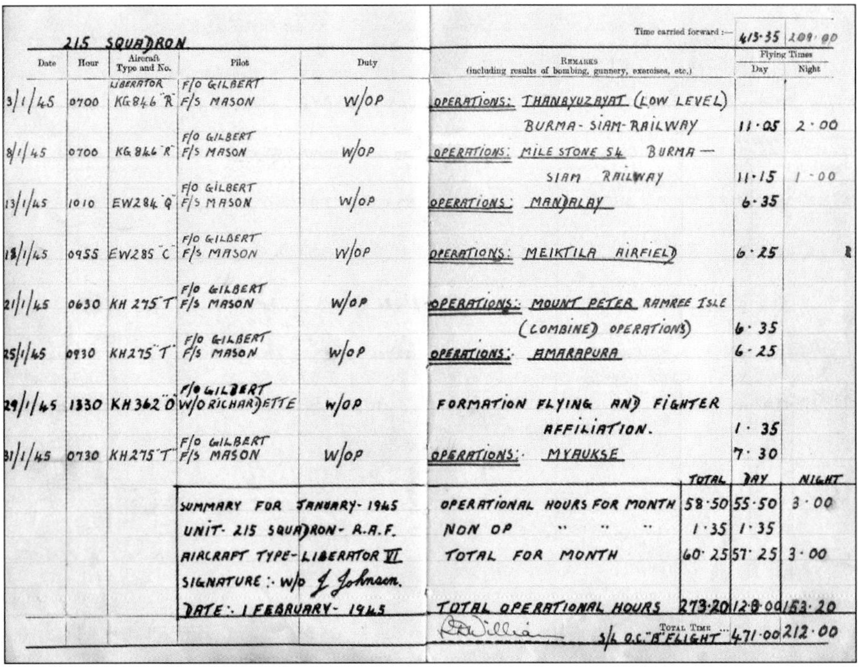

215 SQUADRON

Time carried forward :— 413·35 209·00

Date	Hour	Aircraft Type and No.	Pilot	Duty	Remarks (including results of bombing, gunnery, exercises, etc.)	Flying Times Day	Flying Times Night
3/1/45	0700	LIBERATOR KG846 'R'	F/O GILBERT F/S MASON	W/OP	OPERATIONS: THANAYUZAYAT (LOW LEVEL) BURMA-SIAM-RAILWAY	11·05	2·00
8/1/45	0700	KG846 'R'	F/O GILBERT F/S MASON	W/OP	OPERATIONS: MILE STONE 54 BURMA — SIAM RAILWAY	11·15	1·00
13/1/45	1010	EW284 'Q'	F/O GILBERT F/S MASON	W/OP	OPERATIONS: MANDALAY	6·35	
18/1/45	0955	EW285 'C'	F/O GILBERT F/S MASON	W/OP	OPERATIONS: MEIKTILA AIRFIELD	6·25	
21/1/45	0630	KH275 'T'	F/O GILBERT F/S MASON	W/OP	OPERATIONS: MOUNT PETER RAMREE ISLE (COMBINED OPERATIONS)	6·35	
25/1/45	0930	KH275 'T'	F/O GILBERT F/S MASON	W/OP	OPERATIONS: AMARAPURA	6·25	
29/1/45	1330	KH362 'O'	F/O GILBERT W/O RICHARDETTE	W/OP	FORMATION FLYING AND FIGHTER AFFILIATION.	1·35	
31/1/45	0730	KH275 'T'	F/O GILBERT F/S MASON	W/OP	OPERATIONS: MYAUKSE	7·30	

SUMMARY FOR JANUARY-1945
UNIT- 215 SQUADRON- R.A.F.
AIRCRAFT TYPE- LIBERATOR VI
SIGNATURE :- W/O J Johnson.
DATE :- 1 FEBRUARY- 1945

	TOTAL	DAY	NIGHT
OPERATIONAL HOURS FOR MONTH	58·50	55·50	3·00
NON OP " " "	1·35	1·35	
TOTAL FOR MONTH	60·25	57·25	3·00
TOTAL OPERATIONAL HOURS	273·20	120·00	153·20

S/L O.C. 'A' FLIGHT — Total Time ... 471·00 212·00

Above: The two January 1945 pages from the logbook of 215 Squadron W/Op/AG Jack Johnson. Note that 31 January's target is erroneously spelled 'Myaukse', not 'Kyaukse'. (*Matt Poole*)

Below: On 3 February 1945 215 Squadron attacked the Jumbhorn, Thailand, railway yards. This image is cropped from a bomb-strike photo taken from Roy's future skipper Bill Waddington's KH372. Aboard another 215 Squadron Liberator, KH324, Roy flew his eighteenth op. (*Simon Jervis*)

Above: 215 Squadron Liberator KH352 'M', piloted by Roy's future skipper, Bill Waddington, is seen on 25 January 1945 heading home after bombing its Amarapura, Burma, target. Roy flew on this op, his fifteenth. Circled is the destroyed Ava Bridge crossing the Irrawaddy River. Roy flew two ops aboard KH352 – 2–3 March and 7 March 1945. (*Simon Jervis*)

Below: In this 31 January 1945 strike photo from 215 Squadron Liberator KH320 'D', at left bombs erupt on the Kyaukse, Burma, target, attacked in support of British 14th Army ground actions. Roy participated on this op, his seventeenth, aboard KH324. (*Simon Jervis*)

Above: An excellent frontal view of a Mk VI Liberator. In this 21 January 1945 photo, a 356 Squadron Liberator is seen above Ramree Island after the squadron bombed its assigned Operation MATADOR target, Black Hill, covered in smoke and dust in the background. Allied naval forces can be seen at upper right. (*Crop of C 4941, Imperial War Museum*)

Below: On 25 January 1945 Roy flew his fifteenth op aboard Liberator KH398 in an attack upon Amarapura, Burma. In a photo taken that day from a 356 Squadron Liberator, smoke can be seen to rise from the bombed target. (*Simon Jervis*)

Above: 356 Squadron Liberators depart Ramree Island, Burma, on 21 January 1945. Black Hill, their Operation MATADOR target, is the left-hand smoke and dust plume in the background. On this op, Roy's fourteenth, 215 Squadron targeted Mount Peter (the right-hand plume). Nearest the camera is KH272 'D', *DAEDALUS*, later shot down in Thailand. Note the telltale 'X', 356 Squadron's identification, painted on each of its rudders. (*Crop of C 4939, Imperial War Museum*)

Below: As part of Operation MATADOR on 21 January 1945 215 Squadron bombed positions atop Mount Peter, roughly two miles inland. Three Liberators of 356 Squadron, having already attacked their separate target, are seen overflying the Mount Peter area after Roy's KH398 (his fourteenth op) and eleven other 215 Squadron aircraft had bombed that target. (*C 4940, Imperial War Museum*)

Above: An 8 January 1945 photo recce image of the Anankwin, Burma rail bridges on the Thailand-Burma Railway. The lower bridge is the main steel-and-concrete one, while the upper bridge is a wooden bypass. Possibly the main bridge was breached before this photo was taken. At lower left are zigzag slit trenches and camp buildings. (*Matt Poole, via US National Archives and Records Administration*)

Opposite above: Photo recce imagery taken on 8 January 1945, the same day as Roy's tenth op to attack the Thailand-Burma Railway in Burma. The bridge in the photo crosses the Winyaw River at Shitpyit, Burma. The damage seen in the photo is from an earlier raid. (*Matt Poole, via US National Archives and Records Administration*)

Opposite below: An undated aerial photo of Zayatkwin, Burma, aerodrome, located twenty-five miles north-east of Rangoon, is seen here. On 16 January 1945 Roy bombed Zayatkwin on his twelfth op, aboard KH324. Note the numerous taxiways to remote aircraft revetments. (*Edward M. Young*)

Above: 215 Squadron aircrew, including Wing Commander James Sindall, the squadron CO (3rd from the left). Far left: pilot Bill Waddington, Roy's final skipper. 2nd from the right: bomb aimer John 'Smokey' Williams. Waddington became Roy's captain after three Canadians on 215 Squadron (Williams, pilot 'Mac' Gardner – Roy's skipper at the time – and pilot Eddie Gilbert) died in a non-combat flying accident on 13 March 1945. (*Squadron Leader Tim Sindall*)

Below: Men bomb-up a 215 Squadron Liberator. The unknown RAF serial number, obscured by the starboard wing and no. four engine, was painted on the upper rear fuselage behind the beam gun window (on each side). Seen on the outer starboard rudder is one of the two horizontal stripes – 215 Squadron's identification. (*Crop of PR5352, Air Force Museum of New Zealand*)

Above: In a 4 September 1944 photo recce image rail cars are seen at Bangkok Noi railway station, located near the wide Chao Phraya River in Bangkok, Thailand. Roy's squadron bombed this station on the night of 4-5 March 1945, but he was not on the op. (*Matt Poole, via US National Archives and Records Administration*)

Below: 215 Squadron RCAF W/Op/AG Harold Irvine in front of Liberator EW285's nose art. Not seen is the word CLARENCE painted above the animal. On 1 December 1944 Roy flew his fifth op in this aircraft. Irvine was killed with his crew on 3 January 1945 when KH214 was shot down while attacking a Thailand-Burma Railway target. (*Crop of PL60048, Library and Archives Canada*)

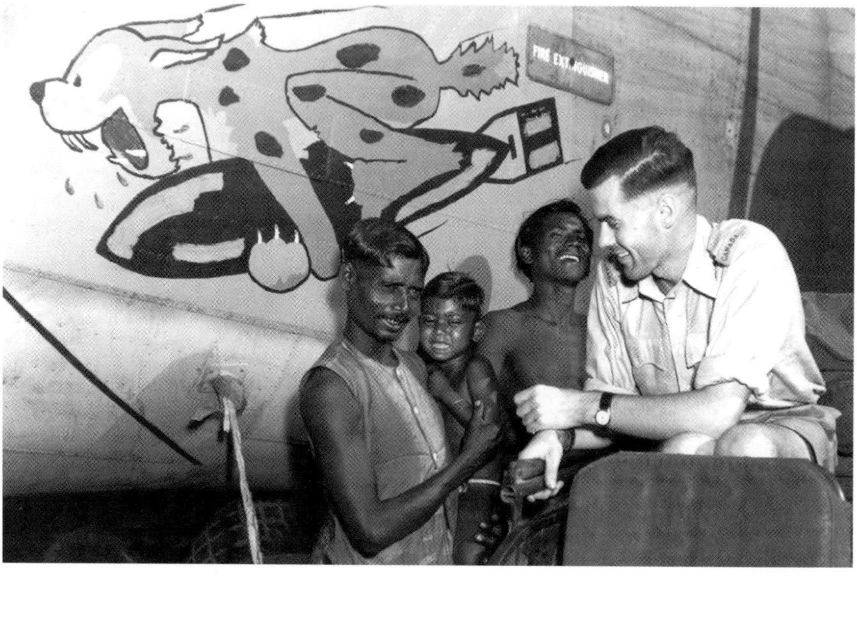

Liberators) and 356 (fourteen aircraft) Squadrons would share a unique target. This would be a big show for the heavy bombers.

The assignment given to 215 Squadron was to knock out the big guns and defensive positions atop Mount Peter roughly two miles inland. The Libs of 99 Squadron would attack a separate target just above the beach closer to Kyaukpyu town. The combined 355 and 356 Squadrons force would target gun positions on Black Hill, a thickly wooded terrain feature, 236 feet above sea level, adjacent to the Bay of Bengal near Adams Point. The American heavy bombers were directed to assault a Japanese supply area.

The island's topography, though not severe, afforded the Japanese defenders relatively higher ground locations upon which to site guns and amass troops. Additionally, from some sites such as Black Hill the enemy benefitted from sweeping vistas over Kyaukpyu town, the invasion beaches and out to sea. Kyaukpyu's airfield and strategic port were important objectives for the invaders.

Following 99 Squadron, ten aircraft from 215 took off between 0605 and 0621 on the morning of 21 January starting with Roy's own Liberator. After getting airborne at 0630 and 0640, respectively, the last two B-24s from 215 were able to catch up and join their squadron's formation.

Thus, Dhubalia's contingent of twenty-eight bombers from two squadrons safely climbed to cruising altitude and headed eastward.

While 99 Squadron was forming up in the vicinity of Sandwip Island at the north-easternmost point of the Bay of Bengal, two of its Libs, KG974 'D' and KH254 'N', collided and violently exploded at 5,000 feet. The time was 0705, in the early light of morning – when visual acuity was sometimes challenging to the human brain and, thus, rendezvous activities could be a strain. Later it was confirmed that all twenty-three men aboard the two Liberators died.

ROY: The timing of the combined offensive juggernaut in the Ramree Island vicinity was impeccable and impressive. Approaching from the north in clear conditions, 215 Squadron's airmen observed naval ships shelling from west of the island. This shelling stopped as bombers went in to attack their assigned targets. Our squadron headed inland perhaps three minutes before 99 Squadron's fourteen surviving aircraft crossed the coast.

MATT: Circa 0929 Roy's squadron's Libs then made the run upon Mount Peter in level flight formation from an altitude of around 6,000 feet. Each of 215 Squadron's dozen Liberators dropped 10,000 pounds of explosives. Included in the total for eleven of these Libs, Roy's among them, were four 1,000lb air burst anti-personnel bombs designed to decimate the enemy troops below. Certainly Roy wouldn't have wanted to be on the receiving end of those air burst bombs.

ROY: It was very difficult to determine the exact crest of Mount Peter, really just a hill, when flying over it. Mount Peter's summit would have been a challenging pinpoint for any bomb aimer to hit, but in toggling bombs on the leader's sign 215 Squadron scored a close concentration of burst on the crest and seaward slopes of the hill. Specific results couldn't be ascertained through the dense foliage and the smoke and dust from the explosions, but the British Army later deemed our results an essential achievement.

MATT: In the excellent weather conditions the airmen aboard the other Liberators, both RAF and US, also succeeded in pounding their assigned targets on Ramree Island.

Other Japanese defensive positions were attacked by fighters and medium bombers, particularly along the invasion beach. No Allied Liberators met opposition, in part owing to this ground strafing, and to the effects of the naval bombardment, as well.

As the British and American aircraft left the island, naval shelling resumed. The movements of landing craft approaching the northern shore were timed to discharge Allied troops and equipment at the cessation of the aerial assault and naval shelling.

ROY: Having never seen a landing before, I was keen to take in the action below from my perch in the sky. Watching a large warship, standing offshore, as it fired landward was thrilling. When the ship fired a broadside it heeled over, stirring up the sand in the shallows around the ship. Then, from behind the ship came landing barges racing for the shore. In the sunshine the choreographed movements of the invading force looked tremendous. Hollywood couldn't have recreated the scene!

MATT: The aerial bombardment, ground strafing and naval shelling enabled the invading forces to secure a valuable beachhead, which quickly led to the capture of Kyaukpyu. Roy expressed intense pride at being a part of it all. While Operation MATADOR wasn't nearly on the scale of D-Day in Europe, neither was the war in the Far East comparable in size to the epic battles on and over the European continent. Warfare was relative, and the fighting in the Far East was grim, ferocious and uniquely challenging in its own right.

The twelve 215 Squadron Libs routinely made their way back to Dhubalia and safely touched down between 1240 and 1300. The Bingham crew's 'H', one of three aircraft to land at 1300, had been airborne for six hours and fifty-five minutes. In fact, all of the RAF and US B-24s involved in the day's actual bombing safely returned to home bases.

Roy and his 215 Squadron mates would have heard that one of the American B-24s crashed on take-off at Pandaveswar airfield in India, killing the entire crew. Then came the tragic loss of the two 99 Squadron Liberators when forming up prior to bombing. With the realisation that three crews were wiped out 'just like that', and reflecting upon the reality of flying, Roy and his fellow 215 Squadron airmen would have acknowledged that even when enemy gunfire wasn't aimed their way, and even when the weather didn't pummel the aircraft, their occupation was inherently dangerous.

An account of the Ramree Island invasion, found in the 23 January 1945 edition of the newspaper *Advocate* from Burnie, Tasmania, would have been typical of the historic Operation MATADOR's print coverage:

> RAMREE ISLAND INVADED
> AFTER TERRIFIC SHELLING
>
> CALCUTTA, Monday – After a terrific bombardment by British, Australian and Indian warships and Liberators and Mitchells carrying Australian and New Zealand crews, South-East Asia Command troops to-day [no, it was Sunday, not Monday] invaded Ramree Island, an important Japanese defensive position and supply staging point on the Arakan coast. This third amphibious attack in the Burma war against an island 45 miles by 15 takes 15th Corps forces another 60 miles down the coast from Akyab and improves their chances of cutting off the remaining Japanese troops in the Arakan.
>
> The operation was perfectly timed. The crews of the bombers, nearly all of which carried Dominion crews, saw as they approached the island in the morning sunlight warships belching smoke and flames. Fire ceased as the bombers went in to attack. Ten minutes later the bombers pulled away, the ships resumed the bombardment and landing

craft went in in two lines. As the troops swarmed up the beaches fighters went on with the task of silencing machine-gun nests and attacking transport.

Squadron Leader D.K. Macdonald, of Randwick (N.S.W.), who led his squadron of fighters in a deck-level attack on the beaches and town of Kyaukpyu, saw the Liberators bombing the area around Ondaw.

"I have never seen a more frightening thing in my life," he said. "I was flying beneath the Liberators when I saw their bomb doors open and stick after stick of bombs come down till they smothered the entire target, and it was amazing to watch huge columns of smoke with flames sparkling in the middle. I was so close that I could hear the bombs exploding. We watched the troops swarm up the beaches and then went ahead and strafed some machine-gun nests."

"We made a lovely bomb pattern over our target" said Flying Officer Leo Kenney, of South Yarra, Victoria, bomb aimer in a Liberator captained by Flying Officer J.E. Haycock, of Nelson, New Zealand. "Everything was over in a minute, and by the time we turned for base landing craft were under way for the shore."

On his last operational flight of the tour was Flight-Sgt. George E. Tucker, of Footscray, Victoria. His parents were killed in an air raid in England. Two friends from Shepparton, Victoria, were Flight-Sgts. Errol Wallace and Rex George. Another Australian in the same crew was Flight-Sgt. Foreman, of Beach Road, Bunbury, West Australia.

Ramree, which is slightly bigger than the Isle of Wight, is a dagger pointed at Taungup, 20 miles away [a fair description, but Ramree Island was not quite pointed at Taungup]. Supplies from Prome were staged at Taungup to Kyaukpyu, a port on Ramree Island, from which they were distributed through the western Burmese river system.

Thursday, 25 JANUARY 1945
(Roy's fifteenth op)
Amarapura, BURMA – railway and industrial installations
(daylight bombing)

In a posted Battle Order on Tuesday, 23 January, twelve 215 Squadron crews, including Roy and his crew, were notified of an upcoming op scheduled for the following day. They then learned of the mission details at the 1500 briefing that afternoon. In conjunction with 99 Squadron the scheme originally was to send 215 out across the Bay of Bengal for a daylight attack upon the railway cutting at Milestone 54 of the Thailand-Burma Railway, south of Thanbyuzayat, Burma. As was the norm of late Roy would fly as first W/Op in the crew skippered by Bingham and with Flight Sergeant Raby as the second pilot. Their Lib would again be KH398 'H', the same as on the previous op. Each of 215 Squadron's participating Libs would be loaded with ten 500lb bombs (5,000 pounds per aircraft).

Due to adverse weather conditions, however, the op was then postponed for a day, until the twenty-fifth, and the target was changed to the railway and industrial installations at Amarapura, Burma – just south-west of Mandalay, and, like Mandalay itself, east of the Irrawaddy River. The added day of rest would be refreshing and rejuvenating to Roy; having been on five of the last six 215 Squadron ops, he had accumulated thirty-five hours and twenty-three minutes of operational time over this recent short period.

On the twenty-fifth, and with the return of fine weather, the op was on. First to take off from Dhubalia was 99 Squadron; twelve of its Liberators successfully climbed into the morning sky. Then, between 0930 and 0945, 215 Squadron's twelve chosen Libs and crews took to the air for the unit's latest incursion into enemy airspace; 'H', Roy's bomber, was the first of its squadron to lift off.

As the distance to the revised target would now be hundreds of miles shorter than to the original Thailand-Burma Railway destination, the bombloads on all of 215's participating Liberators were significantly increased; now each bomber would carry 10,000 pounds of high explosives – double the original weight.

Suffering an engine malfunction, one 99 Squadron Liberator turned back for Dhubalia at 1025, but the eleven other aircraft from the squadron reached the target, also the rail facilities at Amarapura, just over half an hour before 215 Squadron's arrival. Eleven 355 Squadron Liberators and twelve 356 Squadron Libs also hit railway and industrial targets in Amarapura that day.

As planned, without fighter escort 215 Squadron bombed between 1233 and 1236 from an average altitude of just under 6,000 feet, leaving a well-concentrated bomb pattern on the target. Roy's Liberator released its load at 1235 from 6,400 feet.

Smoke and dust from bomb bursts covered the entire western and northern areas of the target. After bombing, three fires with red and orange flames sprang up in a north-south line along the western portion of the target, one giving off black smoke, suggesting burning oil. Subsequent post-raid photographic analysis revealed large areas of devastation in the town on either side of the railway track, including heavy damage to barracks, storage sheds and residential-type buildings.

The attacking aircraft had been routed to the target from the south-west in order to avoid passing over known heavy anti-aircraft batteries at Sagaing and Myitnge. Though the route taken was favourable, it didn't shield the Liberators from all enemy ground fire. Bursts of heavy ack-ack, of moderate intensity, were generally reported as accurate for height but inaccurate for direction. Accurate light anti-aircraft fire was encountered, as well, but, really, in an area that was typically a hotbed of defensive activity the attacking Liberators ran the gauntlet in fine shape with only three aircraft receiving superficial splinter damage.

No Japanese fighters were even seen in the sky. The enemy aircraft response was tellingly feeble for such a major Japanese-held locale.

Roy was comfortably seated at the Officers' Mess back at Dhubalia, drink in hand, by early evening, having landed at 1602 after another six hours and thirty-two minutes of flight time. His Liberator was the seventh 215 Squadron aircraft back from the raid; the twelve touched down at Dhubalia between 1554 and 1608.

Despite anti-aircraft damage to several bombers in the attacking force from four RAF squadrons there were no human casualties among any of the airmen. All aircraft from these squadrons returned safely to their bases.

Sunday, 28 JANUARY 1945
(Roy's sixteenth op)
Kangaw, BURMA – troops and fortifications *(daylight bombing)*

Nearly one month after 215 Squadron's relocation to Dhubalia a Battle Order was posted announcing a planned 28 January bombing sortie. Roy's tour of ops would continue as the first W/Op to Bingham, the skipper, and to Flight Sergeant Raby, again flying as second pilot. Roy and his crew would be back aboard 'their' personal aircraft, Liberator KH324 'B'.

ROY: At the 1500 briefing on 27 January, details were spelled out. The British Army had again requested RAF Liberator support, and we were psyched at the opportunity when called upon to bomb the most easterly of three small wooded hill features almost fifty miles north of where the Allies had landed during Operation MATADOR on the twenty-first. The hill in question, near the hamlet of Kangaw, Burma, was interspersed with numerous strongpoints: Japanese bunkers, foxholes, trenches and gun positions.

MATT: The most westerly of the three hills was occupied by Allied troops, while the middle hill was 'No Man's Land' between the opposing combatants. Given the presence of British 14th Army forces so near to the Japanese, and atop a feature similar to that occupied by the Japanese, it couldn't be stressed enough to Roy and the others at their briefing that accurate bombing was essential, despite the fact that ground detail would make pinpointing the correct hill from above a challenge. In addition, each of 215 Squadron's twelve participating Libs would be dropping a sizeable load – 11,000 pounds, consisting of ten 1,000lb and two 500lb bombs. Placed accurately, that's a frightening total; placed on their own troops, that's a frightening total!

The attack was planned as another daylight formation bombing foray. The airmen were directed to approach the target from the south so as to best be able to view landmark features and also to minimise the chances of hitting their own troops. Aircraft were briefed not to bomb unless certain of the correct target.

Though the issue of avoiding British and Commonwealth troops added pressure to the assignment, this op would be as close to a milk run as was ever handed to the Liberator airmen. A dozen Liberators from each of 99 and 355 Squadrons and eight aircraft from 356 Squadron would join 215 on the attack. Bombs released from forty-seven Liberators would rock the earth, kill, maim and destroy, as if the RAF aircraft were dropping explosive exclamation marks to demonstrate their prowess.

The aircraft of 215 Squadron took off between 0641 and 0656 on the twenty-eighth. Roy's B-24 was one of two airborne at 0645 as the third and fourth bombers to take to the sky. Unescorted by fighters and under conditions of good visibility, the 215 Squadron Liberators formed up, trailed by 99 Squadron's aircraft.

Imbued with the intensity and focus needed to 'get it right', the dozen 215 Squadron bomb aimers identified the target and then accurately toggled their loads. The assigned target zone was well-covered by bomb bursts dropped between 0953 and 0954 from an average height of approximately 3,000 feet. The crew of EW284 'Q' reported seeing hewn timbers, presumably from Japanese revetments, flying into the air as bomb bursts wreaked their havoc. Though Roy expressed the feeling that he was, and had always been, a compassionate soul, the enemy's shocking and sickening record of brutality made it relatively easy to accept, with little anguish, the airmen's role in raining terrible carnage down upon their Japanese adversaries. This attack was fundamentally different than ops where Liberator bombs must have damaged and destroyed the physical property and lives of innocent civilians.

After 215 Squadron's initial attack, 99, 355 and 356 Squadrons bombed, and with similar accuracy.

No Japanese fighter opposition was encountered, nor was anti-aircraft fire an issue. Tactical surprise was evidently achieved on this op. It was logical to assume that the enemy would use its available fighter strength for defence of ground positions, under attack, if sufficient warning of impending operations could be obtained. However, no doubt over 500 RAF Liberator airmen in the sky that day felt a sense of relief in there being no aerial opposition, and no anti-aircraft fire from below.

Far removed from a metropolitan area or a known enemy facility like an aerodrome, the defensive response hardly compared to that typically faced when the flyers hit Rangoon or Mandalay, or an airfield like Mingaladon. Despite the ease in prosecuting their attack, the airmen were well aware that complacency was potentially dangerous; they never knew when an anti-aircraft projectile might have some of their names on it, or when one of the few Japanese Army Air Force fighter pilots still flying would flex his muscles and risk dying for the Emperor in an attack upon the bombers.

An hour before Roy landed he received over the wireless the following message of congratulations to the RAF from British Army ground observers in the area regarding the accuracy and effectiveness of the attack: 'The bombing was first class, and the whole show went like clockwork.' It must have been gratifying to Roy and his crewmates to have their efforts acknowledged.

The twelve participating Liberators from 215 Squadron touched down at Dhubalia between 1257 and 1310; Bingham set 'B' down at 1300 after six hours and fifteen minutes aloft. Most of 215's airmen were friends after what amounted to a relatively short and safe op like this. All knew that future assignments wouldn't be as easy, and certainly not as brief as this one's average of six hours and thirteen minutes of flying time per 215 Squadron bomber.

All forty-seven of the participating Liberators from the four RAF squadrons returned safely to their bases.

Wednesday, 31 JANUARY 1945
(Roy's seventeenth op)
Kyaukse, BURMA – Japanese administrative headquarters and stores
(daylight bombing)

The Allied war machine was in high gear at this stage of the 1945 dry season. Via the terrible punishment being meted out from above the Liberator crews kept up their part in 'encouraging' the Japanese to further fragment and to cede control over geography they'd claimed as their own and people they'd subjugated – and, in some cases, tortured and/or murdered. The highest-level RAF planners weren't about to let 215 Squadron ease up now; it was well-recognised that Liberators flown by dedicated airmen could do a lot of good by doing a lot of bad with their bomb bay payloads, often delivered across tremendous distances.

Roy and the other 215 Squadron airmen learned at a 1600 briefing on 30 January that one more op would be squeezed out of them before the month ended. The Bingham crew – with Flight Sergeant Raby as second pilot aboard KH324 'B' and Roy as first W/Op – would be one of 215's twelve Libs to be sent out during the day on 31 January to attack the Japanese administrative headquarters and stores in Kyaukse, Burma, twenty-five miles south of Mandalay. The op would be their second consecutive British Army support action, and most of the 215 Squadron airmen chosen for the op would have been more than willing to again offer assistance.

Adding to the RAF's offensive punch, as on the last op, would be twelve 99 Squadron Libs, twelve aircraft from 355 Squadron and eleven from 356 Squadron. A small force of American B-24s would be involved on this op, too.

Each of 215 Squadron's aircraft would release 10,000 pounds of explosives (eight 1,000lb and four 500lb bombs).

Eleven of 215's twelve scheduled bombers took off between 0729 and 0742, and the twelfth was airborne at 0818 after a temporary issue was sorted out; Roy's Lib, functioning smoothly, was up and gone at 0739. Soon thereafter 99 Squadron also put its contingent of twelve aircraft into the sky from Dhubalia, but their force was reduced to eleven Libs when one turned back with engine troubles long before bombing. A partly cloudy sky marked the Dhubalia take-offs and then the route in towards the target, but a cloudless vista of five to ten miles in the Kyaukse area with only slight ground haze afforded all bomb aimers in the first attack wave easy identification of the aiming point in the built-up portion of the town west of the Zawgyi River.

The approach by 215 Squadron was from the north-west.

The Japanese headquarters complex, consisting of buildings among shade trees, was plastered with a good concentration of bombs, first by 99 Squadron's eleven Libs from between 1109 and 1111 and followed less than two minutes later by 215 Squadron's twelve bombers between 1112½ and 1115 from an average of nearly 5,600 feet. Roy's Lib, 'B', bombed at 1113 from 6,100 feet.

Many buildings and a canal bridge were seen to disintegrate, and fires were started in the area, but billowing smoke and dust prevented further observation. From above the attacking airmen witnessed one large conflagration that, clearly showing through the haze, emitted black smoke to 3,000 feet.

Once again, even with no fighter protection, aerial opposition was non-existent. The Japanese Army Air Force, a worthy adversary on occasion in Burma, was, by this date, chiefly concentrated in the vicinity of Rangoon, and interception of incoming Allied sorties over central and northern Burma was generally dependent upon adequate advanced warning. However, the attacking Libs had been routed so as to give the enemy the briefest possible warning of their presence over Japanese-held territory.

Although 215 Squadron had been first to depart from Dhubalia that morning, the Liberators of 99 Squadron were the first to return, followed between 1455 and 1507 by 215's bombers. No. 215 Squadron followed, safely putting down between 1455 and 1507. Roy's KH324 'B' landed at 1502 after a flight time of seven hours and twenty-three minutes.

The sortie – one more feather in the RAF's cap – was much appreciated by the British Army. It amounted to another relatively easy op not just for Roy and his crew, but also for the other participating RAF and US Liberators; all returned safely, although one 355 Squadron aircraft was superficially damaged by the 'meagre but accurate' heavy ack-ack.

An assessment at the end of JANUARY 1945

These army cooperation ops tended to mesh well with the pre-dinner social scene in the 215 Squadron Officers' Mess. Though the boys must have been weary from a heavy January schedule of flying ops, morale appeared to be running at a high level not just among Roy and his fellow officers, but throughout the entire squadron. It helped that the daily reports of progress against the enemy in this theatre were mostly heartening, and all ranks had been encouraged by dreams of going home sooner rather than later. Hope must have sprung eternal in their young minds.

The advent of Australian meat in 215 Squadron's Messes and the final disappearance from the menu of the wretched soya links (imitation sausages) certainly were greatly appreciated; morsels and morale went hand in hand.

ROY: By the end of January I'd finished approximately half of my 215 Squadron tour of ops; I no longer have access to my logbook to view the exact numbers. The 300-hour or thirty-op measuring stick wasn't set in stone for defining a tour's length. The limits, for example, could be voluntarily exceeded. Certainly the numbers were on the minds of all airmen.

MATT: Some statistics on 215 Squadron flying times for January 1945 are worth repeating, because Roy and the others on the squadron accomplished plenty, despite the challenges. Although 215 Squadron's men knew that flyers from many other units faced difficulties that dwarfed their own, they must have been proud of the dogged tenacity they displayed in January; even decades later Roy retained tremendous esteem for the exploits of 215's members, both on the ground and in the air. Here are a very few stats for January:

Operational sorties: 105
Operational hours flown:
  Day – 762 hours 18 minutes
  Night – 83 hours 12 minutes
Number of bombs dropped during the month:
  1,000 pounders – 509
  500 pounders – 657
  250 pounders – 3

The weight of the 1,169 bombs dropped in January totalled 838,250 pounds, with 11,000 pounds having been the heaviest load carried by an individual Liberator on an op that month. This was most impressive for a squadron that was only introduced to the complex Liberator in the second half of 1944, didn't begin bombing ops until the night of 2-3 November 1944 and which was also put to the test by having to relocate from Digri to underprepared Dhubalia.

On the ground January had been a month of planning and feverish activity to regain a state of comfort and organisation at Dhubalia comparable to Digri. Most had settled down quite happily – 'happily' being a relative term – by 31 January. This marked approximately one month on station at Dhubalia, a point by which Roy and the others on his squadron had made great strides towards improving their haunts, including the setting up of activities to keep them engaged in things other than pure aviation and war-related matters.

Dhubalia was theirs, and 215 Squadron's members, no different than the lads of any unit, loved life and sought activities on base that were entertaining and, in some cases, diversional. After all, they were out in rural India, in a difficult climate, preoccupied with a deadly serious task, and mostly not long removed from the embraces of loved ones back home and levels of comfort that had become but memories. Making Dhubalia feel even the tiniest bit more comfortable was essential to keeping in good 'fighting trim'; naturally, it was different for each man.

Although it was expected that 215 Squadron would be required to relocate from Dhubalia to another new aerodrome at some point, to have wasted any time thinking about that future ordeal would have been frowned upon. A man might be dead by then. Or posted elsewhere. Or even fat and happy back home following the war's conclusion, or after separating from the air force and once again being on 'Civvy Street'. And maybe a move wouldn't even happen, after all. So, few men likely muddied their brains with thoughts of future moves.

A very useful setup at Dhubalia was the squadron's library and writing centre. An unused room was in the process of being converted into a quiet space for writing and reading. Having been painted by the end of January, the room awaited the imminent arrival of required furniture. Already some four hundred books from 231 Group Welfare had been donated to establish a library in the quiet room, and 215 Squadron's members had also contributed numerous books. With a dedicated librarian lending a hand, the endeavour was sure to be very popular.

Sport was popular among young men at every establishment, even in Bengal, where the weather could be brutal. Naturally, a major move to Dhubalia meant that sporting endeavours couldn't be prioritised, but much sport-related organisation was in the cards, when time allowed in-between the myriad activities that took precedence – like taking the war to the enemy.

Roy and the others on 215 Squadron weren't about to let sporting activities wither on the vine. Already by the end of the month a football field had been prepared, and local on-station matches with 99 Squadron had occurred. It's no surprise that interest in ramping up intersectional league play between, say, 215 Squadron 'A' Flight ground crew and 215 Squadron 'B' Flight airmen was high. The Liberator men at Dhubalia were on a great footing here; football had a way of uniting all.

Cricket, a popular sport, had not developed, only because the construction of a pitch had not yet been possible. It was just a matter of time and effort. With badminton requiring very little in terms of playing fields, and following the erection of nets all over the camp, the game proved to be exceedingly popular.

Even the construction of a golf course was under careful consideration.

One example of 215 Squadron's work to establish Dhubalia as a more functional site could be seen in a report at the end of January by the Electrical and Instrument Section. A considerable amount of overtime had been spent to bring new workshops into a serviceable condition following the move from Digri. A specialist section was being set up internally to deal with items of equipment such as auto-controls, gunsights and bombsights, in the hope that this would enable the unit to keep free of many former minor troubles.

The section was still working under extreme difficulty due to a lack of transport. Dhubalia's other Liberator-flying inhabitant, 99 Squadron, had three times the amount of transport, yet 215 Squadron's Electrical and Instrument Section required many times the mileage accumulated in the same job by 99 Squadron. As 1945 advanced 215 Squadron's transport issues would continue to be lessened.

It's worth noting that many men on the squadron preferred Dhubalia to Digri because of the comparative ease in which Calcutta could be reached on a forty-eight-hour pass. The benefit of being within easy and timely reach of Calcutta would also pay dividends in the form of frequent visits by ENSA and RAF road shows to Dhubalia. Already the 215 Squadron Welfare lads were working on arranging these visits. Having 99 Squadron on the same station, in this regard, was also a great plus, as the travelling revues liked to 'kill two birds with one stone' by performing for more than one squadron at the same station.

All clubs on 215 Squadron were subjected to the inconveniences in losing personnel, mainly through changes such as postings to other assignments (following, for example, the successful conclusions of airmen's tours of ops) and much more rarely due to illness, injury or death. A positive point was that at any time there were still many who willingly organised tournaments. By late January, activities were in full swing again. These seemingly little things certainly would have made life at Dhubalia so much more bearable for Roy and his mates.

Chapter 15

215 Squadron, India: FEBRUARY 1945 *(Part 1)*

215 Squadron's February 1945 summary

February was another busy month for 215 Squadron, in order to both take advantage of the dry season's weather window of opportunity and because the prowess of the Liberators and their crews was much in demand. Fifteen bombing attacks were flown by the squadron in February, and Roy was on nine of them.

The tactical ops in support of the British 14th Army's ground actions dominated 215 Squadron's assignments through 25 February. Undertaken sometimes daily, these tactical raids, primarily aimed at Japanese headquarters, administrative buildings and stores, were typically to areas in Burma close to the fighting fronts. The bombing attacks contributed to rapid advances by Allied ground forces, and aircrew and ground crew on the squadron would have taken great interest in watching the geographic positions of the fronts expand in the Allies' favour. Thanks to the diligence and keenness of the ground crews serviceability was maintained at a very high level on the squadron, and morale of both air and ground crews was seen by unbiased visitors as being remarkably high.

Roy had previously flown on other 215 Squadron ops in support of ground troops, so to continue to be called upon to offer the squadron's unique tactical services to the fighting forces down below must have truly been an honour to him. However, the squadron still embraced its strategic bombing role, and Roy and the fellow members of his unit would have also considered their participation on these strategic bombing raids to be a matter of tremendous pride.

A nearly complete lack of Japanese air opposition now marked 215 Squadron's sorties over northern and central Burma, strong evidence, as previously noted, of the enemy's weakness in the air. Only once during February, at Rangoon on the eleventh, were Roy's squadron's aircraft intercepted. On that occasion at least one Tony fighter and possibly two fighters were shot down without the enemy having inflicted any damage on the squadron's formation. No casualties were sustained by squadron crews during the entire month of February, yet a year earlier the same ops would have been considered much more hazardous due to the enemy aerial defences.

Further fun in the Officers' Mess

ROY: The bar in the 215 Squadron Officers' Mess at Dhubalia continued to bring us essential fun and relief, as it had at Digri. Leading Aircraftman Taffy Humphreys, our barman both at Digri and Dhubalia, hailed from Merthyr Tydfil in southern Wales. What else would we call a southern Welshman but 'Taffy'?

Every night after our baths we officers adjourned to our Mess for drinks before dinner. We inevitably finished up playing a game called liar dice, which required the ability to deceive and to also detect an opponent's deception. The object of this drinking game was to outbluff one's opponents, but if a player lost a challenge he 'lost a life', and a match was placed in front of him. After a player had accrued three matches he had to buy the other members a round of drinks.

By the time we went into the dining room for dinner I'd possibly had three drinks to consume. Hence, I was pretty high by then. This, of course, was if we weren't flying the next day.

I played the riotous game of saddle-me-nag at every station I'd attended, always in an environment characterised by laughter and fun. We were young and foolish in some of our bar activities, but every moment I remember brings a smile to my face. What grand times those were!

Our antics weren't without a minor casualty in Doc Steele-Perkins. On one occasion while participating in saddle-me-nag fun our Medical Officer raced for the line of backs, misjudged the angle somehow and crashed through the wall of the Mess, damaging his arm. Despite roughhousing in this manner and physically ending up somewhat worse for wear, he took it all in stride. It was marvellous fun, not all that dissimilar from getting bashed playing rugby, though perhaps Doc needed to see a doc afterwards!

And yet we knew our serious roles as air force men, not all of which were performed at altitude aboard Libs in flight. For example, there was Doc, of course, who was ground bound and ever so important for the welfare of all squadron personnel. As another example, I was made Officer in Charge of aircrew rations. Because our flights, including some training sorties, were typically of long duration, the crews had to be fed. Rations were made up by the cooks and placed aboard the aircraft for such trips. It was my job to see that this provisioning was always carried out; such assignments came with an officer's rank.

Saturday, 3 FEBRUARY 1945
(Roy's eighteenth op)
Jumbhorn, THAILAND – railway yards *(daylight bombing)*

MATT: Roy and his crewmates were mentioned on a Battle Order posted on 2 February, in advance of an op on the third, three days after their last sortie. Presumably the short break helped Roy to clear his head following a busy January, but he also likely looked forward to more flying as he inched further along the path to completing a full tour of ops. On the Battle Order for 3 February's op Roy was listed in his usual position as first W/Op to Bingham, the skipper, aboard Liberator KH324 'B', with Flight Sergeant Raby as the second pilot. Twelve crews were named.

At the 1500 briefing on 2 February, it was learned that the target would be the Jumbhorn, Thailand, railway yards, far down the Kra Isthmus 240 miles south-south-west of Bangkok. For this op 215 Squadron would fly once again in a long-range strategic bombing role.

Engineering work initiated by 159 Squadron's CO in the second half of 1944, legendary Wing Commander James Blackburn, had revolutionised the Liberator's range and bomb-carrying capabilities. For the 3 February 1945 op 215 Squadron was being asked to take the war further south than they'd ever been before. Because of the distance to be flown to Jumbhorn and back, 215's crew sizes on this lengthy flight had been reduced from eleven men to nine, allowing for an increase in each bomber's petrol and bombload capacities. The number of crewmen per Lib returned to eleven for 215 Squadron's next fourteen ops.

The load for each of the 215 Squadron Liberators on the 3 February op was announced on the Battle Order as being nine 500lb high explosive bombs (4,500 pounds). The petrol amount per aircraft, which included fuel carried in a temporary bladder in each Lib's bomb bay for the long flying distance required, would be 2,654 gallons.

The twelve participating Liberators from 215 Squadron took to the sky between 0820 and 0842 on the morning of 3 February; 'B' was the sixth Lib to climb into the air, at 0835. Twelve Libs from 99 Squadron trailed 215 in departing Dhubalia, bound for the same target, with their take-offs starting at 0855. Although one 99 Squadron aircraft turned back with engine trouble less than two hours later (it safely landed back at Dhubalia) the eleven other 99 Squadron Libs followed 215 Squadron to the target.

In what became the standard procedure on long ops to the south, aircraft flew low and were routed as far as possible over water to avoid the Japanese radar at Rangoon and Moulmein. It was believed that this would lessen the risk of fighter interception from these areas. Although enemy fighter strength was at its weakest since Japan conquered Burma in 1942, it still made sense to be on guard. Further south from Moulmein the radar at Tavoy, Burma, also had to be avoided, as best as possible, by staying low and far out over the water.

The weather en route was good from Dhubalia to about the 20th parallel of latitude, which was only 115 or so miles south of the Sundarbans at the top of the Bay of Bengal. South of this line the Liberator airmen encountered considerable low clouds but only minor local rainstorms – nothing to worry them.

The target area itself was clear and easily identified. Having crossed the Kra Isthmus to a coastal landmark thirty-four miles from Jumbhorn, 215 Squadron attacked from a northerly direction.

Bombing was well-concentrated on the yards and adjacent buildings, and a very bright fire, and other smaller fires, broke out amongst buildings just south of the yards. Rolling stock was seen to be hit in all parts of the yards; wagons were derailed and thrown into the air by the bomb blasts. (The times of 'bombs gone' weren't noted in 215's ORB, but certainly the attacks came in daylight; photographs verified this.)

Trailing 215 Squadron and pummelling the same target were the eleven 99 Squadron Libs, twelve from 355 Squadron, ten from 356, and a number of US 7th Bomb Group B-24s. While the Jumbhorn railway yards were being attacked one group of American B-24s from the 493rd Bomb Squadron carried out a successful Azon bomb attack against a bridge on the Bangkok-to-Singapore railway line close to Jumbhorn, leaving the bridge unserviceable.

Surprise was evidently achieved, as there was no ack-ack reported, and there were no sightings of enemy aircraft on the whole of the flight. While air gunners would have craved a little bit of excitement now and then – and they tended to enjoy making noise by squirting off a few rounds of ammo – they also, no doubt, appreciated being alive, uninjured and free, and not PoWs of the Japanese. The lack of enemy fighters (and the lack of ack-ack), then, wouldn't have annoyed too many of the men on the op.

All of the aircraft on the flight returned safely from this highly successful operation after being airborne for a long time; each 215 Squadron Lib, for example, averaged fourteen hours and forty-eight minutes aloft. Roy's aircraft 'B' was in flight for the least amount of time of 215's twelve B-24s – a 'mere' fourteen hours and twenty-three minutes. The squadron's Libs landed back at Dhubalia between 2258 and 2347; KH324 'B' was the first to return. The last of the returning Dhubalia-based bombers, a 99 Squadron aircraft, touched down at 0040, into the first hour of 4 February.

Airmen from 99 Squadron were told that this raid was the longest formation sortie of the war, with a round trip of roughly 2,400 miles. The Americans noted that it was the longest mission they'd ever flown.

Subsequent photo reconnaissance revealed that the railway staff quarters just north of the yard had been completely annihilated, five locomotives and sixty wagons were either destroyed or else derailed and in poor condition and there had been extensive heavy damage to tracks. The station buildings and goods sheds were also completely destroyed. The RAF Libs plus the sizeable force of American B-24s left their calling cards with a vengeance.

From a newspaper cutting came this brief review of the op:

AIR OPERATIONS

> Air: Heavy bombers of Eastern Air Command in strength yesterday made their longest formation flight to attack Chumphon [Jumbhorn], on the Isthmus of Kra, Siam. They started fires in railway buildings, damaged the tracks and a bridge, derailed trucks and strafed trains.

Monday, 5 FEBRUARY 1945
(Roy's nineteenth op)
Madaya, BURMA – stores, barracks and administrative headquarters, Area 'B' ***(daylight bombing)***

With February being such a busy time for flying, Roy didn't have to wait for long after the 3 February op before he was sent out again. On the fourth he learned that he and his crewmates were on the posted Battle Order for the next day's sortie. Aboard KH324 'B', one of twelve Liberators scheduled on the op, he was listed as first W/Op to Bingham, the skipper, with Flight Sergeant Raby as the second pilot.

At the 1700 briefing on 4 February the 215 Squadron airmen scheduled for the op were informed that their attack would be upon Area 'B', an enemy stores, barracks and administrative headquarters site just west of the railway sidings at Madaya, fifteen miles north of Mandalay, Burma. All twelve of 215 Squadron's aircraft chosen for this British Army support op would carry the same load: twelve 500lb high explosive bombs per aircraft (6,000 pounds, total). Also from Dhubalia, 99 Squadron would send out six Libs. From Salbani twelve 355 Squadron Libs and twelve from 356 Squadron were also destined for Madaya, but their assaults – upon Area 'A' – would precede the attacks by 215 and 99 Squadrons by roughly five hours.

At 1348 on the fifth, Liberator 'B', Roy's aircraft, was the fourth of the squadron's bombers to take off, although the first two aircraft had departed over fifty minutes earlier. All twelve scheduled 215 Squadron bombers took to the sky, including aircraft EV989 'K' (erroneously coded as 'A' in some records), the last to go aloft twenty-seven minutes after the eleventh Liberator's take-off. Six Libs from 99 Squadron also departed Dhubalia, starting at 1400, and the eighteen aircraft of 215 and 99 Squadrons proceeded to the target unescorted by fighters.

The generally good weather en route afforded the flyers moderate visibility; cumulus clouds over Burmese hills weren't a hindrance.

Above central Burma, some nine miles north of the target, three of 215 Squadron's aircraft prematurely released their loads, over thick jungle. That was 18,000 pounds of explosives wasted! When the bomb aimer on Liberator 'Q', EW284, accidentally operated the release mechanism instead of his intercom two other bomb aimers, aboard EV989 'K' and EW125 'P', toggled their loads upon seeing bombs from 'Q' falling.

Had Roy's own bomb aimer, Nick Nicholas, been at fault, the wrath of his crewmates at that moment would have been merciless; these airmen risked their lives every time they took a Liberator aloft, and to have had their bomb aimer stumble so obviously over enemy territory, miles short of the target, would have enraged them. But Nicholas did his job well, as usual. Those at fault on 5 February were aboard other aircraft, but nevertheless, Roy and his crewmates likely raised holy hell within their own Lib when they witnessed or heard of the premature bomb releases.

In good, though hazy, weather conditions, following the error by the three Libs, 215 Squadron's remaining nine bomb-laden aircraft had an excellent cloud-free view of the town and identified the barrack buildings, the railway coming up from Mandalay to the south and the wooded area to the west. Between 1709 and 1710 the nine Libs released their bombs from an average height of 5,900 feet. The six aircraft from 99 Squadron toggled their bombs from a slightly lower altitude, averaging just under 4,400 feet, from 1709 to 1715.

The 215 Squadron Libs, including Roy's aircraft 'B', scored many bursts on the target area, with observed hits on the railway line and adjacent buildings to the east. Several secondary explosions, characterised by much dark smoke, were observed after bombing. One large fire and several smaller fires contributed to a pillar of smoke rising to 4,000 feet.

After bombing from a northerly heading the 215 Squadron Libs turned away to the west before coming within range of the ground defences in the Mandalay and Sagaing areas. But those on the ground in these locales must have been unprepared. Apart from some light machine-gun fire harmlessly directed skyward in the neighbourhood of the target 215 encountered no Japanese opposition – and never any aerial foes.

A large explosion from the target area was reported fifteen minutes after leaving Madaya.

Devoid of any unusual incidents, the homeward flights by 99 and 215 Squadron Libs were almost mundane – and the lack of enemy intervention would have been appreciated. All of the two units' participating Libs landed safely back at Dhubalia. Roy's aircraft was the fourth 215 Squadron Liberator to touch down at 2044, after registering a flight time of six hours and fifty-six minutes.

The twenty-four 355 and 356 Squadron Liberators, having bombed Madaya approximately five hours before Roy's group, had safely returned to their Salbani base. The arrival of 215 and then 99 Squadron Libs over Madaya must have been quite the shock for the Japanese below, who, no doubt, had thought the onslaught from above had already come and gone hours earlier in the day. No, Round Two was shoved in the faces of the enemy by more Liberators.

Back home afterwards the majority of the 215 Squadron airmen who'd flown the op, by then composed and reticent, must have comprehended that the three bomb aimers who'd been hanging their heads in shame for the past hours had given their best. 'Nobody's perfect' is the adage, though errors in their line of work admittedly could have dire consequences and couldn't have been allowed to be repeated. The honest wrongdoings of these three airmen were said to have motivated Roy and his fellow flyers, in a positive way, to be even better at their jobs. Consequently, it was believed that 215 Squadron became an even tighter-knit fighting unit after the 5 February op.

ROY: Certainly, we dropped bombs and incendiaries and killed and maimed people, but we never saw what pain we caused or anything of the sort, because we were high in the air and moving fast.

There was one op that did particularly upset me, and it still comes back to haunt me and raise my sense of guilt. We were bombing a village, maybe as a secondary target, because I can't believe that we'd have been sent to bomb such a vulnerable place.

My job, as usual, was to open the bomb doors. We weren't very high, but high enough so that our own exploding bombs wouldn't physically harm us or our Liberator. 'Open the bomb doors, Chico,' ordered the bomb aimer, which I did, and down went the load.

The bomb doors were still open, as they sometimes were if we weren't too high, and I could see the eruptions of detonating bombs. I saw huts smashed and going up in the air, and palm trees flying skyward and falling down again on their sides. And great clouds of dust.

Even then I was aghast at the destruction as we flew away. I looked back and saw this huge dust cloud slowly settling down. That had a terrible effect on me. It came back to me years later when I heard a piece of music I believe is called *London Concerto*, where there is a solo piece played on a single violin, and now every time I hear that piece, I remember that village. I don't like thinking about it.

MATT: Although Roy didn't identify a specific geographic site or give an attack date in the above snippet from his memoir, he did reveal his emotions regarding the consequences of bombing, impersonally, from the air. He'd briefly broached the subject in relation to his eleventh op to Mandalay, Burma, back on 13 January 1945. His enduring sense of guilt pertained to the ordeals of the innocent, far more than to those of the enemy.

The plight of innocent locals down below would have also played upon the minds of at least some of Roy's fellow 215 Squadron airmen, all of whom knew that a lack of precision could have had unintended negative consequences: the deaths and maiming of innocent victims and the destruction of or damage to their property. The men flying far above simply vowed to do their very best to defeat a wretched enemy, for the overall good of the people. What Roy and his fellow airmen were doing was to them a necessary task, and most would have felt they belonged as participants. 'Good versus evil' was a philosophy which led many men to accept the enormity of their duties and would have greatly helped to dissipate at least some of the anxiety that came with the job. As Roy described, however, the guilt in possibly harming innocent people was undeniable.

Thursday, 8 FEBRUARY 1945
(Roy does not fly on this op)
Singu, BURMA – Japanese-occupied area *(daylight bombing)*

Onward the airmen fought in tactical support of British 14th Army ground units. Some at Dhubalia perhaps bemoaned the fact that 215 Squadron wasn't being allowed to express itself as part of a strategic fighting force that independently 'did its own thing' – but this would have been a false belief, because even the tactical bombing efforts were coordinated within the scheme of the overall war plan.

Roy had affirmed that he was fine with continuing to uniquely aid Allied troops on the ground in the ongoing struggle to bash the Japanese and kick them out of Burma, with his only regret being that sometimes innocent victims likely suffered. But he understood the big picture very well. Roy approved of the overall strategy of focusing the Allied offensive bombing intensity upon Japanese headquarters, supply dumps, artillery positions, airfields, railway facilities, troop concentrations, or whatever the tactical assignment. 'Bring it on,' he would have said with conviction.

In his book, *TO BURMA SKIES AND BEYOND*, 356 Squadron skipper Reg Jordan summed up the nature of these tactical ops:

> The Fourteenth Army was approaching the river Irrawaddy along a front of over two hundred miles, and for their part the Japanese gave every indication of offering stubborn resistance along this defensive feature. With both sides aware that from early May the Irrawaddy would increase substantially in width and speed, the stage was set for an opposed crossing at an early date.
>
> From this point until the end of February, SAF [the Strategic Air Force] switched a good deal of effort from the long-range interdiction

of strategic supply routes to operations in direct support of our army in the field.

On 8 February Roy and his crewmates didn't participate on the tactical daylight op flown by twelve other 215 Squadron crews to Singu, Burma; instead, they rested, and their Lib was serviced on the ground at Dhubalia. Those airmen sent on the op were briefed at 1630 on the seventh. Singu town was four miles north-east of Chauk along the same east bank of the Irrawaddy River in Burma and on the northern end of an oil production belt mainly running from Chauk to Yenangyaung. The Singu attack was in support of the establishment of a British Army bridgehead across the Irrawaddy River near Pakokku, another thirty miles to the north, on the relentless march to victory over the Japanese in Burma.

The entire target area was well-patterned with bursts from 215 Squadron's bombs, and several fires broke out after the bombing. Liberators from 355 and 356 Squadrons also bombed Singu, while 99 Squadron targeted Yenangyaung.

Later analysis of photo reconnaissance imagery revealed heavy destruction in the entire Singu town area; 215, 355 and 356 Squadrons had done their jobs well on 8 February, without even a scratch being suffered by any airman. Libs from 99 Squadron also raised many large fires in their target area.

All participating Liberators returned safely to their bases.

Sunday, 11 FEBRUARY 1945
(Roy's twentieth op)
Rangoon, BURMA – supply dump, Area 'F' ***(daylight bombing)***

ROY: On 10 February, at 1600, my crew attended a briefing for the next day's op: a massive tactical attack upon the Rangoon dump holding an estimated fifty to seventy-five per cent of the Imperial Japanese Army's supplies in Burma. We were scheduled to participate.

MATT: An ongoing Allied campaign to destroy bridges was severely disrupting the flow of supplies. Now the destruction of a major dump complex in Rangoon would add to the negative impact upon the Japanese forces. This would be the heaviest bombing attack to date in the Burma-area war.

Roy was pencilled in to be the first W/Op aboard KH324 'B', one of twelve 215 Squadron Liberators to be sent out to Rangoon along with Libs from three more RAF units (99, 355 and 356 Squadrons), B-29 Superfortresses from the US Army Air Forces' 20th Bomber Command and B-24s of the US 7th Bomb Group. Bingham would pilot Roy's aircraft, with its eleven-man crew, and Flight Sergeant Raby would again fly in the second pilot's seat. The participating 215 Squadron aircraft would each carry a load of six 1,000lb and five 500lb high explosive bombs.

On 11 February, KH324 was the next-to-last 215 Squadron Liberator to get airborne, taking off at 0937. Including 99 Squadron, which followed 215 into the air, twenty-four aircraft departed from Dhubalia.

The outward journey, flown without incident, was characterised by good visibility and a decrease in clouds as the target was approached.

No clouds blocked the siting of the dump, though 215's specific aiming point was obscured by heat haze and dense black smoke from previous bomb detonations.

Having been routed to avoid known flak concentrations, the bombers still expected heavy anti-aircraft fire from Mingaladon (three miles north of the target) and from positions in the northern sector of Rangoon.

In the minute before 'bombs gone' the flak opened up. The ORB for 215 Squadron referred to it as 'moderate to intense H. A. A. accurate for height and direction'. Four of the squadron's aircraft and seven of 99's bombers received slight shrapnel damage. Later it was heard that six of the twenty-three Libs sent out by 355 (twelve aircraft) and 356 (eleven) Squadrons also suffered superficial ack-ack damage; nothing was serious and nobody was injured.

Along with 99, 215 Squadron attacked the target, already burning fiercely from the earlier B-29 attack. The specific focus of 215's attention, the northerly portion of the dump area, was bombed from an average altitude of just above 13,100 feet. Approaching from due west, as did all of the Liberators from 99 and 215 Squadrons, Roy's bomber dropped its load at 1328 and then joined in turning to port for the journey home.

Most of 215's bombs fell across the northern part of the dump, as planned. Nick Nicholas, Roy's bomb aimer, reported that their aircraft's salvo hit the northern part of the dump's north section, and 215 Squadron's post-op Sortie Report stated that the 'whole target area' was covered with a particularly good concentration in the northern half of the area – 215's assigned target.

The combined RAF attack by 355 and 356 Squadrons upon the southern half of the dump resulted in the greater part of their target being covered by a good bomb pattern.

The US 7th Bomb Group's B-24s, following the RAF Libs over the target, fortunately faced only ineffective anti-aircraft fire, and their bombing results were considered excellent. Like the RAF Liberators, the American B-24s also turned for India after bombing.

It's a safe conclusion that the American B-29s also bombed with accuracy and success.

Some of 215 Squadron's bombs fell across the mental hospital north of the dump and also onto the grounds to the west of the hospital. The hospital was reputedly being used for ammunition and petrol storage, not as a hospital. An especially brilliant group of fires was burning at the site of the hospital.

RAF P-47 Thunderbolts of 134 and 258 Squadrons and a top cover of US 459th Fighter Squadron P-38 Lightnings escorted the bomber formations from Ramree Island (220 miles north-west of Rangoon) to the target. Approximately one minute after 215 Squadron's bombing four Japanese fighters – three Ki-61 Tonys and a possible Ki-43 Oscar – were sighted 2,000 feet above the formation, and ahead. One aircraft identified as a Tony dived in towards Roy's Lib and flew under and to the rear of the formation to gain position for a beam attack. At three o'clock the Tony levelled out but was destroyed by concentrated fire from 215's gunners before its attack developed. After the pilot baled out the aircraft, about 200 yards from Roy's formation, emitted smoke and was seen to fall earthward.

Several other enemy aircraft were seen being chased around the sky by Thunderbolts, but no other assaults threatened 215 Squadron's formation or any of the other attacking bombers. No further sightings of enemy aircraft were made after 215 departed the Rangoon area, and none of its aircraft suffered any damage from fighters.

The Liberators of 215 Squadron were intercepted only this one time during the entire month of February, further indicating how poor the Japanese aerial response had become.

Dense black smoke rose to 10,000 feet after the attack, with many fires visible.

All RAF and US bombers and fighters returned safely to their bases, completing what 215's ORB deemed 'an exceptionally successful operation'. Roy's KH324 'B' was the last 215 Squadron Lib to land back at Dhubalia, at 1801, after being airborne for eight hours and twenty-four minutes.

The tonnage of bombs dropped on 11 February made the headlines of a news story highlighting the sortie:

HEAVIES DROPPED 700 TONS OF BOMBS
ON RANGOON ON SUNDAY

SUPERFORTS "DRENCH" 530-ACRE
SUPPLY AREA NORTH OF CITY

SE ASIA COMMAND HQ, February 12. – Nearly 700 tons of bombs were dropped in Sunday's raid (already reported) on supply dumps in the Rangoon area by USAAF 20th Bomber Command Superfortresses and RAF Liberators and USAAF B-24s of Strategic Air Force, Eastern Air Command. It was the heaviest bomb load yet dropped on any objective in Burma. The dump area, covering 530 acres, contained petrol and ammunition stocks.

RAF Thunderbolts and USAAF P-38s provided escort and cover for the bombers. Japanese fighters were met near the target area: preliminary reports show that two were destroyed, one probably destroyed and two damaged.

A Press Note today from HQ, Eastern Air Command, says: Photographic reconnaissance pilots flying high over the Rangoon area yesterday groped their way through clouds. They were dense, black and pungent clouds, smoke from vast accumulations of burning oil fired by the heaviest bombing attack ever carried out in the Burma theatre.

It was an attack on a scale new to Burma. At mid-day Superfortresses of USAAF 20th Bomber Command drenched an area nearly 530 acres in extent near Victoria Lake, north of Rangoon, with high explosive bombs. An hour later a strong force of RAF Liberators of Strategic Air Force, Eastern Air Command, with fighter cover, rained 1,000-lb bombs into the same target and minutes behind them came the USAAF 7th Bombardment Group B-24s with hundreds of heavy incendiary bombs.

"Observation of results after that," as one pilot put it, "was impossible." The whole stores area was aflame and belching black smoke.

Each element of the Strategic Force went in in V formation close together and salvos patterned the entire dump, with the greatest concentration of all right in the centre. Fires immediately sprang up and at different points over the entire target explosions flashed up the success of the attack to the crews in the bombers.

By the time they were leaving the target the smoke was up to 11,000 feet and crews, looking back from 50 miles away, could still see the black shadow of their handiwork on the horizon.

Anti-aircraft opposition, both heavy and light, was intense but although one or two aircraft were hit all returned safely to base.

A brief, but memorable spot of bother

ROY: On one of the trips around this time I went to the aircraft's rear without problem, but it was coming back that caused me no end of trouble. There was a narrow walkway between the bomb racks. In order to pass through the bomb bay one had to move sideways when wearing flying gear. Like all airmen who flew over water, I wore an uninflated Mae West life preserver in case I found myself in the drink. The vest included two small cartridges of fluid carbon dioxide, which, when activated, caused carbon dioxide gas to fill up the vest's air pockets. As I moved along through the bomb bay my release lever for the life preserver got caught in the bomb rack, and the vest inflated. There I was, stuck in the bomb bay! I couldn't move forwards or backwards, and my arms were raised so that I couldn't uninflated the vest.

I yelled and yelled for help, but no one could hear me above the roar of the engines. And it was really cold. I must have been there for twenty minutes before somebody asked, 'Where's Chico?' Was I pleased to see them come to get me out!

Chapter 16

215 Squadron, India: FEBRUARY 1945 *(Part 2)*

Monday, 12 FEBRUARY 1945
(Roy's twenty-first op)
Near Myinmu, BURMA – Area 'A', gun positions *(daylight bombing)*

MATT: There was no slowing down during this prime flying and fighting weather. On the day following the Rangoon op eight Libs and eighty-eight 215 Squadron airmen, including Roy and his crew, were scheduled for another op. At the briefing held at 1000 on 12 February they learned that this time their target would be Japanese gun positions just inland from the shore of the Irrawaddy River near Myinmu, Burma, a town on the banks of the Irrawaddy situated west of Mandalay. Roy would again fly as first W/Op, with Bingham as skipper and Flight Sergeant Raby as second pilot. Their eleven-man crew would take KH372 'H'. Each aircraft would be loaded with twelve 500lb bombs (6,000 pounds).

In need of tactical support, the British Army was directly across the Irrawaddy from the Japanese. The aerial attack was planned to silence enemy positions associated with ten 75mm and four 105mm guns. No. 99 Squadron was assigned Area 'B', while 215 Squadron's specific target would be Area 'A'. Because target identification would be difficult crews were briefed to look for signs of the actual gun emplacements, such as track activity and marks of muzzle blasts, but knowing the Japanese skill at using natural camouflage, it was felt that little would be seen from on high.

At the time of take-off 215 Squadron's force had been reduced to seven Liberators and seventy-seven airmen, while 99 Squadron put up eight Libs. Roy's KH372, at 1342, was the fifth 215 Squadron Lib to lift off from Dhubalia.

Sixteen Libs from 355 and 356 Squadrons (eight Libs from each unit) would be the first to bomb, followed shortly thereafter by eight aircraft from 99 Squadron and then 215's Libs. US 7th Bomb Group B-24s would also contribute.

The weather en route to the target was good, and there was little or no cloud over the target.

Roy's squadron approached from a northerly direction.

Attacking in formation between 1624 and 1626 from an average altitude of just under 5,000 feet, 215 Squadron was pleased to find that British Army gunners had marked the target area with white smoke shells fired from the opposite bank of the Irrawaddy. Roy's bomb aimer, Nick Nicholas, released his Liberator's load at 1625 from 5,000 feet.

The post-op Sortie Report said this about KH372's bombing accuracy: 'Bursts in centre of area.' While Roy couldn't take the credit, he'd have been immensely pleased to know that Nicholas had once again delivered.

Bomb aiming by 215's participants had been complicated by, and damage observations were hindered by, smoke, red dust and impact craters from previous attacks. Nevertheless, almost all of the squadron's bomb bursts were seen within the marked area, and an exceptionally vivid flash accompanied the bursting of the stick of bombs put down by the 215 Squadron aircraft flying behind Roy's Liberator (either KH362 'O' or EW284 'Q', but not KH362 'Q', as erroneously noted in 215's ORB).

Assessment of this attack acknowledged the fact that when Allied troops crossed the Irrawaddy shortly afterwards not one of the Japanese guns targeted by the Liberators was fired at them. Captured enemy documents subsequently confirmed that the bombing attack had been completely successful.

No enemy opposition was encountered throughout the flight by any Liberator, and all aircraft sent out that day safely returned to their respective bases. However, 215 Squadron's aircraft EW285 'C', with engine trouble, had opted to land first at Chittagong before returning to Dhubalia on the following day.

After an uneventful flight home Roy's Lib touched down at Dhubalia at 2113 on the twelfth. Though 'H' had been the fifth 215 Squadron aircraft to take off, it was, by twenty-three minutes, the unit's final aircraft to land at Dhubalia that night. Roy and his crewmates, though safe, were tired after being airborne for seven hours and thirty-one minutes.

Thursday, 15 FEBRUARY 1945
(Roy's twenty-second op)
Nyaungwun, BURMA – administrative headquarters *(daylight bombing)*

During a two-day break from combat sorties following his twenty-first op, Roy decompressed from his stressful recent flying schedule. However, still far from the end of his tour of ops, Roy would have itched to get back into action; he was wired that way. His return was to come on 15 February when 215 Squadron once more flew a tactical op in support of the 14th Army.

A posted Battle Order announced a 1530 briefing on the fourteenth. Roy and his crew were called upon to fly this one. Again, they were assigned KH324 'B', to be skippered by Bingham, co-piloted by Flight Sergeant Raby and with their skilled bomb aimer, Nick Nicholas, aboard. Roy was to fly in his customary role of first W/Op.

At the briefing those in attendance learned that eight 215 Squadron Libs had been detailed for a day bombing attack upon what was believed to be a local Japanese administrative headquarters in the village of Nyaungwun, Burma, four miles north-west of Kyaukse. A different village, Nyaungwe, on the northern (opposite) side of the Kyaukse-Sagaing Road from Nyaungwun, would be simultaneously attacked by eight 99 Squadron Libs.

Loads on 215 Squadron's Liberators would consist of ten 1,000lb and two 500lb high explosive bombs per aircraft.

Eight 99 Squadron aircraft were airborne just prior to 215's take-offs. Roy's Lib led the way for 215 Squadron, going aloft at 0811. The eighth and last 215 bomber lifted off the Dhubalia runway at 0819.

En route to the target the weather was fine with good visibility. Closer to the target visibility was still good and observation wasn't impeded.

The direction of the attacks by 99 and 215 Squadrons was from the north-west, the Initial Point being the Mu River road and rail bridges, twenty-six miles due west of Mandalay and immediately north of the confluence of that river with the Irrawaddy. Approaching the target, the Liberators saw the town of Kyaukse ahead. The road network was plainly visible, too.

Finding their specific target to be clear, seven of 99 Squadron's aircraft bombed from 1111 to 1112, covering Nyaungwe village with hits. The eighth 99 Squadron aircraft jettisoned its bombs 300 yards south-east of the target due to a technical failure.

Unfortunately, a suspected electrical malfunction led one of 215 Squadron's aircraft (likely either EV989 'K' or KH372 'H'; the records were conflicted) to release bombs 200 yards south-east of the target at 1113, but despite no longer carrying its load this bomber stayed with the attacking force. Flying in a two-box formation of four aircraft each, with Bingham in 215's lead aircraft, the squadron's Liberators attacked their long and narrow target area in one run. Aboard Roy's Liberator Nick Nicholas toggled his aircraft's bombs at 1112, aimed at the north edge of the village, from a height of 6,480 feet and on a course of 129 degrees. The altitude of the squadron's aircraft at 'bombs gone' – the last bombs having been released at 1113 – averaged nearly 6,500 feet.

Nyaungwun was straddled by the explosives dropped by 215 Squadron. Several of 215's aircraft certainly secured hits on the village, but in many cases bombs partially overshot.

The results of bombing the target, per 215 Squadron's ORB:

KG830 'A':	The bomb pattern fell across the village.
KH324 'B': (Roy's Lib)	About one quarter of the bombs overshot the target, but the remainder of the stick impacted down the eastern edge of the target;
KH320 'D':	All bombs fell across the target in the eastern section;
EW125 'P':	Bursts were seen straddling the target;
EW284 'Q':	Almost all of its bombs were seen to explode across the target, with only the end of the stick overshooting;
KG846 'R':	Two bursts were seen in the village, while the remainder overshot;
KH275 'T':	The majority of bursts were in the target area.

Numerous bright secondary explosions believed to be ammunition cooking off were seen by 215 Squadron airmen twenty miles after leaving the target on the return trek to Dhubalia.

Although eight 355 Squadron Liberators had taken off from Salbani, only seven bombed the squadron's assigned target – Japanese stores and administrative personnel in Kyetsha village, five and a half miles north-west of Kyaukse – around 1115; the eighth Lib, aircraft 'D', didn't attack, having jettisoned its bombs to maintain height due to an engine malfunction. Eight 356 Squadron Liberators bombed Japanese personnel and the stores area at Uyingyi, again north-west of Kyaukse.

Despite the close proximity of the different targets and with 'bombs gone' times of four RAF Liberator squadrons being within a few minutes of one another, there were no visibility issues due to exploding bombs or dust clouds, and the risk of one squadron interfering with another's performance was negligible.

For the thirty-two RAF Liberators that overflew the Kyaukse vicinity there was no opposition encountered, either from enemy aircraft or anti-aircraft fire from the ground.

All aircraft returned safely to their respective home bases; Roy's Lib touched down at Dhubalia at 1454, having been airborne for six hours and forty-three minutes.

Saturday, 17 FEBRUARY 1945
(Roy does not fly on this op)
Aungban, BURMA – airfield *(daylight bombing)*

Roy's crew didn't fly on this next 215 Squadron sortie, a daylight raid on Aungban, Burma's airfield in central Burma, situated ninety-seven miles south-south-east of Mandalay and eleven miles south-west of the major regional Japanese airfield at Heho. Roy felt that it was OK this time to take a break, as it gave his hearing a chance to rebound; their bombers were loud, and being a W/Op and, consequently, having to endure a variety of radio noise didn't help matters, either.

A force of RAF Liberators, including 215 Squadron, was tasked with attacking different airfields, all in support of the British 14th Army's relentless and inspiring advance towards Rangoon. The briefing for 215 was held at 1545 on 16 February.

Aungban airfield was surprisingly difficult to identify. Hangarettes, though, were visible on approach, and the runways became apparent.

The six attacking 215 aircraft made individual bombing runs from varying directions, the object being to crater the runways. Photographic reconnaissance flown after the op revealed that the east-west runway was rendered unserviceable, with seven direct hits, and there were three craters on the south end of the main north-west to south-east runway.

Thankfully, the 17 February 1945 sortie was a quiet op with little excitement for 215 Squadron. All participating aircraft, from all squadrons, safely returned.

Sunday, 18 FEBRUARY 1945
(Roy's twenty-third op)
Yenangyaung, BURMA – concentration of vehicles and troops *(daylight bombing)*

No airman still on an RAF Liberator squadron in India at this time had a long break from action during his tour of ops, and so Roy and his crew were once again called upon to fly on the 18 February op. The posted Battle Order indicated that Roy would fly as first W/Op aboard his eleven-man crew's usual

KH324 'B', skippered again by Bingham and with Flight Sergeant Raby as second pilot.

Those gathered at the briefing were informed of the target: a concentration of Japanese armoured fighting vehicles, other motor transport, servicing equipment and troops in the Yenangyaung, Burma, oilfields. Located on the east bank of the Irrawaddy River 130 miles south-west of Mandalay, the Yenangyaung oil belt was one of the most heavily defended sectors in South-east Asia.

Each of the eight 215 Squadron Libs earmarked for the op would carry ten 1,000lb and two 500lb high explosive bombs. Roy's squadron would join forces with three other RAF Liberator units (99, 355 and 356 Squadrons) and B-24 squadrons of the US 7th Bomb Group for this combined attack. Each other RAF squadron would also contribute eight Libs.

Following the successful take-off of 99 Squadron's participants the eight 215 Squadron Libs took to the sky from Dhubalia between 0809 and 0818, with Roy's aircraft being the sixth 215 bomber to take off, at 0815. On 215 Squadron's flight to the target the weather and visibility were good; the sky was clear over the sea and over Burma. The 355 Squadron ORB noted slight ground haze and visibility fifteen miles in the target area, although 356 recorded thick haze in the vicinity of the Yenangyaung oilfields. Despite some haze, atmospheric conditions, by and large, were decent.

The particular target assigned to 215 Squadron was heavily defended by thirty-two heavy and thirteen light anti-aircraft guns. The siting of these guns, imparted to 215's participating airmen by their intelligence officer at the pre-op briefing, called for an approach from the west in order to safeguard the incoming bomber force from hazardous anti-aircraft fire for the maximum possible period to and from the target. Nevertheless, Roy and his fellow flyers were under no illusion of escaping danger.

The bombers of 215 Squadron came into the range of accurate and intense to moderate anti-aircraft fire just before crossing the Irrawaddy River prior to releasing bombs. Several 215 Squadron crews, including Roy's, were shaken by anti-aircraft bursts, and two of the unit's aircraft, but not Roy's, were hit by shrapnel. The harm to the squadron's attacking Liberators was superficial.

After readily picking up the Initial Point prior to the anti-aircraft fire, 215's Liberators went in to bomb the target between 1104 and 1105, following 99 Squadron. Roy's 'B' toggled its bombload at 1105 from an altitude of 6,700 feet and a heading of fifty-five degrees; the average 215 Squadron bombing altitude and heading were just over 7,900 feet and nearly sixty-eight degrees.

The area attacked by Roy's squadron was situated just north of one of the watercourses draining into the Irrawaddy. The eroded nature of the terrain made for a confusing pattern of gullies and ridges, and the similarities between the many watercourses entering the Irrawaddy made target identification difficult.

Furthermore, because 215 Squadron wasn't the first unit to release bombs, it was of no surprise that dust and smoke from the previous attack on the area obscured ground detail. The 215 Squadron bomb aimers could only estimate the position of their target. Bombs disappeared into a thick pall of dust that obscured the bursts and prevented their impact positions from being pinpointed.

To the disappointment of 215 Squadron personnel, subsequent photographic examination after the squadron's return to Dhubalia revealed that the main concentration of bursts were identified just south of the target area. It was well understood, however, that even though aiming was slightly errant the bombloads weren't wasted, and that the might of the squadron was still helpful in vanquishing a despised enemy.

The eight Liberators from 215 Squadron landed at Dhubalia between 1400 and 1408. The sixth to land, at 1405, was Roy's KH324 'B', having been airborne for five hours and fifty minutes. All participating aircraft from the other B-24 squadrons, of both air forces, returned safely to their bases. Although several Libs from these other units had felt the sting of Japanese anti-aircraft fire, none received anything more than light, inconsequential hits – just as with 215 Squadron. In fact, the damage to the two Libs from 355 Squadron that had reported hits was said to have had no impact upon flying characteristics, per the unit's ORB.

There were no injuries among the RAF airmen, and only one wound was reported by the Americans – a 492nd Bomb Squadron navigator's damaged eye.

No opposition from enemy aircraft was encountered at any time by the attacking bombers, even though the B-24s lacked fighter escorts to tackle any potential aerial onslaughts.

From a newspaper cutting saved by Roy:

HEAVIES DROP 200 TONS IN THE YENANGYAUNG AREA

HQ, EASTERN AIR COMMAND. – RAF Liberators and USAAF B-24s of Eastern Air Command on Sunday dropped more than 200 tons of bombs in the Yenangyaung area, 130 miles south-west of Mandalay.

Objectives were troops, equipment, 30 tanks and motor-transport and oilfield installations.

Tuesday, 20 FEBRUARY 1945
(Roy does not fly on this op)
Singaingmyo, BURMA – military installations, stores and personnel
(daylight bombing)

Roy wasn't a participant on this op. In support of advancing Allied ground forces, the op was a 'town blitz' directed against Japanese troops and installations in Singaingmyo, on the railway line seventeen miles south of Mandalay. The attack wasn't limited to any specific areas in the town. Apparently the op, initially scheduled for 19 February, had been postponed for one day. The main briefing was held at 1545 on the nineteenth. As was the norm, 215 Squadron's bombers were only one component of the combined Liberator attack and were joined by three other RAF squadrons (99, 355 and 356) and by US 7th Bomb Group B-24s.

Because 215 Squadron followed other units, it was of no surprise to learn that Singaingmyo town, already burning, was covered by a pall of smoke and dust from the earlier attacks when 215's seven Libs approached. Despite the visual hurdles, 215 Squadron's bombing results were considered excellent, as were the overall results for the combined bomber force.

No casualties or aircraft losses were incurred by 215 on the op, and the same held true for the other squadrons involved, both RAF and US.

Wednesday, 21 FEBRUARY 1945
(Roy's twenty-fourth op)
Myittha, BURMA – stores buildings and personnel, Area 'D'
(daylight bombing)

On the Battle Order posted on 20 February 1945, Roy was scheduled to be Bingham's first W/Op aboard Liberator KH372 'H', and the second pilot again would be Flight Sergeant Raby. The briefing for the sortie, a daytime op to be flown on the twenty-first, was set for 1830 on the twentieth. Eight 215 Squadron Liberators would be carrying identical loads – ten 1,000lb and two 500lb bombs.

This being his twenty-fourth op, Roy was truly an old-timer among his fellow 215 Squadron airmen.

At the briefing the attendees learned that 215's Liberators were destined to attack Japanese occupied areas of Myittha, Burma. Located thirty-six miles south of Mandalay, the target was an area of ten enemy stores buildings in the south-western portion of the town near the river. Once again 215 would be part of a combined attack in support of the 14th Army's efforts to capture Mandalay, this time joined by seven 99 Squadron Liberators, eight from 355, eight also from 356 and B-24s from two US 7th Bomb Group units (the 436th and 492nd Bomb Squadrons). Roy's squadron's specific target would be Area 'D'.

On the twenty-first, eight 215 Squadron Libs took off between 0805 and 0821, following 99 Squadron's successful take-offs. Roy's KH372 was the fifth of 215's aircraft to take to the sky, at 0809.

The weather throughout the trip was mostly clear, with no clouds in the target area and very few clouds elsewhere. The 355 Squadron ORB did note that thick haze in the target area decreased visibility significantly.

The town contained no known anti-aircraft defences, though the attacking Liberators approached the target aware of the possibility of mobile light anti-aircraft fire. Only two bursts were seen by the 215 Squadron crews, and no ground flashes were detected.

The contingent of aircraft from 215 Squadron attacked in level flight in a south-easterly direction at altitudes ranging from 6,000 to 7,100 feet, having begun their bomb run from the Initial Point at Myotha village, on the Myingyan-Paleik railway line thirty-two miles north-west of Myittha. Roy's aircraft 'H' released its full bombload at 1106 on a heading of 148 degrees.

Owing to an electrical failure all bombs hung up on 215 Squadron aircraft 'V', but they were eventually released in open country four to five miles south of the target. The attack by the remaining seven 215 Squadron aircraft was well-concentrated on the target, with the bomb aimers obtaining a good distribution of bursts over the area and with secondary explosions evident. Roy's bombs were seen to impact across the south-eastern part of their target, with a large flash seen when one specific building was hit. Damage Assessment Report PM(S) 512 later stated that only the shells of three storage-type buildings remained; the other seven buildings were completely gutted. Again, Roy's bomb aimer, Nick Nicholas, did his job well, thus ensuring that their attack was successful.

The 356 Squadron ORB noted that smoke from the burning town could still be seen fifty miles away on the return flight.

Apart from superficial damage to the starboard wing of 215 Squadron's 'S' caused by the meagre anti-aircraft fire encountered over the target, the entire flight was routine and uneventful for Roy and the other airmen from the squadron.

Roy's 'H' landed back at Dhubalia at 1455, the sixth of 215 Squadron's eight participating bombers to do so. Despite having released its bombs away from the target, Liberator 'V' was in ideal flying form and stayed with the seven other 215 Squadron aircraft all the way home.

As far as operations went this one seemed most satisfactory. The flying and bombing weather was favourable, anti-aircraft opposition was almost nil and the cooperation with other squadrons was impressive. Fighter attacks were again non-existent, and all Liberators on the op safely returned home.

In fact, the overall attack was assessed as being very successful.

Having flown on this sortie, Roy added another six hours and forty-six minutes to his tour of ops total. Following this flight he'd accumulated in the vicinity of 200 hours of combat flying time, well on the way to completing his required 300 hours or thirty ops, whichever came first. (Because Roy's flight logbook is missing and 215 Squadron's records don't specifically state his Liberator's time aloft for eight of his first nine ops, a precise summation of hours flown by Roy is unknown.)

Chapter 17

215 Squadron, India: FEBRUARY 1945 *(Part 3)*

Thursday, 22 FEBRUARY 1945
(Roy does not fly on this op)
Paganyat (near Sagaing), BURMA – fortified Kaungmudaw Pagoda area *(daylight bombing)*

Roy wasn't on this op, but it was a special one for the airmen who participated: a bombing attack upon a Japanese military contingent occupying the area around the landmark Kaungmudaw Pagoda in Burma. From here, north of the Irrawaddy and five miles north-west of Sagaing, the enemy protected Mandalay's western approaches. The Japanese force was centred at the large and distinctly-shaped pagoda, an important Buddhist religious site previously off-limits for bombardment. This gen was imparted to the participating crews at the 0700 briefing on the morning of the op.

The 22 February sortie, another combined effort, called for participants from 99, 215, 355 and 356 Squadrons on the RAF side and the 7th Bomb Group's 9th Bomb Squadron on the American side. The front line was just over a mile to the west of the target.

Landmarks over Burma and near the target, including the Irrawaddy, railways, road junctions and the lofty golden dome of the pagoda, stood out exceptionally well despite haze.

Minimal opposition inflicted neither aircraft damage nor injuries.

Damage Assessment Report PM(S) 510, summarising the attack by all five Liberator squadrons, stated:

> The area is seen to be saturated with heavy crater formations which extend well beyond the limits of the target on every side. Several small buildings within the pagoda grounds have been destroyed or damaged. There have been several near misses to the pagoda, which, however, remains intact.

All participating aircraft, including the American B-24s, safely returned to their respective airfields in India.

Despite an imperfect bombing pattern the op was considered successful.

For propaganda purposes the results were blatantly hyped to tout the precision capabilities of RAF and US bomb aimers and bombardiers. When Roy and his mates saw how the op was written up in Calcutta's newspaper, *The Statesman*, they recognised the readiness with which the Allied propaganda machine seized upon the non-destruction of the great pagoda as evidence of bombing accuracy and of the Allies' choice to spare religious and cultural buildings. The 215 Squadron men had a laugh over it – because the pagoda had been an aiming point!

The exaggerated wording of the newspaper story is worth repeating:

> Mandalay Front – The pagoda of the Royal Benefaction at Kaungmudan [Kaungmudaw] – the Monte Cassino of the Buddhist Husana five miles north [north-west] of Sagaing, stands this evening among the blasted ruins of the village surrounding it – a monument to the accuracy of the RAF [and US] Liberator bombers of Eastern Air Command.
>
> Two hundred tons of high explosives and incendiaries were put down into the area in half an hour today without touching this 1200 year old shrine which is revered by Buddhists throughout the world. A difficult and critical decision had to be made when it became known that the Japanese were using the area surrounding the shrine as an HQ and an artillery observation post. Unmolested they were able to direct accurate gunfire on to our positions.
>
> An appeal had been made by the religious authorities that the pagoda should be spared destruction. It was a case of risking the ruin of the most holy place in the country or exposing any more of our men to death.
>
> Reluctantly it was decided that the risk must be taken. The religious authorities were told the bombing would take place from 8000 feet in daylight and that all crews would be instructed to avoid the pagoda. A guarantee could not be given that the pagoda would remain intact.
>
> The enormous explosion of salvoes of 1000 lbs [sic] bombs from the first formation of eight Liberators and the roar of the ammunition dump on which they had scored a direct hit, began the attack. Smoke rose in a thick column to 8000 feet and huge fires broke out in and around it.

> The second wave came in and after their load had fallen only the great dome of the pagoda, shaped like a woman's breast, could be seen shining in the sun. After the fourth wave the whole landscape was obscured by smoke suffused with fire. The pagoda could no longer be seen.
>
> Japanese anti-aircraft guns put up shells but they were wide of the mark. After the Liberators had left nothing could be seen for fifteen minutes. When the smoke thinned the pagoda was still there.

Friday, 23 FEBRUARY 1945
(Roy's twenty-fifth op)
Mahlaing, BURMA – Japanese-held Area 'D' ***(daylight bombing)***

The Battle Order in advance of 215 Squadron's next op listed eight eleven-man Liberator crews and one reserve crew. The Bingham crew, with Roy as the first W/Op, would take Liberator KG830 'A' on the op. Each of 215 Squadron's participating Libs would carry ten 1,000lb and two 500lb bombs.

The men learned at the 1630 briefing on 22 February that the squadron would attack Area 'D' at Mahlaing, Burma, located twenty miles north-west of Meiktila. They would be joined by RAF Liberators of 99 (eight aircraft), 355 (seven) and 356 (eight, but only seven bombed) Squadrons and also by US 7th Bomb Group B-24s.

First into the sky from Dhubalia was 99 Squadron, between 0849 and 0855, followed by 215's eight bombers, from 0900 to 0908. Roy's 'A' was the third 215 Squadron Liberator to take off, at 0902½. The weather was clear to and from the target. En route, 215's Liberators began their run-in to the target from an Initial Point at Myingyan, near the confluence of the Chindwin and Irrawaddy rivers, and followed the railway running south-east for the thirty miles between Myingyan and Mahlaing. However, in the Mahlaing area the bombers met heavy altocumulus clouds, some dull drizzle and slight ground haze.

This didn't affect the bombing. With KG830 flying on a heading of 162 degrees, Nick Nicholas toggled his aircraft's load at 1202 from an altitude of 5,600 feet. In formation 215 Squadron bombed from 1202 to 1204 from an average height of 5,275 feet. Of the Liberator units, 215 was the last one to attack Mahlaing, chronologically following, in order, the US B-24s, then the main force of 356 Squadron, then 355 and finally 99. The majority of 215's bombs fell across the target area, starting numerous fires. Three individual Liberators – one each from 99, 355 and 356 Squadrons – bombed after 215 Squadron's attack.

The overall bombing results by the combined Liberator force were considered good, but not great.

All participating aircraft, both RAF and US, returned to their bases. The Libs from 215 Squadron landed back at Dhubalia between 1532 and 1539, following 99 Squadron's arrival. Roy's Liberator was the first of its squadron's bombers to touch down, having been airborne for six hours and twenty-nine and a half minutes.

None of the Liberators, RAF or US, were damaged, nor were any airmen injured. There was no opposition encountered, either from anti-aircraft guns or from enemy fighters. Especially because the bombers on this op flew with no fighter escort, their crews must have been relieved that the Japanese Army Air Force, once a formidable adversary, made no appearances.

Again, the airmen did what was asked of them, in support of the British 14th Army's march to defeat the Japanese in Burma.

Roy makes a necessary change: Bingham and crew are out and Gardner and crew are in

ROY: I'd been flying with Bing as my skipper since December 1944, after he'd been promoted from second pilot to aircraft captain with the departure of our tour-ex pilot, Jackson Grouse, but I regret to say that there were reasons why I didn't enjoy flying with Bing. It was time for a change, although he'd been my skipper on seventeen safe ops and one lengthy exercise over India, and though I'll forever be grateful for his skill, leadership and friendship. Approaching the Flight Commander, I requested a release from Bing's crew and a transfer to Canadian pilot Murray 'Mac' Gardner's crew, where a first W/Op vacancy had come up.

Mac, a very likeable 28-year-old, had accumulated a huge number of flying hours aboard Liberators. I felt very comfortable with him at the helm, given his vast experience in the B-24.

My request was granted, with no lingering hard feelings between Bing, my old crew and me. Mac was pleased, even relieved, to add me to the crew, especially given my own experience.

Saturday, 24 FEBRUARY 1945
(Roy's twenty-sixth op)
Myingyan, BURMA – stores and headquarters, Area '3' ***(daylight bombing)***

MATT: Following quickly on the heels of his twenty-fifth op Roy's next sortie, and first with skipper Mac Gardner, would be flown on 24 February. On the Battle Order for what would be Roy's twenty-sixth op, posted on the twenty-third while he was airborne (for the last time) with Bingham, Roy was scheduled to fly as Mac Gardner's first W/Op aboard Liberator KH372 'H', with Flight Sergeant W.F. Hill in the second pilot's seat. (Hill flew as Roy's second pilot ten times.)

The op of 24 February would be Roy's fourth combat flight in seven days. Previously he'd flown four ops in eight days between 11 and 18 February.

The Battle Order recorded that each of 215 Squadron's eight participating Libs would carry ten 1,000lb and two 500lb bombs to the target.

At the 1700 briefing on 23 February, less than ninety minutes after Roy's return to Dhubalia from his final op with Bingham, the participants learned that they'd be flying in support of Allied ground troops fighting to capture Mandalay. Joining three other RAF Liberator units (99, 355 and 356, each of which would contribute eight aircraft) and US B-24s, the eight 215 Squadron aircraft were scheduled to specifically attack Area '3' of the Japanese stores and headquarters at Myingyan, the town that had been the Initial Point for the previous day's op. Myingyan was fifty-seven miles south-west of Mandalay and just east of the Irrawaddy, near its junction with the Chindwin River.

From Dhubalia 99 Squadron took off first on 24 February, between 0807 and 0814 215's eight aircraft followed, taking to the sky between 0817 and 0823½. Roy's KH372 was the fourth 215 Squadron Liberator into the air, at 0819½.

Apart from a generally hazy visibility of five to ten miles the flying weather was decent, with no clouds. The Initial Point had been at the Mu River road and railway bridges, just over four miles immediately north of where the Mu flowed into the Irrawaddy and forty miles north-east of Myingyan.

The plan had called for each Liberator squadron of the attacking force to hit the target at four- or five-minute intervals. Due to a slight error in timing 215 Squadron arrived over the target almost two minutes late, while

355 Squadron, the next unit scheduled to attack, was three minutes early. Consequently, as 215's aircraft approached the target, 355 Squadron was observed coming in to bomb at a greater height (6,300 to 6,700 feet) and on a different heading, but at nearly the same time. Flight Lieutenant Shaw, 215 Squadron's formation leader, turned the unit's Liberators off target to avoid any possibility of being struck by 355's bombs, and after flying a circuit the aircraft made a fresh bombing run on Area '3'.

On this second run strong air currents, possibly due to disturbances caused by preceding aircraft and by updraughts from the many fires already burning, forced the 215 Squadron formation to starboard, away from the correct line, despite efforts to maintain course.

Undaunted by smoke and dust from the other B-24 assaults, 'H' released its bombs at 1119 from 4,800 feet while flying on a heading of 185 degrees. Most of these bombs were seen to burst in Area '3', as planned, but some overshot into buildings outside of this specific zone.

Sticks of bombs from four 215 Squadron aircraft mostly fell in the *chaung* just west or north-west of the target area, while the remaining sticks from the squadron, including the bombs from 'H', fell squarely across the target. After 215's bombing run a large fire was evident in the southern part of the town, and numerous small fires were seen over the whole area. It was reported by 355 Squadron that black smoke up to 6,000 feet was visible sixty miles away on the return flight.

As was the norm, the attacking Liberators met no fighter opposition that day. In fact, there was no anti-aircraft fire, either. Airmen from 355 Squadron described one single-engine aircraft taking off from Lethit landing ground on the north side of Myingyan, but it wasn't seen again.

Roy's squadron was the second to land back at Dhubalia, between 1454 and 1500; 99 Squadron, the first to return, touched down between 1431 and 1446. Roy's Liberator, arriving at 1459, was the seventh of the eight 215 Squadron aircraft to come to rest, having been airborne for six hours and thirty-nine and a half minutes.

All aircraft returned to their home bases. None of the participating Liberators was damaged, nor were there any casualties.

The operation, even though imperfect in some ways, was deemed successful, and the efforts by the bombers was gratefully acknowledged by the 14th Army.

Sunday, 25 FEBRUARY 1945
(Roy does not fly on this op)
Taunggyi, BURMA – army headquarters and supply dump *(daylight bombing)*

Neither Roy nor his new crew flew on this op to the Japanese army headquarters and dump at Taunggyi, Burma, located 100 miles south-east of Mandalay. Joining 215 Squadron for this sojourn into enemy airspace were three other RAF Liberator units (99, 355 and 356) and US 7th Bomb Group B-24s, as was learned at 215's 1200 briefing on 24 February.

The 355 Squadron ORB noted considerable damage throughout Taunggyi. The 7th Bomb Group's Operations Officer stated that it was a 'marvelous (spelled the preferred American way) mission.'

From all of the Allied Liberators flying on this op there were no injuries or aircraft losses; each bomber and crew returned safely to its home base.

Wednesday, 28 FEBRUARY-Thursday, 1 MARCH 1945
(Roy does not fly on this op)
Korat, THAILAND – railway sidings and installations *(daylight bombing)*

At last, the tactical ops flown in direct support of the British 14th Army had ceased, not that a return to strategic bombing assignments would be any easier. However, strategic targets were farther from the India airfields where the participating Liberators were based than were tactical targets, which meant more time in the air. Flying was a challenging endeavour regardless of the enemy's defensive actions, especially given the occasionally formidable dangers associated with the area's climate and the reliance upon sometimes erroneous maps. The gross generalization, then, was that the longer an aircrew was in the sky the greater was the potential for difficulty; ack-ack and interception by enemy fighters were only two risk components to be considered.

The Gardner crew (with whom Roy now flew) didn't fly on this op, to attack the railway sidings and installations at Korat, Thailand, located 1,064 miles south-east of Dhubalia. Korat, now more commonly known as Nakhon Ratchasima, was situated 130 miles north-east of Bangkok. This was the first Allied attack on this important railway junction and marshalling yard on the enemy's line of communication with French Indo-China.

The briefing for the op was held at 1830 on 27 February.

On this lengthy strategic bombing op twelve 215 Squadron Liberators joined three other RAF B-24 units: 99, 355 and 356 Squadrons.

One of the fundamental differences between tactical and strategic sorties was that each squadron's force tended to include a greater number of participating aircraft on strategic ops than on tactical ops. When an airman was called upon to fly shorter tactical ops (that, for Roy, were mostly six to seven hours in duration), he could more readily handle the physical and emotional loads with minimal rest breaks between ops. However, the men especially needed to rest after a long, noisy, exhausting strategic flight. Thus, it was recognised that an airman could reasonably fly fewer strategic ops than tactical ops in the same time frame.

Also, shorter tactical ops meant less accumulated wear and tear per airframe, and less frequent standard servicing interruptions (like 100-hour inspections). The machines (with rare exceptions) could be prepped for future use more quickly after tactical ops than after much longer strategic ops.

Because the Japanese were being pushed to the south and east, out of Burma, and because the distance flying capabilities of the Liberator had greatly improved in 1944, strategic flights to distant targets were generally lengthier than in the past and much further afield than were typical tactical flights.

At Korat the atmospheric conditions were favourable for the attacking Liberators.

The attacking Liberators had been routed north of Phitsanulok, Thailand (210 miles north of Bangkok), in part to give a wide berth to Bangkok's Don Muang airfield. Consequently, no enemy aerial opposition was encountered, which was fortuitous, since the Liberators were unescorted by Allied fighters.

After readily identifying ground detail, an excellent concentration of bursts was obtained on the target, causing heavy damage to the marshalling yard and surrounding buildings. Before dust and smoke obscured the view crews reported seeing two trains derailed, with orange flashes from secondary explosions in the yard and numerous fires. The through-lines and sidings were cut in many places. In all, forty-four RAF Liberators devastated the enemy at the Korat railway facilities.

All forty-eight aircraft that had taken off safely returned to Allied control.

A message to bolster the spirits of 215 Squadron's men

Air Commodore Francis J.W. Mellersh CBE, AFC sent 215 Squadron a congratulatory message dated 28 February 1945, in recognition of the role played by RAF Liberator units, including 215, in the numerous recent tactical bombing operations. His message read:

> On completion of the recent sustained effort put out by the Strategic Air Force in support of the 14th Army during their crossing of the Irrawaddy River in their operations for the capture of Mandalay, I want to send you my thanks and congratulations for the really fine show all squadrons have put up. The fact that you have succeeded in meeting all our demands, and have carried out the tasks given you with such skill and precision, has been most gratifying to me personally and reflects the very greatest credit on your personnel, both aircrews and groundcrews. I shall be glad if you will pass on my congratulations to all concerned and will let them know that I realise what a great deal of hard work this has meant for them, and how much I appreciate their efforts.

It was noted in 215 Squadron's ORB that the message 'gave much satisfaction to the squadron, and was reflected in the high standard of work and morale which was maintained.'

Chapter 18

215 Squadron, India: MARCH 1945 *(Part 1)*

215 Squadron's March 1945 summary

Improvements to 215 Squadron infrastructure at Dhubalia continued in March. In mid-month the squadron's headquarters, the offices for 'A' and 'B' Flights and several sections moved into satisfyingly solid and spacious new facilities, situated to the west of the single north-west to south-east runway (that had been built on a 318 degree/138 degree alignment). Furniture in the new spaces added to the men's satisfaction.

Among the developments was the manner in which Liberators were prepped for action. On the day prior to an op there was no longer a need to taxi the aircraft to a separate marshalling strip for bomb loading, fuelling and other work required to prepare a bomber for action. Instead, all prep work was done in the new dispersal pens, although the 'running up' of engines in the pens created clouds of dust that permeated the offices behind the dispersals. Roofs were liable to be taken off and small stones were thrown around.

Mandalay, Burma, fell to attacking Allied forces on 20 March, in small part due to 215 Squadron's tactical bombing efforts in support of the 14th Army ground forces. The squadron was back to flying strategic bombing ops in March, with an emphasis on Rangoon – the next major objective in the theatre – and, even further afield, Thailand.

In a month of heavy operational commitments, the squadron operated on every second or third day throughout the month with only one exception: a gap between Rangoon dump attacks on the eleventh and then a return to the Rangoon dump on the seventeenth. Roy participated on seven of the eleven ops flown by 215 Squadron in March.

As always, not enough credit went to the ground crews, who, working with their typical focus and speed in a then dry and dusty part of India, maintained a high standard of serviceability throughout March.

'More than a fair share of flies and mosquitoes', plus too many snakes, scorpions, centipedes, rats and other pests was how Dhubalia was described in March entries found in 215 Squadron's ORB, but the wonder spray of the time, called 'the all-powerful DDT', helped to reduce infestations and to make life much more comfortable.

The weather turned hot at the end of the second week of March, averaging between 95° and 100° Fahrenheit. The relatively cooler winter months became only memories, but the return of the monsoon rain was still not expected for weeks.

Despite the alarming upswing in temperature and humidity in March sport – particularly football – was still popular.

Judging by the amount of outgoing mail, all of it requiring inspection and censoring, letter writing continued to be essential for the well-being of squadron personnel.

The squadron's library was so popular that the stock of books held was insufficient to meet the demand. Consequently, an appeal was made for books to be donated, and this was expected to help until a further stock of books could be obtained. With hot weather the need to equip points of congregation, including Messes and the reading room, with more fans was prioritised.

An ENSA show was on for two evenings during the month, and although the consensus was that it wasn't first-rate, 215 Squadron's men found it to be a rewarding change from their usual cinema options. There was also a drive to obtain donated gramophone recordings from private collections, but it was understood that should squadron members give up any of their personal discs there would be less music in the billets. Had this drive been organised back when Jackson Grouse was still in Roy's *basha*, perhaps some of his classical music, including those with the oboe soloes that especially offended his mates in the billet, would have been donated – behind Jackson's back, no doubt.

Friday, 2 MARCH-Saturday, 3 MARCH 1945
(Roy's twenty-seventh op)
Bangkok, THAILAND – Makasan railway workshops *(night bombing and strafing)*

ROY: The sortie to be flown on the night of 2-3 March 1945 – my first night op and my second flight as Mac Gardner's first W/Op – would be my twenty-seventh op.

MATT: A new mission was announced via a Battle Order posted on 1 March. Roy's KH352 'M', with Gardner as the skipper and Flight Sergeant W.F. Hill as the second pilot, would be one of ten 215 Squadron Liberators sent out to the target the following night.

The crew listing indicated that Roy's aircraft would carry only nine men into battle – minus the usual second W/Op (who primarily occupied a beam gun) and the nose gunner – to save weight; fewer gunners were needed because the Japanese fighter presence had significantly diminished. With distances to many strategic targets on the rise, less weight in crewmen, guns and ammo for these weapons meant that more bombs and/or petrol could be carried.

Likewise, each of the nine other 215 Squadron Liberators would be crewed by nine airmen, also eliminating both a second W/Op and a front turret gunner. The diminished crew sizes plus the amount of petrol to be carried per Lib, 2,484 gallons, indicated that the 2-3 March op would be another long strategic bombing sortie.

Those named on the Battle Order and in an amendment giving some substitute airmen's names learned at the noon briefing on 2 March that the target would, indeed, be a faraway location, the Makasan railway workshops in Bangkok, Thailand. This important target had been bombed before, but an attack now was even more relevant.

At 215 Squadron's briefing the airmen present learned that ten of their Liberators would be joined by forty-seven B-24s from four other RAF squadrons: 99 (twelve aircraft), 355 (twelve), 356 (eleven) and 159 (twelve, including three Libs that were assigned minelaying duties in the Chao Phraya River, the broad waterway snaking its way through Bangkok).

The 215 Squadron airmen were also told that two of their aircraft, 'H' (KH372) and 'U' (EW151, not EW125 as the ORB had erroneously recorded), would take off early to act as 'pathfinders'. In this role the two, along with similar pathfinder Liberators from the other RAF squadrons, would mark the target at very low altitude; each squadron chose two crews for this daring role, so ten Libs would perform pathfinder duties. It was planned that all ensuing Libs in the main force (excluding the three 159 Squadron aircraft tasked with mining duties only) would then easily be able to locate the target, accurately marked (presumably) by the pathfinders despite the darkness of night.

The eight non-pathfinder Libs from 215 Squadron would each be loaded with three 1,000lb and six 500lb high explosive bombs, while the squadron's two pathfinder aircraft would drop their full loads of incendiary bombs (3,900 pounds per Liberator) on the target. The eight additional pathfinder Libs, from the four other participating RAF squadrons, would also only release incendiaries.

As darkness increased on 2 March 215's 'H' and 'U' took off – at 1757 ('H') and 1759 ('U') – from Digri, not Dhubalia, and then headed for Thailand. At Dhubalia 99 Squadron's two pathfinders lifted off first, at 1758 ('R') and 1800 ('H'), followed by ten more 99 Squadron bombers between 1807 and 1830. Then 215 Squadron's additional eight participating Liberators took to the sky from Dhubalia between 1838 and 1848. Roy's bomber, KH352 'M', was the fourth of these eight to lift off, at 1841.

In a clear night sky illuminated by a bright moon, and with a visibility of ten to fifteen miles, RAF Liberators individually (not in formation) made their way over water, then across the southern Burma landmass into Thailand. In the vicinity of Bangkok the sky was still clear and bright, though a slight ground haze was reported.

In the moonlight, and now into the early morning hours of 3 March, the pathfinder Libs, hitting the target first, were able to easily identify Makasan via numerous visual clues. Consequently, these leading Liberators precisely set the target alight from very low altitudes (300 feet for 215 Squadron's 'H' and 'U' and roughly 400 to 500 feet for other pathfinder aircraft) with their incendiary bundles in an ideal demonstration of successful target marking. Their seemingly fearless work greatly simplified the main bombing force's task of dropping high explosives on the pinpoint location at night.

In his book, *TO BURMA SKIES AND BEYOND*, 356 Squadron's Reg Jordan, one of the pathfinder skippers, described his experiences that night:

> Our performance...was a textbook operation. We arrived within striking distance of the target with time in hand, and having loitered for a few minutes, we ran in precisely on time and placed our bombs squarely on target on the first run: all very satisfactory, but no more than I would have expected. Nevertheless, it gave me a certain elation as I banked steeply after our attack and looked back, to see our incendiaries burst into flame and illuminate the target. So much so that, on impulse, and knowing that the main force was not due to attack for several minutes, I circled the target area at a few hundred feet encouraging my gunners to silence the tracer fire from the ground.

I had found this combination of low flying and tangling with the defences quite exhilarating after the long outward flog.

The daring and exceptional night-time target marking by the pathfinder aircraft, including the two from 215 Squadron, allowed the conventional bombloads of the main Liberator force to be accurately dropped onto the Makasan railway workshops in individual runs. It was reported in 215 Squadron's ORB that crews in the main bombing force were 'delighted to see the target so clearly indicated'. Among the elated would have been Roy and his crew.

Of the eight 215 Squadron aircraft from the main force to toggle their loads, between 0114½ and 0147, Roy's was the third to do so, at 0128, on a heading of 275 degrees. The squadron's bomb release altitudes, excluding the two pathfinders, varied between 2,100 and 3,000 feet; Roy's Lib bombed from 2,400 feet.

Similarly, the high explosives-carrying Liberators from other squadrons also bombed from what were considered low altitudes, just not as low as the pathfinder aircraft.

ROY: In Bangkok, as we approached Makasan, we could see the kites ahead of us doing their run-ins to the target. Searchlights came on, flak was sent skyward in the hope of hitting the attacking bombers, us included, and tracer bullets also streamed towards the Liberators from the ground. My memory tells me that when a kite was in the target vicinity, all the city lights would go out temporarily, until the next kite arrived.

After my Liberator, KH352 'M', had climbed to 2,400 feet, and approaching the time of bomb release, Flight Lieutenant Messer, our bomb aimer, exclaimed, 'Bomb bay doors open, Chico.' I lost my nervousness then, because I had something to do. I sat just outside the bomb bays and watched the load go down and the fires go by.

Our attack height was low enough for our machine guns to be put into action. The defensive bullets from the ground seemed to come up right between our eyes, and only at the last minute would they miss us and zing past the aircraft. Back on the flight deck with nothing to do, I was very nervous standing in between the two pilots. Flight Sergeant Parkes, our rear gunner, shot out one of the searchlights – a very difficult undertaking from a moving Liberator at any time, day or night.

MATT: The three 159 Squadron aircraft tasked with mining the Chao Phraya River successfully deployed their loads.

One of the high explosives-dropping Liberators from 159 Squadron suffered engine problems and opted to attack the secondary target of Moulmein, Burma. However, the aircraft abandoned its raid after enduring an engine fire near Moulmein. Consequently, its bomb aimer successfully jettisoned its load into the Andaman Sea west of Moulmein, and the Liberator made a safe return to India.

Forty-four high explosives-dropping bombers added to the devastating Makasan conflagration started by the ten pathfinders' incendiaries, although detailed observation of the bombing accuracy was restricted at the time due to the fire, smoke and dust and the fierce glare of searchlights. It was certain, however, that further fires were started by the main Liberator force among buildings, walls were seen to collapse and burning debris was thrown into the air following a number of explosions. An excellent concentration of bursts was reported, with a large blue secondary explosion being observed in the west end of the railway yard following the completion of 215 Squadron's bombing runs.

When the Liberators departed Bangkok, many fires were burning inside the workshops, illuminating them brilliantly through holes in the roofs and the sides of the buildings.

The meagre and ineffective heavy and light anti-aircraft fire caused neither damage to 215 Squadron Liberators nor interference with the bombing runs of its aircraft.

Some of 99 Squadron's B-24s suffered minor damage, with one Liberator choosing to divert to Cox's Bazar with a fuel leak. Likewise, several 159, 355 and 356 Squadron bombers also sustained slight damage from anti-aircraft fire, but there were no casualties among any of the bomber crewmen across all five RAF squadrons.

The 355 Squadron ORB mentioned another curious observance: alternate green and red signals on the ground that possibly related to enemy fighter control. In addition, a circular patch of light four feet in diameter appeared on the ground below one 355 Squadron aircraft and followed it to the target, but then the light was extinguished. Nothing has materialized to explain this.

The chief threat on the flight over Thailand was from the concentration of enemy fighters at Don Muang airfield, twelve miles north of the target. In fact, few opposition aircraft (Japanese Army Air Force and/or possibly Royal

Thai Air Force machines) were sighted during the RAF incursion over enemy territory, but 'few' weren't 'none'.

ROY: Parkes, in the rear turret, barked out, 'Bandit, six o'clock!' Mac Gardner dived for the deck, which was standard for an attack of this sort, because it forced the fighter to break off the approach earlier than it would have at a higher altitude. We flew across Bangkok so low that I was looking into the second floor windows of some buildings.

MATT: With this move by Mac Gardner, Roy's skipper, working well, the Liberator succeeded in safely escaping from the fighter.

Other enemy fighter aircraft were encountered, as well, but not once did the enemy prevail versus the RAF Liberators. Over Thailand a 99 Squadron aircraft saw a single fighter with an inline engine cross its path, but the fighter didn't spar with the Liberator. While on its bombing run an unspecified 215 Squadron B-24 identified two fighters – each characterised by a single radial engine – that steered clear of the Lib. Another 215 Squadron bomber, KH275 'T', spotted a Ki-61 Tony fighter 800 yards ahead, in the vicinity of the target. KH275's mid-upper gunner fired a burst that seemed to have warded off an attack. A twin-engine aircraft seen by an attacking 355 Squadron bomber switched on brilliant white lights located near its engines, but there was no attempt by this fighter, or three or four single-engine fighters also spotted, to fire upon the bomber.

A 159 Squadron Liberator reported that a low-wing enemy monoplane made three passes at them north of the target, after the Lib had released its bombs. On the fighter's third pass the bomber took evasive action per the command of the rear gunner, who fired off a burst when the enemy aircraft approached to 700 yards. No strikes on the fighter were observed, and the defending fighter never again was seen. While crossing Bangkok's Chao Phraya River north-west of the target a 159 Squadron gunner fired a short burst at a single-engine fighter 900 yards away. The fighter broke away and disappeared – it was the smart thing to do, in terms of self-preservation.

Two Liberators from 356 Squadron observed enemy aircraft, as well, in Bangkok. A twin-engine aircraft heading south passed fifty feet below one of the bombers, but it didn't fire. In another encounter a single-engine fighter believed to be a Ki-44 Tojo passed a Liberator, and once again the enemy chose not to attack.

Not one Liberator in the combined force, including the pathfinders, was damaged by enemy aircraft, which was fortuitous, since on this op the bombers were unescorted by Allied fighters.

A clear sky and the bright moon characterised the return flight to India. Numerous fires burning fiercely in Bangkok were visible for sixty miles on the return journey. The two pathfinder aircraft from 215 Squadron successfully landed at Dhubalia, but after inclement weather closed in landings there were deemed too risky. KH352 'M', Roy's Liberator, along with four of the other 215 Squadron high explosives-carrying bombers, instead opted to set down at Digri, 215's former home field; Roy's aircraft landed in daylight at 0858. Another 215 Squadron bomber, KG846 'R', put in safely at Bishnupur, seventy-seven miles south-west of Dhubalia and seventeen miles north of Digri, while one 215 Squadron Lib, aircraft KH275 'T', chose to land at Chittagong.

Aircraft 'M' was airborne for a long fourteen hours and seventeen minutes. Though the op was relatively straightforward and turned out to be safe, the lengthy time aloft would have been exhausting; the much shorter tactical assignments were generally easier on mind and body (and on the aircraft).

The scattered 215 Squadron Liberators all returned to Dhubalia from Digri, Bishnupur and Chittagong on the afternoon of 3 March. In fact, all fifty-seven bombers that had set out from India on the evening of 2 March came home.

Subsequent photographic reconnaissance revealed heavy damage to the Makasan railway workshops. A general remark in 215 Squadron's 'Reports on Operations' for the 2-3 March 1945 op summed up the mission in this manner: 'An exceptionally successful operation. Crews had no difficulty in finding target, and the bombing was concentrated.' Damage Assessment Report PM(S) 547 described complete destruction to, or very heavy damage to 'the Carpenters' Shop, Carriage Repair Shop, Woodworking Machine Shop, Carriage and Wagon Building Shop, Paint Shop, Smithy, Machine Shop, Bench Shop, Wheel Shop, Tool Shop, Works Stores and Offices, Erecting and Boiler Shops and other buildings'. Additionally, there was heavy damage to tracks and other railway infrastructure.

A short newspaper story publicised the 2-3 March 1945 op:

> 200 Tons on Bangkok
> Rail Workshops
>
> HQ, EASTERN AIR COMMAND – Marked clearly with flares dropped by Pathfinder aircraft, the big Makasan railway workshops at

Bangkok stood out clearly in the midnight moonlight when they were heavily attacked on Friday night by RAF Liberators of Strategic Air Force (Eastern Air Command).

An hour later, when about 200 tons of high explosive and incendiary bombs had fallen among the closely-built brick buildings, the whole area was covered with smoke, flame and dust.

It was the heaviest attack yet made on any target in Bangkok.

The Makasan workshops, the largest of their kind in Siam, cover nearly 62 acres. Makasan has been bombed by Strategic Air Force on previous occasions but never on a sufficiently heavy scale to put the workshops and yards out of act on [sic] for an appreciable time. The last attack was in Nov 1944.

Sunday, 4 MARCH-Monday, 5 MARCH 1945
(Roy does not fly on this op)
Bangkok, THAILAND – Bangkok Noi railway station *(night bombing and strafing)*

This op was challenging because of its length, but the relatively youthful Liberator airmen were getting acclimatised to such long sorties, by necessity.

The Gardner crew wouldn't be among them, but Roy and his crewmates would have been pulling for those flying on the op, another rare night-time sortie, to do well and to safely return to Dhubalia.

At the 1100 briefing on 4 March the participants learned that the target was the Bangkok Noi railway station adjacent to the wide Chao Phraya River on the western fringe of Bangkok, Thailand.

Joining 215 Squadron's seven Liberators were aircraft from four other RAF Lib units: 99, 159, 355 and 356 Squadrons. The US 7th Bomb Group targeted two areas nearby: the Klong Toei docks, also on the Chao Phraya River, about seven miles south-east of the RAF's target, as well as a supply dump at Klong Bang Chak, bordering the same river another couple of miles further south-east of the RAF's focus.

An escort of P-51 Mustangs from the 2nd Air Commando Group joined the Liberators on the way to Bangkok.

The 215 Squadron force found that the results of their independent bombing runs, believed to be good, were difficult to observe due to the existing haze and the intense smoke and flame arising from a target already burning fiercely.

All Liberators and their crews, both RAF and American, returned to Allied control after bombing Bangkok.

Subsequent photo reconnaissance revealed severe damage to Bangkok Noi railway station and adjacent areas. The nearby US B-24 attacks, similarly, met with success.

Wednesday, 7 MARCH 1945
(Roy's twenty-eighth op)
Martaban, BURMA – railway jetties and sidings, Area 'C' ***(daylight bombing)***

On 6 March a posted Battle Order again listed Mac Gardner as skipper of Liberator KH352 'M'. Roy would once more be his first W/Op with Flight Sergeant W.F. Hill as second pilot. This upcoming op would be Roy's twenty-eighth.

Unlike their op of 2-3 March, this time the Gardner crew would be comprised of eleven men, not nine. In fact, nine of the ten 215 Squadron Liberators earmarked for the op would be crewed by eleven men, while one Lib, KG830 'A', would carry a twelfth crewman – a bomb aimer screening another bomb aimer under training.

Each of 215's ten aircraft would be loaded with two 1,000lb and ten 500lb high explosive bombs.

The briefing at 1800, also on 6 March, provided further details. The squadron's Liberators would attack the railway jetties and sidings in Martaban, across the wide Sittang River from Moulmein, Burma. At this point the Sittang interrupted the rail line coming up from the south (which included transport along the Thailand-Burma Railway), necessitating the barging of railway cars across the river between Moulmein and Martaban, then their reconnection to the rail line, in order to continue the journey further through Burma. Following this major attack, it was hoped that the Moulmein/Martaban vicinity, already vulnerable, would become an even more severe bottleneck in the transport of Japanese soldiers and materials towards Burma battle zones.

Because all the bombers would be routed over southern Burma in daylight, forty Allied fighters would rendezvous with them over Ramree Island, now in Allied hands, and shepherd them to and from the target. Flying independently in a one-unit formation, 215 Squadron would be joined on the op by twelve

Liberators from each of three RAF squadrons (99, 355, and 356) and by B-24s from three squadrons of the US 7th Bomb Group. Seventy-four bombers would be sent out on the op.

Roy's KH352 took off in daylight at 0838 on 7 March, the eighth 215 Squadron Lib to go aloft. The squadron's nine other participating aircraft departed Dhubalia between 0830 and 0840, followed immediately by the take-offs of the twelve 99 Squadron Liberators.

The weather on the outward leg of the op was good.

On the way to the target, over Burma near the Irrawaddy River, crewmen aboard Roy's 'M' observed a group of buildings surrounded by protective earthworks, plus tracks leading from these buildings to a nearby road, suggesting the existence of a storage dump. After the op this was shared with the 215 Squadron Intelligence Officer, who forwarded it to military planners for future consideration.

Trailing 355 and 356 Squadrons, 215's attacking force approached Martaban from the north. There were clouds seen as the target was approached, but these weren't a hindrance during the attack. Haze, however, restricted visibility in the target area to roughly four to five miles.

KG830 'A' of 215 Squadron accidentally released its bombs approximately six miles north of the target but continued on the bombing run in formation, taking photos. Ironically, this was the Liberator carrying the experienced screen bomb aimer overseeing the inexperienced bomb aimer under training.

The target zone in Martaban had been divided into areas to attack, the northernmost one being assigned to 355 Squadron. Consequently, in approaching Martaban from the north, although some ground detail was identified by 215 Squadron's bomb aimers, views of their specific target segment, Area 'C', were obscured by dust and smoke when Roy's squadron attacked between 1335 and 1336. His Liberator bombed from 7,400 feet, the highest release point of the squadron's aircraft (the lowest being 6,000 feet). Roy's bomb aimer, Flight Lieutenant Messer, simply reported 'bursts across area', which was a positive appraisal of his results, though it was essentially a guess due to the smoke and dust.

All attacking Libs were briefed to turn to starboard after releasing their loads, to avoid, as much as possible, the known anti-aircraft batteries at Moulmein, but, nevertheless, heavy ack-ack guns in the northern part of Moulmein town over a mile away opened up with accurate flak of moderate intensity. Fortunately, no 215 Squadron Liberators were damaged. Minor light anti-aircraft fire was reported, as well, but this was ineffective against 215's formation. One bomber from 99 Squadron sustained slight ack-ack damage.

En route back to Dhubalia after bombing, 215 Squadron's Libs passed near Mokpalin, Burma, where a few rounds of heavy anti-aircraft fire were encountered, with inaccurate results.

No enemy fighters were encountered either to or from the target by any of the squadrons. Good flying weather continued throughout the op, and all bombers from the participating RAF and US B-24 squadrons returned to India with their crewmen safe. Reaching Dhubalia before 99 Squadron, 215 successfully landed in fading daylight between 1758 and 1806½; Roy's Liberator, the tenth and final 215 Squadron aircraft to touch down, was airborne for nine hours and twenty-eight and a half minutes.

Post-sortie Damage Assessment Report PM(S) 568 gave a favourable summary of results:

> There has been damage to transshipment sheds in this area, one measuring approximately 30' x 20' has been completely destroyed, one measuring approximately 30' x 60' has been 75% destroyed, and a third shed of similar dimensions has been completely destroyed, and a fourth one severely damaged. At least 2 direct hits were registered on the tracks in this area. Immediately west of the area a direct hit was seen on the loop track, and a second hit on the main road. There is subsidiary damage to several small buildings west of the road.

Chapter 19

215 Squadron, India: MARCH 1945 *(Part 2)*

Friday, 9 MARCH 1945
(Roy does not fly on this op)
Rangoon, BURMA – supply dump near Victoria Lake, Area 'B'
(daylight bombing)

An op was on for 9 March, per a posted Battle Order, but the Gardner crew, including Roy as its first W/Op, wasn't to be part of it. Each of twelve Liberators from the squadron (carrying 132 airmen – eleven per aircraft) would drop 7,500 pounds of high explosives (three 1,000lb and nine 500lb bombs).

Details of the upcoming op were shared at the 1600 briefing on 8 March. This would be the first of three consecutive 215 Squadron attacks focused upon the supply dump near Victoria Lake in Rangoon, Burma, a town that in the past had been a fearful hellhole to Allied airmen. Previously, back on 11 February, 215 Squadron had targeted the dump, but the time had come to attack once again. It was considered essential to destroy as many dump supplies as possible on this and ensuing raids, thus denying their use to the Japanese.

The dozen 215 Squadron Libs plus B-24s from three other RAF Liberator units – 99 (twelve aircraft), 355 (twelve) and 356 (eleven) Squadrons – and the US 7th Bomb Group would attack in daylight, a challenging time to encroach upon this heavily-defended location. The bombers would be escorted by P-51 Mustangs of the 1st and 2nd Air Commandos.

In the morning light of 9 March eleven 215 Squadron Liberators took off between 0814 and 0826, followed by the twelfth, EW151 'U', at 0842. Rendezvousing over Ramree Island, Burma (across the Bay of Bengal), the bomber force, watched over by the patrolling Mustangs, headed to Rangoon in what was called a 'javelin formation', led by 215 Squadron. This formation afforded one of the heaviest concentrations of defensive fire possible, and it had the additional benefit of group bombing precision.

Weather en route was fair. The approach to the target was begun from the Initial Point at Maubin, Burma, thirty-three miles west of, and a little further south of, Victoria Lake on a course of approximately seventy-five degrees.

After Maubin the clouds thickened, obscuring much essential ground detail during the last ten miles of the run-up to the target. Moderate ground haze added to the confusion. When the bombing and sighting mechanism aboard KH372 'H' (the command aircraft skippered by Zoot Beadon) failed completely three minutes from the target, the leadership of the formation was handed over to Liberator KH322 'V', piloted by Eddie Gilbert. To avoid the negative effects of low cumulus clouds the bomb aimer aboard 'V' called for an unplanned turn south and then northward preceding the release of bombs.

Initiating the attack, 215 Squadron bombed between 1235 and 1238, and from an average altitude and heading at 'bombs gone' of 12,100 feet and nineteen degrees. Despite the complexities experienced on the run-in and the general visibility issues, 215's bombing was reported as being well-concentrated on the target, although smoke and haze prevented accurate observation of details.

The other Liberator squadrons followed in quick succession, with mixed results; a lack of visibility due to the haze, drifting clouds, smoke from previous bomb detonations and the disruption of the overall formation due to the challenging last-minute heading changes adversely affected accuracy, but reports stated that the dump area was still well-covered by bursts.

It was known that some B-24s from the 7th Bomb Group, unable to effectively sight and bomb their specific area of the dump, continued on to the alternate target, a Prome, Burma, supply dump 150 miles to the north-west of Victoria Lake. The Prome dump was peppered with incendiaries.

Because of the unorthodox approach course to the Rangoon target, which undoubtedly resulted in some confusion for the ground defences, certain surprise was unintentionally achieved. Immediately after the release of bombs, the formation led by 215 Squadron made a turn to starboard to successfully avoid the known flak batteries around Mingaladon airfield (nine miles north of the Rangoon waterfront), and then a course for home was regained by a wide turn to port, around the northern end of Hlawga Lake, nearly eighteen miles north of the waterfront.

Sunday, 11 MARCH 1945
(Roy's twenty-ninth op)
Rangoon, BURMA – supply dump near Victoria Lake, Area 'E', within Area 'B' ***(daylight bombing)***

Roy's squadron was alerted for an op to be flown on 11 March. This time the eleven-man Gardner crew, with Roy as first W/Op and Flight Sergeant W.F. Hill as second pilot, was on the Battle Order, and they'd fly aboard Liberator KH118 'G'. Thirteen Libs and crews were listed, including a reserve aircraft and crew; the plan was for only twelve bombers to take off.

The 1545 briefing on 10 March set out details for the op. The supply dump in Rangoon, bombed one day earlier, would once again be the focus of attention on the eleventh. Two areas of special activity within Area 'B' were chosen for the attack and designated Area 'C' and Area 'E'. At the time of the briefing the twelve 215 Squadron Libs were scheduled to join 99 Squadron in hitting Area 'E', while 355 and 356 Squadrons were designated to attack Area 'C'. Joining the RAF in attacking the dump would be B-24s of the US 7th Bomb Group.

With each of 215's Liberators loaded with three 1,000lb and nine 500lb high explosive bombs – the same tonnage per aircraft as carried on the previous dump attack on 9 March – twelve of the squadron's machines took off on the eleventh between 0700 and 0712; Roy's KH118 was the fifth 215 Squadron Lib into the air, at 0704. Preceding these Dhubalia take-offs, twelve bombers from 99 Squadron went aloft between 0646 and 0657.

Because the Libs of both 355 and 356 Squadrons were unable to take off from Salbani due to adverse weather conditions, a decision was made to split the 215 Squadron bombers into two separate forces: Six, including Roy's 'G', would still target Area 'E', as planned (as would 99 Squadron's twelve Liberators), while the other six aircraft from 215 would switch to bombing Area 'C', the section originally assigned to 355 and 356 Squadrons.

Although Salbani's local weather conditions led to the cancellation of the flights by 355 and 356 Squadron Libs, the Dhubalia contingent had no such problem with take-offs. The force of bombers was escorted to and from Burma by forty P-51 Mustangs.

The daytime weather en route to Rangoon was good. The target was found to be clear of clouds, but the atmosphere was hazy.

Approaching from the west, six 215 Squadron Liberators – Roy's KH118 and five other aircraft – followed 99 Squadron from the Initial Point, again over Maubin, the same IP as two days earlier. Bombing the clearly seen target between 1056 and 1057, after 99 Squadron, the 215 Squadron Libs obtained a good concentration of bursts in the centre of Area 'E'. On a heading of 120 degrees Roy's bomb aimer, Flight Lieutenant Messer, released the load of explosives at 1056 from 9,150 feet, with buildings claimed as hit.

The remaining six 215 Squadron Libs, flying as an independent formation, also approached from the IP at Maubin and attacked Area 'C' with accuracy, except for one stick of bombs that overshot and exploded on the edge of Victoria Lake. According to the 215 Squadron ORB, these six aircraft bombed between 1055 and 1057.

Subsequent photo reconnaissance revealed that both Area 'C' and Area 'E' had been severely mauled by the attacking Liberators.

Again that day there were no enemy aerial fighters seen. In fact, much of the Japanese fighter strength had been withdrawn to airfields in Thailand or elsewhere, and allegedly the number of enemy aircraft based in Burma had been halved since mid-February.

There was, however, ack-ack encountered on 11 March, but it wasn't felt until a minute before bombing. As Liberators crossed the Hlaing River on the western fringe of the Rangoon area, heavy and light anti-aircraft batteries opened up; most crews reported accurate fire that was more concentrated than what was experienced two days earlier. This anti-aircraft opposition continued as the bombers attacked and for some two minutes after.

Three unspecified 215 Squadron Libs received slight shrapnel hits; one aircraft later required a fuel cell change, one suffered stringer damage and the third reported aircraft skin damage. Nine of 99 Squadron's Liberators were struck, as well. One of 99's aircraft, EW178 'X', suffered serious Category III damage, including an engine fire, and the rear gunner was wounded; there was speculation that an anti-aircraft shell had made a direct hit on a bomb falling from this Liberator, resulting in the injury and the Category III damage.

US 7th Bomb Group airmen described the anti-aircraft fire as being intense and accurate, with one American squadron, the 436th, reporting five of its aircraft damaged and one crewman wounded. The US 492nd Bomb Squadron, which escaped unscathed, recorded that '…the flak was as close as possible without being fatal to any of our planes.'

Coming off of the target a wide sweep was made to avoid the defences at the various airfields in the region. From Ramree Island courses were set for home bases in India. Making the long Bay of Bengal crossing, crewmen aboard a

99 Squadron Liberator accompanying the badly damaged aircraft 'X' watched in wonderment, intrigued as to how the bomber could still remain airborne, but 'X' was nursed back to Dhubalia for a safe, but challenging, landing, never to take to the sky again.

Flying at 8,000 feet with 99 Squadron Libs, 215's bombers landed in daylight at Dhubalia between 1526 and 1539 following 99 Squadron's touchdowns; Mac Gardner's KH118 was the seventh 215 Squadron aircraft to return, at 1534, after being airborne for eight hours and thirty minutes.

Despite the various degrees of damage all RAF and US Liberators made it back to their respective home airfields, having taken advantage of clear weather for the returns to India.

The op was deemed very successful with almost all bombs having been dropped on the targets. Considering the intensity of the opposition flak the fact that formation flying was maintained was especially seen as being impressive.

Roy loses his skipper: the non-combat deaths of Mac Gardner, Smokey Williams and Eddie Gilbert *(13 MARCH 1945)*

ROY: After changing crews in late February 1945, I flew only four combat sorties with skipper Mac Gardner, the final one being my twenty-ninth op, the 11 March attack on the supply dump in Rangoon. Two days later, as far as I was concerned, one of the worst events I ever experienced on 215 Squadron happened.

Two Liberator pilots and one bomb aimer from our Mess took a light aircraft (a single-engine Fairchild Argus II, serial number FZ786) down to Calcutta. They were my skipper, Mac Gardner, and two others: pilot Eddie Gilbert and bomb aimer Smokey Williams. Rumour had it – and it was vehement denied, too – that the three got plastered while in Calcutta, and when it was time to go back to Dhubalia clearance was denied, as they were in no condition to fly.

As the story goes there was no way Mac was going to be prevented from returning home. With him at the controls the Argus made a perfect take-off from Red Road in Calcutta, as one would have expected of Mac, and headed for Dhubalia, about sixty-five miles north of their Red Road location. Allegedly, Mac missed the correct turn off for the approach to Dhubalia, and the three men flew on, searching for the base after sunset until they ran out of gas.

In forcibly landing Mac struck a railway embankment and jumped an earthen wall separating borrow pits created in the construction of the embankment.

The Argus, landing on its belly, burst into flames. Wing Commander Sindall, who inspected the crash site, believed that the men were dead from the effects of hitting the embankment. Mac and the other two victims were Canadians; Mac and Gilbert were members of the Royal Canadian Air Force (RCAF), and Williams, from Vancouver, was in the RAF. It was an awful event – the needless loss of three very popular and talented guys.

MATT: Rumour can be cruel, especially to loved ones of deceased victims who can never defend themselves. It's wrong to focus upon excessive alcohol consumption as having been of any factor whatsoever in the loss of the three Canadians; whatever the cause or causes, they died in a horrible accident that likely could have befallen any men, even teetotalers. Any speculation about alcohol is just that, speculation, not backed by fact, as far as is known.

ROY: Once more, I was without a skipper, but I was soon able to join Bill Waddington's crew in my capacity as a first W/Op; Bill was a Canuck, and a fine pilot. Most of the airmen with whom I'd flown ops on Mac's crew also joined the Waddington lineup, replacing men who were reassigned to the CO's crew.

Unlike after I transferred from Bing's crew to Mac's, I wasn't put back on ops right away; my first op with Bill wouldn't come until 22 March.

Bill would be my fifth Liberator skipper since I joined 215 Squadron: Jackson Grouse (one ASR op, one long exercise that counted as an op, one long exercise not counted as an op and four regular bombing ops before finishing his tour in December 1944), Jack Hadaway (only two ops as my skipper, but Jackson was screening him from the second pilot's position both times), Bing Bingham (one bombing op when he was screened by Jackson, then sixteen ops as the true skipper, plus one long non-op exercise), Mac Gardner (the four ops, before his untimely death) and then Bill (six ops ultimately).

MATT: One more take on the loss of the three men came from 215 Squadron skipper Wally Frazer, another Canadian, in his book, *A TREPID AVIATOR*:

> Bad news! We've lost three more Canadians – Ed Gilbert, Smokey Williams, and Mac Gardner. From enemy action? No, Eddie took the little single-engine Argus into Cal on some errand for the CO. Just an hour into Cal, then right back after lunch. Mac and Smokey went

along to keep him company – Eddie was a guy who always liked lots of company – or maybe just for the lark.

Did they perhaps do too much larking over lunch? Whatever, they were late getting back to Dum Dum airport, apparently picked the wrong rail line to follow back to Dhubalia. But there's little twilight in these latitudes; the sun dips below the horizon and it's like someone switched off all the lights. They ran out of gas, tried to land in the dark, didn't make it.

Today I had breakfast with Bill Waddington. He looked up from his fried eggs to ask, "When you and I came to 215, Wal, how many RCAF in the [Officers'] Mess?"

"Nine."

"Right. Not counting new arrivals, how many are left?"

"Two. Just us."

Bill took a long swig from his cup, finally looked up at me and said, "Keep your fingers crossed."

"Yeah, Bill… you too."

Saturday, 17 MARCH 1945
(Roy does not fly on this op)
Rangoon, BURMA – supply dump near Victoria Lake, Area 'A', within Area 'B' *(daylight bombing)*

Roy didn't fly on this sortie, although his future skipper, Bill Waddington, was on the op. It's not known whether Roy had yet been reassigned to Waddington's crew following Gardner's death on the thirteenth.

The briefing for the op was held at 1545 on 16 March.

As one component of a major attack, eleven 215 Squadron Liberators bombed a Rangoon supply dump servicing the entire theatre of war, near Victoria Lake. The squadron's Liberators, flying with eleven-man crews, joined three other RAF squadrons (99, 355 and 356). US 7th Bomb Group B-24s and US Twentieth Bomber Command B-29s also attacked the Victoria Lake dump.

While ack-ack was predicted to be lighter than in the past, the target was still in Rangoon, a destination that had sent many a shiver down the spines of airmen at briefings. American 7th Bomb Group crewmen who'd never been to Rangoon before were still initiated into the 'Goon at Noon Club', a relic from earlier in the war, when enemy aircraft often made brutal daylight attacks in numbers, and when there was no, then still inadequate, protective fighter cover.

Greeting the incoming bomber force over Ramree Island was a reassuring escort of P-38 Lightnings, P-47 Thunderbolts and P-51 Mustangs.

The green Target Indicators dropped by 356 Squadron were very helpful to the main force of attacking Liberators, although the Superfortresses, slightly ahead of schedule, had begun bombing prior to 356's release of red Target Indicators.

The B-29s, attacking from between 27,000 and 30,000 feet (higher altitudes than the Liberators), concentrated bombs upon their primary assignment.

Overall, impaired target visibility hindered few bombers, despite clouds, haze and the usual smoke, dust and debris thrown skyward by the explosions below.

All crews over Rangoon that day reported the ack-ack as meagre, only moderately accurate and tailing away quickly as aircraft passed over the target. However, some Liberators were damaged, but no crewmen were injured. The 215 Squadron aircraft were unharmed.

All bombers from all units returned safely to Allied control.

With no airborne Japanese aircraft spotted over the course of the entire flight, the Allied fighter escorts had little to excite them; this type of boredom may not have suited too many of these escorting pilots, but the bomber boys would have appreciated the sense of security in having these 'little friends' around.

The Rangoon operation of 17 March largely went according to plan and was considered a success. Preliminary Damage Assessment Report PM(S) 591 stated that there were many direct hits and near misses on stacks of stored materials at the Victoria Lake dump, together with a heavy cratering of roads. At least seven stores buildings surrounded by blast walls had been completely destroyed, and two others severely damaged.

Monday, 19 MARCH 1945
(Roy does not fly on this op)
Na Nien, THAILAND – railway yards, Area 'C' *(daylight bombing)*

Although Roy and the other members of his crew didn't fly, twelve other 215 Squadron Liberators, along with aircraft from three other RAF units – 99, 355 and 356 Squadrons – attacked the railway yards at Na Nein, Thailand, on the Kra Isthmus six miles east of Jumbhorn, a round-trip of over 2,400 miles.

The 215 Squadron briefing for the op was at 1545 on the eighteenth.

At Na Nien, despite generally good visibility the cumulus coverage varied from 3/10ths to 6/10ths; this didn't stop 215 Squadron from completing its duties. Roy's squadron reported a good concentration of bursts on the yards and in the vicinity of a landing strip. Rolling stock and buildings were seen to disintegrate after being hit by bombs, and many fires erupted as a result of the bombing. One train in the centre of the area was seen blazing from end to end, and a large oil fire, with black smoke rising to 3,000 feet, broke out in the western portion of 215 Squadron's designated target zone.

Three of 215 Squadron's aircraft put in for fuel at Chittagong (between 2141 and 2210). This was probably unnecessary, but the decision to take on petrol at Chittagong, in the name of safety, was understandable and acceptable.

With the exception of 355 Squadron aircraft 'A' (EW180), tragically shot down by flak solely attacking the Prome, Burma, secondary target, all of the Libs returned safely to their home bases in India. These included the American B-24s and also the RAF aircraft that had first landed at Chittagong.

In general, the 215 Squadron portion of the operation was considered 'fairly successful'. Preliminary Damage Assessment Report PM(S) 598 – which analysed the attacks by four Liberator squadrons, not just 215 – described the bombing as extremely well-concentrated, with severe damage to all installations in the railway yards. Numerous fires from rolling stock and supply stores, and general damage throughout the area, were a testament to the successes of bomb aimers from 215 and from the other three RAF Liberator squadrons.

In what was believed was the longest B-24 mission flown in formation in the Second World War, aircraft of the American 7th Bomb Group attacked railway targets over ninety miles south of the RAF's target. The flight, it was said, was roughly equivalent to an aerial excursion in the US from Boston, Massachusetts, to Kansas City, Missouri, and back.

Chapter 20

215 Squadron, India: MARCH 1945 *(Part 3)*

Thursday, 22 MARCH 1945
(Roy's thirtieth op)
THAILAND – Thailand-Burma Railway targets between Milestone 50 and Milestone 100 *(bombing and strafing in the increasing early light of day)*

ROY: On 22 March 1945, 215 Squadron again raided the Thailand-Burma Railway, scoring direct hits on locomotives. I was a participant on this op. This bombing and strafing attack on the railway line was done at very low altitude. In conducting a 'sweep' for targets along a fifty-mile segment of the railway line allotted to five 215 Squadron Liberators, we flew alongside the line, with the wing nearest the railway angled down so that all the turrets and one beam gun could fire at the locomotives and rolling stock. Though I was first W/Op, I commandeered the beam gun on the 'action' side so that I could fire, too. After all, I was a trained air gunner, and firing off a .50-calibre Browning was invigorating.

When a locomotive was hit an escape of steam would be visible. Of course, at our low attack height almost anything, even rifles, that were fired at us could have hit us, but, remarkably, we made it home without damage or injury.

MATT: It was time for Roy to rejoin 215 Squadron's offensive might on a bombing op, skippered from here onward by Bill Waddington following Mac Gardner's death. This opportunity to again participate on an op was announced in a Battle Order posted on 21 March. With Waddington as skipper and Flight Sergeant W.F. Hill as second pilot, aircraft KH372 'H' would be one of 215 Squadron's twelve Liberators earmarked for the op. Each aircraft, filled with 2,334 gallons of petrol, would carry a load of ten 500lb high explosive bombs.

At the 1800 briefing on 21 March the nature of the op was spelled out for the assembled crews of the participating aircraft. The Allied advance in Burma and the dramatic innovations in Liberator flying and bomb carrying capabilities meant that strategic bombing targets were further from India than earlier in the war. This op would be another long one. Roy's squadron was detailed for an early daylight sweep against locomotives and rolling stock along two separate stretches of the Thailand-Burma Railway. Six Libs were to attack targets of opportunity between Thanbyuzayat, at the western terminus of the railway, and Milestone 50 in Burma, to the south-east of Thanbyuzayat, and six bombers were assigned to the stretch of railway between Milestone 50 in Burma and Milestone 100 in Thailand.

Other RAF Liberator squadrons to be sent to the Thailand-Burma Railway that day to bomb and strafe their assigned stretches of railway line or specific bridges along the same line would be 99, 355 and 356.

The US 7th Bomb Group's 436th Bomb Squadron, based at Madhaiganj, Bengal, India (seventy-one miles west of Dhubalia), would focus upon a different branch of the railway system in Thailand – a northern segment between Nakon Sawan and Uttaradit. The US 7th Bomb Group's 9th Bomb Squadron, with its B-24s based at Pandaveswar in Bengal, India (seventy-eight miles west of Dhubalia), would attack the Cocos Islands (not to be confused with the separate Coco Islands north of the Andaman Islands) in the southern Bay of Bengal.

Eleven Liberators from 99 Squadron lifted off from Dhubalia in the last hour of 21 March, followed by eleven 215 Squadron take-offs between 2359 on the twenty-first and 0041 on the twenty-second; 215 Squadron's op was, technically speaking, flown on two adjacent calendar dates, although only one aircraft, KG830 'A', departed on the twenty-first, in the last minute of the day. For all other 215 Squadron Liberators the raid was only flown on 22 March. Thus, only 22 March is given for the date of the op.

The Waddington crew, with Roy aboard, was the fourth 215 Squadron Liberator into the night sky, at 0010. From Salbani 355 Squadron contributed all twelve Libs, as planned, but 356 Squadron, short of serviceable aircraft, only managed to send ten aircraft skyward.

Because the airmen were initially flying, for hours, on a night decently illuminated by a waxing gibbous moon, the 215 Squadron Liberators on the op flew to their target areas in a very loose javelin formation. Due to the presence of low stratus clouds no pinpoint was obtained on the Indian coast at the Sundarbans, but the course to the Thailand-Burma Railway was, as per usual, checked and maintained by taking astro fixes, radio fixes and drift measurements.

The aircraft of 215 Squadron headed out to Alguada Reef, just off the Burma coast near the mouths of the Irrawaddy River, where the bombers split into two boxes: the six that would target the railway from Thanbyuzayat to Milestone 50 in Burma, and the second box's five Libs, which would cover the stretch of line from Milestone 50 in Burma to Milestone 100 in Thailand. The Waddington crew would be among the attackers going for this latter segment of the railway.

Unescorted by friendly fighters, the frequent low-level Liberator bombing and strafing attacks were made individually. If trains were found to be moving, they'd be stopped by strafing before further damage was meted out, though a majority of the trains proved to be stationary. Because targets of opportunity were so widely distributed, the times when Liberators hit them varied considerably; for 215 Squadron attacks were made over a nearly two-hour period, from 0500 to 0652.

Roy's Liberator, KH372 'H', having approached from the north-west, reversed course 180 degrees in preparation to attack. As the morning light increased, bombing and strafing began.

A stationary train of two locomotives and twenty rolling stock at Milestone 104, slightly beyond the bomber's assigned south-eastern limit at Milestone 100, proved to be a fortuitous encounter. One railway wagon was observed as having already been derailed from an earlier Liberator attack. Roy's 'H' then made three bombing runs from 2,000 feet between 0603 and 0644, but all bursts were fifteen to twenty yards from the train. It was considered that because of the heavy timber used in the railway's construction, the actual tracks would require a direct hit to cause major damage, while a near miss, such as that resulting from the initial attack by 'H', would cause little, if any, damage to the line. Strafing was believed to have the potential to cause more damage.

And so, in pursuit of further damage to the stationary train after KH372's bombs had been released, Waddington's gunners thoroughly strafed it from fifty feet, claiming strikes on the boiler of at least one locomotive; clouds of steam were seen to escape from the damaged engine. A pile of large transshipment cases standing alongside the railway line was also well-shot up.

Continuing in a north-westerly direction along the rail line, on one run and with their three remaining bombs, at 0717 Roy's Liberator attacked a train of two locomotives pulling twelve rolling stock at Milestone 81½, still in Thailand. This time, a direct hit on the train was observed, followed by a burst of flame rising to 500 feet. When this flame died down, two or three rolling stock were seen to have been destroyed in the attack.

The results of Roy's aircraft's attacks were similar to what other Libs reported.

At 0717, just before this successful encounter, at Milestone 82 about 100 men were seen close together in a compound, watching Roy's aircraft. It was assumed that these men were Allied PoWs or else native Asian labourers.

In general, the weather was misty.

No opposition was encountered en route to the Thailand-Burma Railway, or on the return flight, nor were enemy aircraft sighted by any squadron. During 215 Squadron's sweep phase of the op, however, there was opposition at several points along the railway, chiefly from light machine-gun fire.

Some tracer fire was seen near Milestone 101 by 215 Squadron's aircraft 'A', KG830, which also reported flashes from a machine gun sited on a hillside a little further to the north-west. During the attacks by KH320 'D' two machine guns inside a PoW encampment fired intermittent bursts, and flashes were seen from a nearby hillside. As KH118 'G' passed over Milestone 94 in Thailand at 3,000 feet, tracer fire was seen and successfully evaded. A solitary machine gun that opened fire upon EW125 'P' one mile south-east of Milestone 24½ in Burma was effectively silenced by this Liberator's gunners.

From fifty feet crewmen aboard 215's aircraft 'R', KG846, witnessed four light ack-ack guns and machine guns firing upon the Liberators near Milestone 28, and superficial damage was sustained to the bomber, without injury to airmen. During a bombing run Liberator 'S' identified machine-gun fire and occasional bursts of light anti-aircraft fire from the vicinity of Milestone 24½. Flying over Anankwin village in Burma, near Milestone 27, EV963 'S' was lifted by a heavy ack-ack burst, with slight shrapnel damage resulting, but the crew was uninjured. Some members of the crew of KH322 'V' thought they saw flashes from Shitpyit, Burma, near Milestone 37, but no bursts were seen in the air. Finally, during the bombing by aircraft 'M', KH352, near Milestone 99 in Thailand, sporadic, but ineffective, rifle fire was observed from nearby woods.

Meagre machine gun and anti-aircraft fire similar to that experienced by 215 Squadron was reported by other squadrons, as well, but all bombers, including the American marauders, returned safely to their bases. Of the twelve 355 Squadron Liberators to take off eleven completed the op as planned, but one had jettisoned its bombs early on the flight out before returning to Salbani. Likewise, on 356 Squadron, one Lib suffered engine issues and turned for home upon reaching the Tenesserim coast in southern Burma. A safe landing followed at Salbani after its load of bombs had been jettisoned to maintain height.

At Dhubalia 215 Squadron's eleven Liberators uneventfully touched down in the early afternoon between 1210 and 1337. Roy's KH372, the last of its unit to land, was airborne for thirteen hours and twenty-seven minutes.

More trains were seen on the railway on this occasion than was the case during sweeps made earlier in the year.

On this op the sole unit assigned bridge busting duties, 355 Squadron, had extensively damaged the two Thailand-Burma Railway bridges near Thanbyuzayat, Burma, that it had been tasked with targeting.

The overall 22 March operation was considered satisfactory in view of the difficulty in having heavy bombers attack railway targets.

One of the US 9th Bomb Squadron B-24s, serial number 42-73437, crashed into the sea near the Cocos Islands after being hit by anti-aircraft fire, killing its eleven-man crew.

Except for this tragic loss, no other US or RAF bombers were lost on 22 March and no other individuals were killed or known to have been injured.

Flying beyond the 300-hour or thirty-op mark

Typically, an airman's operational tour on an RAF squadron in the Far East was 300 hours or thirty ops, whichever came first. Roy had reached the magic thirty-op mark with his 22 March flight, yet he kept on flying. Upon completion of his thirtieth op the total number of hours he'd flown on operational sorties, while not precisely known (his logbook does not exist, nor were all details spelled out for each of his ops in 215 Squadron's ORB), does appear to be roughly thirty hours short of the 300-hour mark; he'd reached the coveted thirty-op mark before closely approaching the 300-hour limit.

In early 1945, a high-level decision was made to increase the required tour length for an existing Liberator airman in the theatre to four hundred hours or one year, whichever came first, and adding a stipulation that a crewman shouldn't operate through more than one monsoon period without a rest.

Not surprisingly, this ruling was unpopular. Pilot Reg Jordan of 356 Squadron had this to say in his book, *TO BURMA SKIES AND BEYOND*:

> The impact of this decision to extend our operational tours did not reach 356 Squadron until March, by which time a number of us, including my own crew, were on the brink of tour expiry. For most, this was hard to stomach, and aircrew morale generally took quite a knock. For my own part I was able to accept the extension philosophically, but I recall more than one high-calibre person coming close to cracking up at the thought of his tour being extended: a flood of tears from a grown man can be very embarrassing. It was as though such people had subconsciously paced themselves to last a set number of hours, and an eleventh-hour change in the rules was the last straw.

The 13 April 1945 entry in the diary of Eric Kightley, a 355 Squadron air gunner, included the passage, 'Heard that we have to do 400 hrs for tour.'

Skipper Wally Frazer, who was on 215 Squadron when Roy was there, was transferred with his crew to 356 Squadron in late April 1945. He wrote the following in his book, *A TREPID AVIATOR*, soon after joining 356 Squadron to continue flying Liberators:

> An ugly rumour is circulating. The Adjutant on one of the squadrons is saying that crews can forget about being released after doing 300 hours, that we could be kept on the job indefinitely. But I don't believe it. They'd never change the tour requirements at this stage, would they?

However, the powers that be did alter the rules, but as late as April 1945 the change in the length of an operational tour had not yet become official on 215 Squadron. It seems that the new requirements wouldn't have applied to Roy's operational flying on the squadron.

So why did he fly thirty-five ops, not just thirty? It's an unclarified mystery. Roy, perhaps having picked up upon a rumour that 215 would 'soon' switch to a transport role, chose to continue flying Liberator sorties beyond the end of a standard tour's length. Maybe he had volunteered to fly a set number of extra ops, not knowing of the rumour.

The rumour did come true (as will be explained further below), and 215 Squadron's final Liberator op coincided with Roy's final op, flown on 8 April 1945. Roy knew in advance that the 8 April flight would be his last op.

Saturday, 24 MARCH 1945
(Roy's thirty-first op)
Pa-auk, BURMA – one of the three dump areas, and railway locomotive and rolling stock dispersal areas *(daylight bombing)*

Roy would exceed the thirty-op figure with his flight on 24 March 1945. In a Battle Order posted on 23 March he was included as Bill Waddington's first W/Op aboard Liberator KH372 'H' (second pilot: Flight Sergeant W.F. Hill). Eleven men would comprise the crew once again. Roy's aircraft would be one of eleven participating 215 Squadron Liberators, each carrying a load of three 1,000lb and nine 500lb high explosive bombs.

At the 1545 briefing on the twenty-third the assembled crews heard the details of the next day's op, an attack upon the enemy railway locomotive and rolling stock dispersals plus a camouflaged supply dump at Pa-auk, Burma, situated nine miles south of Moulmein. Led by 215 Squadron, three trailing RAF Liberator units, each putting up twelve aircraft, would also attack the target in the following order: 356, 355 and 99 Squadrons. This would be the first strike on Pa-auk's target, which was divided into three specific areas. Separate aiming points were assigned to 99, 215 and 356 Squadrons, while 355 Squadron's focus would be split between 215's area and 356's.

In good weather 99 Squadron, the first unit from Dhubalia to take to the air, could only put up eleven of the twelve aircraft planned for the raid. Next came 215's eleven daylight take-offs, between 0854 and 0907; Roy's aircraft 'H' was the fifth 215 Squadron Liberator to lift off, at 0857.

In a javelin formation 215 set course across the Bay of Bengal. A major navigational landmark before reaching the target was Elephant Point, Burma, where the wide Rangoon River entered the Gulf of Martaban twenty-four miles south of Rangoon. Small patches of stratus clouds were encountered en route.

When landfall on the west coast of Burma was reached at Boronga Point, Burma (twenty-four miles south of Akyab), 99 Squadron's extremely scattered formation was sighted to 215 Squadron's port side. Some ten to fifteen miles distant, also to port, 356 Squadron was seen in good formation. Astern of 215 Squadron, 355 was coming into position.

Further inland, at 1243, when flying at 8,000 feet, the Waddington crew noted twenty freight cars on railway sidings at Gyobingauk, Burma, 105 miles north-north-west of Rangoon.

Twenty-four P-51 Mustangs of the 2nd Air Commando Group escorted the Liberators.

Bypassing the target in order to approach from the east, 215 Squadron, in the lead, reorganised into two boxes for the attack. The Waddington crew's 'H' was in the six-aircraft group headed to the target first. Some low clouds were met on this stretch of flying. The Pa-auk area was found to be very hazy, with target identification being further impeded by drifting smoke from agricultural fires in the vicinity.

Despite visual difficulties 215 Squadron was able to identify its target zone and release bombs between 1355 and 1356½; 'H' attacked from 6,500 feet. This first box of six 215 Squadron Liberators obtained a good concentration of bursts on its assigned area, but trees obscured the target, preventing any accurate observation of damage. Some rolling stock, however, was seen to be derailed. The second box, finding much more ground detail obscured by clouds, haze and drifting smoke and dust, also released its bombs, but with less success. The bombsight of KH118 'G', in this second box, had suffered a malfunction, so 'G' bombed at the same time as did the leader of the box, KH322 'V'.

The three other RAF Liberator squadrons followed in bombing the target: first 356 (nine aircraft had reached Pa-auk), then 355 (all twelve intended Libs attacked), and finally 99 Squadron's eleven aircraft. Results were mixed, primarily owing to visual impairment.

Aerial opposition from enemy fighters was non-existent for the bombers, both to and from the target.

As for ack-ack from below, the Liberators were routed, as per usual, to avoid known defended areas, and it's believed that no RAF aircraft experienced anti-aircraft defensive fire on the inward flight to Pa-auk. A 99 Squadron report recorded meagre inaccurate heavy anti-aircraft fire from just south of Moulmein, near Pa-auk, but presumably this was experienced when homeward-bound, after departing the target area. None of the other three squadrons noted any anti-aircraft opposition from the ground, with the exception of three Libs from 215 Squadron. They reported meagre heavy ack-ack from guns near Prome, Burma, on the return to India, despite the three aircraft having been out of range. In the opinion of 215 Squadron airmen, the inaccurate bursts were a waste of ammunition.

Safe and successful returns to Dhubalia (for 99 and 215 Squadrons) and Salbani (for 355 and 356 Squadrons) were made by all of the airborne RAF Libs that day. Wing Commander James Sindall, 215 Squadron's CO, wrote in his report that the return was 'uneventful'. The eleven 215 Squadron Liberators landed back at Dhubalia between 1808 and 1830, before 99 Squadron's return. Roy's 'H' was the fifth aircraft from 215 to land, at 1811, after traversing 1,745 air miles on a flight of nine hours and fourteen minutes.

Tuesday, 27 MARCH 1945
(Roy's thirty-second op)
Bangkok, THAILAND – Klong Bhang Chak supply dump *(daylight bombing)*

The Battle Order for the upcoming 27 March 1945 op once again listed Roy as first W/Op aboard Bill Waddington's KH372 'H' (second pilot: Flight Sergeant W.F. Hill), but on this op each crew would be comprised of ten men, one less than on most sorties; no second W/Op would be included. Thirteen aircraft and crews were listed on the Battle Order, but one Lib, KH352 'M', was marked as a reserve aircraft; only twelve 215 Squadron aircraft would fly the op. Each of the Liberators would carry a load of nine 500lb high explosive bombs.

At the briefing for the op, held on 26 March at 1545, the details of the raid, to be flown on the following day, were presented to the assembled Liberator airmen. A daylight bombing attack upon a Klong Bhang Chak storage dump close to the northern bank of Bangkok, Thailand's winding Chao Phraya River, was on the agenda. Twelve 356 Squadron Liberators would lead the RAF bombers, followed by twelve 355 Squadron aircraft, then by 215's twelve, and finally by a dozen Liberators from 99 Squadron.

As was usual, each RAF squadron was assigned its unique section of the dump to attack. Differing slightly, the US 7th Bomb Group would independently bomb two targets in the vicinity: the Klong Bhang Chak dump – same as the RAF aircraft – and also the Klong Toi docks only a couple of miles to the north-west, adjoining the same bank of the Chao Phraya River. Later, in darkness on that same day, Liberators from 159 Squadron RAF would mine the river.

Poor weather conditions at Dhubalia made take-offs challenging for both 215 and, next, 99 Squadron; 215 Squadron's twelve participating aircraft lifted off between 0623 and 0638 or 0644 (the records differ), while 99 Squadron's twelve Libs took off from 0637 to 0650. At 0627 Roy's KH372 was the fifth Liberator to take flight. Despite a low-level layer of stratus clouds at 1,000 feet over the airfield 215's Libs were able to assemble into a defensive formation for the flight out to Thailand.

While crossing the Bay of Bengal 215 Squadron met worsening cloud conditions as the day progressed. At 1015 and fifteen miles west-south-west of Alguada Reef (south of the Irrawaddy River delta in Burma) 215 Squadron's EW151 'U' signalled by Aldis lamp that it was abandoning the formation due to an engine issue (later determined to be tied to a faulty carburetor), and it safely returned to Dhubalia early with its full load of bombs. Eleven Libs from 215 Squadron, including Roy's 'H', continued onward, along with bombers from the other squadrons.

The Liberators were, as usual, routed over the sea as much as possible in order to minimise the risk of enemy interference by fighters or ground-based gunfire. The bombers proceeded eastward across the Gulf of Martaban at 5,000 feet before turning south at Pagoda Point off the western coast of Burma near the town of Ye (eighty-seven miles south of Moulmein), and continuing down the Andaman Sea coast. Turning inland, the formations then crossed a narrow portion of lower Burma near Tavoy Island. Gaining altitude to 12,500 feet to overfly the Tenasserim Hills, the incoming Liberators, without dire consequences, passed between banks of cumulus clouds and finished crossing the Kra Isthmus. On the run across the Gulf of Thailand to the Initial Point, south of Bangkok, the aircraft height was decreased to 11,000 feet.

P-51 Mustangs and P-38 Lightnings escorted the bombers to Bangkok.

Eleven aircraft from 356 Squadron led the way over southern Bangkok. (A twelfth, having developed an oil leak on the journey to Bangkok, had jettisoned its bombload and returned to base.) Cumulus clouds marked the target area, but they didn't seriously impede observation. There was a clear patch over the target, and despite hazy conditions below the attacking Liberators, and a good deal of cumulus clouds about, the Klong Bhang Chak target, lying in open country with no attempt at concealment, was readily seen.

The eleven 356 Squadron Liberators, twelve from 355 Squadron, eleven Libs from 215 and then twelve from 99 Squadron made their bombing attacks, in that order. The US 7th Bombardment Group B-24s followed up the high explosive attacks with incendiaries.

Specifically, in daylight from 1325½ to 1328, 215 Squadron's Libs, maintaining formation, dropped bombs, as planned. The Waddington crew's KH372 'H' released its load from 10,700 feet at 1325½ on a course of 279 degrees.

Bombing results for 215 Squadron were excellent. Photographic evidence later confirmed that all sticks were well on target, with the exception of KH118 'G', whose bombsight failed (for the second op in succession) during the run-up; its bursts were seen just south of the allotted area. In the target zone buildings were seen to disintegrate, and two large secondary explosions, characterised by red flashes and grey smoke, occurred after bombing. One covered revetment was seen to go up in flames, and many explosions and fires were observed in other areas upon which 215 Squadron focused its attention. Aircraft KH320 'D' of 215 Squadron photographed two destroyers and a gunboat in a bend of the river.

While in the target zone Allied fighters protected the Liberators, but no enemy aircraft were sighted.

Meagre but generally inaccurate and ineffective heavy flak was fired over the Klong Bhang Chak area from known Bangkok gun batteries, from other positions along the river near the target, from naval vessels moored in the river and also, likely, from merchant vessels. After bombing, two Libs from 99 Squadron received minor shrapnel damage.

An enormous amount of damage to the enemy was meted out in the attack, and large fires could be seen from many miles away.

The Liberators of 215 Squadron split into two boxes to cross the Tenasserim Hills on the westerly run out of Bangkok and climbed to 17,000 feet to get between cumulus clouds, which had greatly increased in size since the run-in to the target. Once clear of the clouds, and now over the Andaman Sea, the Liberators from all of the squadrons made again for Alguada Reef before turning north-westerly for the long, but uneventful, slog across and above the Bay of Bengal back to India. As dusk was approached bombers from the participating squadrons eventually abandoned formation flying and returned individually. Aside from KH362 'O' of 215 Squadron, which landed at Akyab suffering from a main bearing issue in an engine, all attacking Liberators from each squadron safely returned directly to home bases.

Back at Dhubalia 215 Squadron landed before 99 Squadron, setting down in the dark between 1952 and 2019 or 2054 (there is a recording error in one source). At 2019, after traversing 2,540 air miles, Roy's KH372 'H' was the tenth or eleventh (records conflict) 215 Squadron Liberator to land. The aircraft had been airborne for thirteen hours and fifty-two minutes (or thirteen hours and fifty-five minutes in Wing Commander Sindall's summary).

The operation against Klong Bhang Chak by all attacking Liberators from the various squadrons, both RAF and US, was deemed highly successful. The American 7th Bomb Group raid on the nearby Klong Toi docks, however, wasn't successful, as smoke and clouds obscured the target.

Thursday, 29 MARCH 1945
(Roy's thirty-third op)
Rangoon, BURMA – headquarters, Burma Area Army *(daylight bombing)*

Having already surpassed the then standard end-of-tour milestone of thirty ops, Roy continued to put his life on the line by flying potentially dangerous Liberator sorties with 215 Squadron. What would soon be his thirty-third op was announced via a Battle Order posted on Wednesday, 28 March 1945. This time Roy would be in a full crew of eleven men once more as the first W/Op aboard KH372 'H', skippered by Bill Waddington and with W.F. Hill as second pilot.

It was guessed from the crew size and the petrol allotment per aircraft, 2,060 gallons, that the op wouldn't be outrageously lengthy, such as on the over-thirteen-hour flights Roy had endured for his thirtieth and thirty-second ops. However, knowledge of where he, along with 131 other airmen aboard twelve Liberators, would be heading had to wait until the briefing scheduled for 1545, later the same day.

From the Battle Order it was understood that 8,500 pounds of high explosives would be carried per aircraft: five 1,000lb and seven 500lb bombs.

Details from the late afternoon briefing revealed that the squadron would again be headed to what the men still considered their most dangerous target: Rangoon. In the daylight attack 215's Dhubalia stablemate, 99 Squadron, would also be in the mix (tasked with putting up twelve bombers), but no other RAF Liberator units would be in on the action. Instead, over thirty aircraft from three of the four US 7th Bomb Group B-24 squadrons in India would lead the attack.

The target would be an important one: what Allied Intelligence experts believed was the Rangoon headquarters of the Burma Area Army – the Japanese control centre for all of their army's exploits in Burma. In fact, the

Americans in the 436th Bomb Squadron, one of the B-24 units tasked with the sortie, deemed this assignment one of their most important missions ever, because the Japanese army headquarters was 'the focal center of the enemy infection in South East Asia.' The target consisted of a group of buildings located just north-east of Kemmendine railway station on the west side of Rangoon.

Following 99 Squadron's twelve take-offs the dozen chosen 215 Squadron Liberators joined them in daylight between 0800 and 0813. As the second of 215's aircraft to take flight the Waddington crew's KH372 departed Dhubalia at 0801. The weather was good throughout the entire op, with few clouds, making for a much less stressful sortie.

In crossing the Bay of Bengal Roy's squadron reached the landmark of Cheduba Island, off the west coast of Burma. Long-range P-51 Mustangs joined the Liberators near neighbouring Ramree Island and escorted the bombers to the target and back. Partly because of this protective show of force 215 Squadron airmen saw no enemy aircraft from start to finish.

Approaching Rangoon from the west, the bomber force prepared to release its loads. The target visibility, affected by no more than a few scattered puffs of clouds, nevertheless, was moderate due to haze, but this wasn't a hindrance to the attacking force. Thirty-six US B-24s, leading the way from the highest altitude, 14,000 feet, were followed by ten Liberators from 99 Squadron (two of their aircraft had aborted and returned early to Salbani) at about 11,500 feet. Flying in the lowest position, at 10,200 feet, 215 Squadron's twelve bombers brought up the rear.

As anticipated, anti-aircraft fire – meagre to moderate in this case, but accurate – had been experienced as the Liberators crossed the wide Hlaing River on their inbound bombing runs. The American 7th Bomb Group B-24s and 99 Squadron's aircraft, both ahead of 215's Libs, reported only a few bursts, but the flak was well-aimed. In fact, the US 492nd Bomb Squadron's post-mission report put the anti-aircraft fire into perspective by noting, 'Accuracy replaced intensity insofar as flak was concerned.'

As the final formation over the town 215 Squadron seemed to take the greatest concentration of enemy anti-aircraft fire. Few ack-ack bursts appeared anywhere near 99 Squadron's formation.

In addition to standard heavy anti-aircraft guns, the Japanese employed rockets in their defensive arsenal, confirming what had been reported on the Korat raid of a month earlier.

The US B-24s carried fragmentation bombs, while 99 Squadron, like 215, released demolition explosives.

On arrival over the target 215 Squadron found all but the southern portion smoke-obscured from previous bursts, so they swung slightly southward to attack a relatively untouched area and laid down a superior bomb pattern. Aircraft 'H' released its load at 1205 from 10,800 feet, 500 feet higher than any other of its squadron's Liberators. KG830 'A' of 215 Squadron let loose all but one of its bombs on the target, but an electrical failure prevented the last 500lb high explosive bomb from being dropped until approximately one mile beyond the target.

Overall, very heavy damage was inflicted by the mixed US and RAF force in their foray over Rangoon.

A particularly active gun battery located near the railway bridge crossing Pazundaung Creek on the eastern side of Rangoon scored hits on two of 215 Squadron's Libs, aircraft KH352 'M', which was badly holed in the starboard tailfin by shrapnel, and Roy's 'H', which was hit by shrapnel in the bomb bay, severing a hydraulic line for lowering the undercarriage and flaps. Fortunately, Roy's flight engineer, Sergeant R. Hindson, made an ingenious temporary in-flight repair that conserved precious hydraulic fluid by rigging a piece of corrugated tubing from an oxygen mask over the damaged hydraulic line using tape and wire.

For 215 Squadron the anti-aircraft fire continued until its bombers were turning away to the left, in the neighbourhood of the Pegu River east of the target, while withdrawing from the built-up area of Rangoon.

Despite the lack of dense ack-ack fire the US 9th Bomb Squadron suffered its final combat loss of the war on this mission when the B-24 piloted by First Lieutenant Charles Wiley, serial number 44-50335, failed to return from the raid. Just after its bomb release this aircraft dropped out of formation, losing altitude, but all four propellers were initially still functioning. It was presumed that anti-aircraft fire had damaged the aircraft, though this was unverified. Soon number two engine's propeller – on the inboard engine of the port wing – stopped turning.

On the return flight to India the Wiley crew's B-24 steadily dropped further behind until it was lost in the haze and was never seen again. The nine men aboard the bomber were eventually declared dead; they never made it to Rangoon Jail, the region's prison camp, but it was believed that those of the crew still alive on the ground were ultimately executed.

In addition to the perceived fates of this American bomber and her crew at least one other US B-24 had been hit by flak, but the damage was superficial.

Including Roy's KH372 'H' and also the damaged KH352 'M' from 215 Squadron, all of the Liberators on the op except for Wiley's B-24 returned uneventfully to their respective India bases in the clear flying weather. Landing after 99 Squadron's return to Dhubalia, 215 set down in the late afternoon light between 1615 and 1628. Bill Waddington brought KH372 and his crew home for a satisfying conclusion to their challenging op, landing at 1618 as the fifth returnee from 215 Squadron. Having been aloft for eight hours and seventeen minutes, Roy's 'H' had traversed 1,580 air miles and burned an identical 1,580 gallons of petrol.

ROY: On 29 March 1945 we went to Rangoon to attack the Japanese army's Burma headquarters. We were very lucky on this trip because we were hit by flak, but nobody in the crew was injured, the Liberator made it home and everyone survived. While I was standing in the bomb bay there was a terrific bang, and when I looked around there was a hole in the floor just behind my foot. Hydraulic fluid was spraying around the bomb bay from the cut hydraulics. We had to land without brakes when we got back...you go a long way down the runway without brakes! I found a piece of flak in the kite measuring about two inches long and an inch wide. That would have been nasty, had it hit me.

MATT: And so ended March 1945's operational activities. Roy, in surpassing the thirty-op mark that month, accumulated a further seventy-seven hours and six minutes of operational flight time in March on seven ops. In addition to his combat sorties that month, 215 Squadron flew four more ops in March. Although the squadron was in the final months of the war, the dangers were still always there for Roy and his fellow 215 Squadron airmen, as well as for all others who flew against the Japanese – as was evident on this last op of the month.

Chapter 21

In India Roy flies his final ops, 215 Squadron faces a change of aircraft and an impending move and Dhubalia is hit by a storm: APRIL 1945 *(Part 1)*

215 Squadron's April 1945 summary

The world turned upside down for 215 Squadron in April. The month opened with normal Liberator activities, but the squadron received a severe shock on the thirteenth – five days after Roy finished his tour of operational flying – when its personnel were informed by Wing Commander Sindall, himself disappointed, that 215 was to immediately begin converting at Dhubalia from four-engine Liberators to twin-engine C-47 Dakotas, for transport duties. The C-47 was the military variant of the civilian Douglas DC-3. The CO was certainly not responsible for this major switch in 215 Squadron's mission and its conversion to a different aircraft.

Furthermore, it was likely that on this date (or soon thereafter) the CO also revealed that 215 Squadron would be relocating from Dhubalia to the much more primitive Tulihal, near Imphal, India – about 355 miles to the east; the squadron's ORB was unclear on the date when the announcement of the impending move was made. The relocation from a developed RAF station to one lacking many basic amenities would happen early in May and be completed 'by p.m. 5.5.45', per a Movement Order found in 215 Squadron's ORB.

The impact, wrote 215 Squadron pilot Wally Frazer in *A TREPID AVIATOR*, was:

> ...like changing from a Cadillac to a Model-T. Instead of sailing off to faraway places in the Queen of the Skies, we'll be flying the Pack Horse of the Hills, dodging tree tops to deliver groceries.

Complicating matters significantly was the weather. Dhubalia was hit by a severe storm on 10 April when Roy was still a member of the squadron. The storm, which impacted both 215 and 99 Squadrons, led to great hospitality being readily extended to men in need. Those with relatively dry places to sleep offered shared quarters to the needy, but there were also many duties required to quickly repair damaged aircraft and to bring 215 Squadron back up to speed as a functioning flying unit.

With good will among all parties and much hard work difficulties were met and generally overcome as they arose. Although morale was maintained, there was still a certain feeling of discontent, frustration and even fear, especially among the aircrews who'd been flying Liberators.

More details about the storm and its aftermath are in order. From 215 Squadron's ORB came this vivid description of events on 10 April:

> After tea a light wind sprung up from the south-west, and, with little visible warning a hurricane developed. The first indication of anything unusual was a bar of dark cloud on the southern horizon, rapidly spreading, and bringing with it a wind of 60 mph velocity, with frequent gusts to 80-100 mph. When the storm really hit the camp, clouds of dust obscured the declining sun, and empty tar-barrels, bricks, tiles, trees and all kinds of rubbish were seen to be airborne amongst the murk. The electric-light supply failed almost at once, owing to damage to the overhead cables. Within a few minutes buildings on the Domestic site were being demolished – roofs were ripped off almost all, and many walls caved in. Some billets were entirely destroyed, and all kinds of kit – clothing, bedding etc., – went flying through the air.
>
> All personnel worked hard, salvaging kit and equipment, and putting out fires which had been lit earlier to heat water for bathing, so preventing the wind carrying live embers amongst the inflammable huts. With the exception of a small "bush-fire", which was quickly extinguished without damage, these efforts were entirely successful.
>
> As soon as the hurricane began, W/Cdr. J.H. Sindall and the Adjutant (F/Lt. G.T. Williams D.F.M.) with other personnel, left for the airfield. The aircraft were found secure, although many had shifted "into wind", in spite of having a full load of bombs and petrol, and being picketed to heavy weights, in addition. Some damage was inflicted and all aircraft were rendered provisionally unserviceable, for a period of 48 hours, pending a complete check of such damage.

> The new buildings at Headquarters site, and the Flights, weathered the storm fairly well. Some roof damage was inflicted, particularly at "A" Flight offices and the Squadron Intelligence Room, where a door was also blown in.
>
> After about 15 minute's [sic] high wind, heavy rain fell for a quarter of an hour and the wind velocity decreased. The rain was welcomed as cutting down the fire risk, but it completed the dishevelment of roofless billets and offices. Luckily no member of the Squadron was injured.
>
> Everyone took this mishap as something of a joke – it was certainly a memorable experience. Those who had comparatively dry places to sleep "took in" the homeless, and hospitality was given to many officers and airmen of 99 Squadron, whose billets and messes had suffered particularly heavy damage by fire, in addition to the devastation caused by Nature's forces, which was common to all.

The ORB continued with its summary of post-storm activities on 11 April:

> The groundcrews and aircrews "turned to" with a will, to straighten out the mess caused by yesterday's storm, and to repair and flight-test damaged aircraft. Spare time was spent in sorting out personal kit, and retrieving odd items from the surrounding landscape.
>
> Sleeping quarters were again reviewed, advantage being taken of every building with part of a roof still in position. Tents were erected to supplement accommodation in the Senior NCOs' section.

An impressive milestone, having been met on 12 April, was noted in the ORB: 'All damaged aircraft were again serviceable by nightfall.'

On 14 April the first two Dakotas arrived on the squadron, and many more were to arrive at Dhubalia over the next days.

Before the weather hit and the news of the impending move and the switch from Liberator bombing ops to Dakota transport ops was announced there were still three Liberator sorties to fly in early April – 215 Squadron's final Liberator operations.

Monday, 2 APRIL-Tuesday, 3 APRIL 1945
(Roy does not fly on this op)
Kaeng Khoi, THAILAND – railway yards, repair installations and stores buildings *(daylight bombing)*

The Waddington crew, including Roy, didn't participate as one of the twelve 215 Squadron Liberators sent on the next combat operation to the railway yards, repair installations and stores buildings at faraway Kaeng Khoi, Thailand, situated sixty-six miles north-east of central Bangkok and nearly seven miles by rail north-east of Pak Phrio (Saraburi). This op was flown in conjunction with three other RAF Liberator squadrons.

Skipper Wally Frazer in *A TREPID AVIATOR* wrote of 2-3 April, when he captained 215 Squadron Liberator EW125 'P':

> …Another long one. As an experiment, we'll fly in a "gaggle" – in a cluster, but no set alignment. With monsoons nearly upon us, a gaggle may help us squeeze individually through small gaps in the clouds. Also, it's supposed to be easier on gas.

The overall op by the four RAF Liberator squadrons was deemed very successful, and free from injury or death for those who flew it.

Thursday, 5 APRIL 1945
(Roy's thirty-fourth op)
Rangoon, BURMA – dump near Victoria Lake, Area 'K' ***(daylight bombing)***

Back for his penultimate op Roy would again be skipper Bill Waddington/ second pilot W.F. Hill's first W/Op in an eleven-man crew aboard KH372 'H' (likely noted in error as KH352 'H' in 215 Squadron's ORB). On this occasion 'H' would carry no second W/Op, whose role would have mostly been to handle a beam gun, and, instead, an old salt navigator, D.E. King, who knew the ropes and could impart his wisdom as needed, would screen an inexperienced navigator, W.A. Williams. Thus, there would be two navigators and only one W/Op (Roy) aboard 'H' on this upcoming op. The destination would be revealed at the briefing for the nine Liberator aircrews chosen to fly the op. Each aircraft was to carry twelve 500lb high explosive bombs to the target.

The attentive assemblage of airmen at the briefing was informed that 215 Squadron would be a component in a large foray to Rangoon, Burma, to attack a newly discovered supply dump. Area 'K' of the dump would be 215's assigned aiming point. Joining 215 Squadron on this daylight op would be three other

RAF Liberator squadrons (99, 355 and 356, each sending out nine Libs) and US 7th Bomb Group B-24s.

Though the mention of a mission over Rangoon could still evoke worry, with telltale gasps and murmuring from a few men at a briefing, the contrast with the sorties to Rangoon from past years was striking, as was revealed in US 492nd Bomb Squadron records:

> There once was a thing called "Rangoon-jitters", but the feeling has been put away with moth balls for historical purposes only. Our former respect for this Burma "hotspot" has dwindled to a low ebb...

The US 9th Bomb Squadron – originators of the 'Goon at Noon Club' – expressed similar sentiments in their records:

> ...there has been a great deal of satisfaction on the part of all personnel that we are now able to "drive over the Goon" just about any time we feel like it without encountering a swarm of enemy fighters – a situation that used to obtain [sic] during the hectic months of November and December 1943. One begins to see real progress in the war, and our part becomes more real.

In good weather 215's nine Libs departed Dhubalia in daylight from 0810 to 0820, with aircraft 'H' being fourth into the air at 0815. The javelin formation first reached Elephant Point, India, on the east side of the Bay of Bengal nineteen miles south of Cox's Bazar (and not to be confused with Elephant Point, Burma, located twenty-four miles south of the Rangoon waterfront). Onward the 215 Squadron Liberators flew, to the Boronga Islands, south of Akyab on the west coast of Burma, where they met 99 Squadron's nine bombers. Together the two units proceeded further south to Ramree Island, where they formed up with 355 and 356 Squadrons.

From Ramree Island Allied fighters were supposed to escort the bomber formations into Rangoon, although no fighters, friendly or hostile, were actually seen throughout the sortie.

Also, from Ramree Island the course was set for the Initial Point west of Rangoon. The force then turned to port and aimed for the target, and each squadron focused upon its assigned portion of the supply dump.

The approach to the target was found to be largely obscured by a layer of cumulus clouds, and even where there were cloud gaps considerable ground haze marred the visibility. Most crews on Roy's squadron, flying at 10,500 feet, had been able to glimpse the wide Hlaing and Panhlaing rivers as they made their way to the supply dump in the noon hour.

The first to attack was 99 Squadron, followed by 215. Flying parallel courses from the Initial Point, 355 and 356 Squadrons attacked an area of the dump immediately south of Area 'K'. It is uncertain when the American B-24s bombed the dump.

By sheer luck 215 Squadron's aiming point, a conspicuous winding road inside the target area, was identified through a gap in the clouds, but bombing results couldn't be immediately ascertained because of the extensive cloud coverage. Other squadrons faced similar conditions, although 355 Squadron reported achieving good results, in spite of its bomb aimers having been hindered by thick haze and cumulus.

Flak, expected over Rangoon, turned out to be meagre and unremarkable, and no 215 Squadron Liberators sustained damage. Anti-aircraft fire didn't commence until immediately after 215's bombing, when about fifteen bursts were seen just below the aircraft. Additionally, there were a few bursts at the correct altitude but between Nos 1 and 2 three-aircraft vics. Only this one salvo of ack-ack was definitely aimed at 215 Squadron.

The Libs of 99 Squadron also reported only inaccurate anti-aircraft fire. Likewise, 356 Squadron noted ineffective heavy ack-ack; it inflicted no damage whatsoever. While inbound to its target 355 Squadron cited only meagre and inaccurate heavy anti-aircraft fire from the Mingaladon area north of the dump. Among the American B-24s the 436th Bomb Squadron bombers, to their surprise, were met with no anti-aircraft fire over the target, though the 492nd returned with reports of accurate flak at their 9,000-foot bombing altitude that resulted in minor damage to two aircraft.

Immediately after bombing 215's Liberators departed Rangoon by making a wide sweep to port and regaining their defensive formation as the course was set back to Ramree Island. No further ack-ack from below was experienced, and the aircraft were flying higher than enemy rifle fire could reach. On reaching Ramree formation flying was abandoned, and 215 Squadron's aircraft made individual flights across the Bay of Bengal to Dhubalia.

Unlike 215, 356 Squadron maintained its formation all the way back to Salbani, per its ORB. It's uncertain as to whether 99 Squadron, 355 Squadron, or the US B-24s broke formation for the Bay of Bengal crossing and eventual returns to India.

All Liberators reached their home bases safely and without incident. Beginning with Roy's aircraft 'H' 215's bombers set down back at Dhubalia in daylight between 1600 and 1645. The Waddington crew was airborne for seven hours and forty-five minutes.

Despite claims that results had been obscured by clouds, photographs taken during 215 Squadron's bombing were able to reveal that the attack had been well-concentrated in the assigned area, and the raid was deemed 'a very creditable result, gained under difficult conditions' in the 215 Squadron ORB.

Sunday, 8 APRIL 1945
(Roy's thirty-fifth and last op)
Bilin, BURMA, area – road bridges (bombed) and railway rolling stock (strafed) *(daylight)*

ROY: I had only one more trip after the Rangoon op. I was a bit nervous, because, well, it would be my last trip; it would be ironic to have something go horribly awry on one's last scheduled op, but it happened, such as back on 6 October 1944. Skipper Jock McKinnon would have completed his tour of ops had he survived, but he died in the ditching of his 159 Squadron Lib, BZ978 'W', when trying to return to Allied control after being shot up over Thailand. (I was on an ASR sortie afterwards – my first op – in search of survivors of this Lib.)

My last op, on 8 April, was also 215 Squadron's final Liberator sortie. On this flight we dive-bombed road bridges not too far north of Moulmein, Burma. My nervousness was undeniable until I was safely on the ground back at Dhubalia.

MATT: On the posted Battle Order Roy was listed as first W/Op aboard Liberator KH372 'H' (likely noted in error as KH352 'H' in 215 Squadron's ORB for the second straight op) – the same aircraft as previously piloted by Bill Waddington on past recent ops – and for the sixth and final time Waddington would be his skipper and Flight Sergeant W.F. Hill his second pilot. On this trip 'H' would carry only one navigator, D.E. King, and a second W/Op. Each of the eight participating Liberators from the squadron would carry a load of four 1,000lb and six 500lb high explosive bombs.

When and if Roy returned from the op and survived, it would mark the conclusion of his tour of operations with 215 Squadron; he'd have flown thirty-three combat flights, one exercise into enemy airspace and one ASR sortie near the enemy coast, thirty-five ops in all, more than were then required.

At the briefing the target, to be attacked in daylight, was announced to the assembled crews: two road bridges in the Bilin, Burma, area, situated fifty-six miles north-north-west of Moulmein. Joining 215 would be eight 99 Squadron Libs, nine from 355 Squadron and nine 356 Squadron Libs. In an effort to suppress ack-ack prior to the arrival of 99 and 215 Squadrons from Dhubalia, the contingent from 355 would attack known anti-aircraft positions near Hninpale, Burma.

Nine Liberators from 356 Squadron were tasked with bombing three separate bridges (one railway bypass bridge and two road bridges) near Waw, Burma, forty miles north-west of Bilin. Thus, their destination was different from those of 355, 215 and 99 Squadrons.

The airmen of 355 Squadron going on the op had been briefed to fly at 6,000 feet, while the other three squadrons were to eventually fly at 500 feet to avoid radar. When flying at low altitude men from 99, 215 and 356 Squadrons each reported great discomfort from the heat.

All eight of 215 Squadron's scheduled Liberators took off from Dhubalia between 0548 and 0558, with Roy's aircraft 'H' being the sixth into the sky at 0557. In good weather the squadron formed up and set course across the Bay of Bengal and then the Gulf of Martaban in order to approach the target area from the south.

On the way to the target some low stratus clouds were met above the Sunderbans land area at the top of the Bay of Bengal and over the northern Bay of Bengal. Further across the Bay to the Gulf of Martaban there were variable patches of cumulus and stratocumulus, some covering up to seventy per cent of the sky.

Clouds encountered in the Bilin area didn't affect 99 or 215 Squadrons' bombing, especially since their bomb releases, as planned, were made from the low levels of 300 to 500 feet, below the cloud bases; visibility was considered good for the attacking Liberators at their low heights.

Roy's aircraft and three other 215 Squadron Liberators were assigned the more northerly of the two road bridges near rail bridge No. 64, close to the settlement of Kawkadut, Burma, while the other four 215 Squadron aircraft bombed a separate road bridge to the north, but in the vicinity of the same rail bridge. Each Liberator made two individual bombing runs over its target.

Bridges were notoriously difficult targets to destroy from above with conventional high explosives, yet while the southern road bridge remained standing, the centre span of the northern bridge was seen to have been downed in the attack. Without success Roy's 'H' had specifically bombed this northern bridge at 1206 from 400 feet and again at 1214 from 350 feet. The first stick burst in the river thirty yards south of the bridge, and the second stick undershot onto the approach road, cratering it heavily. However, after dust and debris had cleared from the attacks the bridge was seen to have been knocked down, possibly the handiwork of another Liberator.

The three bridge targets assigned to 356 Squadron in the Waw, Burma, area to the north-west were left standing, despite 356's attacks. The squadron's gunners did have a good day in strafing rolling stock, barges and sawmills.

Down in the Bilin area and still at a low level following its second bomb run the Waddington crew's gunners thoroughly shot up two covered box cars near Taungzun.

Fighter cover was provided to the 355 Squadron Liberators, but 99 and 215 Squadrons were unescorted. However, an Allied fighter sweep over railways in the vicinity of the 99, 215 and 355 Squadrons' targets was in progress until after the cessation of the bombing runs, and this could have contributed to the absence of opposition aircraft.

The 215 Squadron ORB stated that no opposition had been expected, and while no enemy fighters were encountered or even seen by any RAF bombers, the hope that anti-aircraft fire would be non-existent when its Libs hit the Bilin area was false, despite the efforts of 355 Squadron to eliminate it.

Their attempt to neutralise the ack-ack sites met with mixed success, hampered by haze and the cumulus regularly encountered at this time of year at the 6,000-foot bombing altitude. During 355's foray over the area the anti-aircraft fire directed at them, both light and heavy flak, was considered meagre, inaccurate and ultimately inconsequential. Their crews had claimed that no guns were situated in the positions they'd been given to bomb, and whether this was true is debatable. Despite dropping their loads across the centre of the light ack-ack site the first of the three 355 Squadron three-Lib vics only inflicted minor damage, but the second vic provided a good pattern of bombs on the heavy anti-aircraft positions, thoroughly plastering them.

For a variety of reasons, including one aircraft's slight engine malfunction, the third vic had reached the area too late to attack its primary target, for fear of hitting low-level Liberators below.

In fact, in the 355 Squadron Commander's Report it was stated that the light ack-ack position had been only 'slightly damaged'.

While bombing its designated bridge 215's aircraft KH275 'T' reported several flashes from one of the gun positions 355 Squadron had targeted, though no fire was directed at 'T'. During the bombing runs by 215 Squadron's KH320 'D' three bursts of heavy anti-aircraft fire were seen, but the guns had apparently been fired at 99 Squadron Libs. In addition, 215's EW151 'U' identified three bursts of inaccurate light anti-aircraft fire emanating from the Kawkadut vicinity during its attacks.

Having arrived too late to target anti-aircraft sites as planned, the three 355 Squadron aircraft of its third vic opted to bomb supply dumps at Prome, Burma, on the way home, with some favourable results and with only meagre and ineffective light anti-aircraft fire aimed at them.

On their return journeys at least two Liberators from 215 Squadron – EV963 'S' and Roy's KH372 'H' – witnessed anti-aircraft fire while passing over Mokpalin, Burma, to the north-west of the Bilin-area targets by over twenty-five miles and less than two miles south of the Sittang River bridge, but the three heavy ack-ack bursts directed at 'S', though accurate for height, were away to starboard.

Atmospheric conditions for all returning RAF Liberators were similar to those faced on the trek to the targets, and every bomber from the four squadrons safely returned to its home base in Bengal, India. It's known that for their long return flights 215 and 356 again formed into one-squadron units after each had individually bombed its bridge target. The presumption is that the 99 and 355 Libs each also returned in a separate squadron formation mode, independent of other units.

The Liberators from 215 Squadron landed in daylight at Dhubalia between 1631 and 1651; the Waddington crew touched down as the unit's fourth returnee at 1642 after a flight time of ten hours and forty-five minutes.

And so ended Roy's first tour of ops; he'd survived without injury.

Chapter 22

In India Roy finishes his 215 Squadron duty with non-operational work, takes his leave in Darjeeling and returns to Dhubalia: APRIL 1945 *(Part 2)* into MAY 1945 *(Part 1)*

Dedicated, brave men on 215 Squadron

ROY: I finished with 319 operational hours. Considering all of the dangers and the potential for catastrophe at any moment of those 319 hours, on other training hops and at any time between my 215 Squadron arrival and my eventual departure, I do feel exceptionally proud to have become a tour-expired airman. And not an expired – as in a deceased – airman who, in death, couldn't have become a tour-expired flyer!

I never saw any cowardice in any of the bods on 215. Not even a hint of it. Everybody I ever knew or witnessed always wanted to go on a raid, and to have stayed behind was maddening. There was routinely a spare kite (and sometimes a crew) waiting in case a Lib designated for an op should be withheld from flying, typically for mechanical reasons, or if it reported a serious issue, like an engine malfunction soon after take-off. Rarely did the standby crew end up flying the op. Usually (not always) the crew expecting to fly the op still had the right to go.

Here is the typical scenario should one of the chosen Libs prove to be troublesome before take-off. If a designated crew climbed aboard their kite in preparation for flying the op and found something wrong, and the decision not to take off in that Lib was made, there would be a mad panic to claim the spare kite. 'Quick! Hurry, get the *gharry*!' would be the mindset. Everybody would be yelling at the slowest airman to get his finger out, and in no time flat the crew would pile onto a *gharry*, head over to the spare Lib, jump aboard and, if the reserve aircraft checked out, away they'd go. If another chosen kite was also found to be faulty, that aircraft's crew would similarly be seen racing in their *gharry* to try to get to the spare first.

When an issue with my crew's planned aircraft arose, and we were faced with grabbing and claiming the spare for flying on the op, we always seemed to win.

The frantic rush to claim another Liberator was quite amusing to watch, because the activity was very rushed, with someone from the crew in question having to get inside to quickly claim the aircraft (in case there was competition from another crew). The last sprint from the *gharry* to the kite, with all the urging on from the rest of the crew, was terrific...not that I enjoyed it when it happened to my crew.

I've read books like *THE CRUEL SEA*, by Nicholas Monsarrat, where men were standing in front of the noticeboard reading their postings. In one of the books, perhaps Monsarrat's, a sailor staggered out saying, 'Submarines, Atlantic!' as white as a sheet. The next did a dance and said he bagged the Admiral's staff in Hawaii. That was the exact opposite of the fellows I knew.

Roy is still a wireless operator at Dhubalia on 215 Squadron for another two weeks after flying his last op

MATT: Before he eventually began his new non-operational posting – something every airman received after completing his tour of ops – Roy still had an obligation to serve in 215 Squadron. The end of his operational flying, and also the cessation of the squadron's Liberator usage, didn't signal the immediate termination of his stint on 215 Squadron. His next posting was announced on 20 April, twelve days after his thirty-fifth and last op. Before he reported for this next assignment in late May, however, he took a much-deserved leave to the hill station of Darjeeling, India, beginning on 22 April. The protocol for leave was to report back to the issuing unit, which, of course, was 215 Squadron at Dhubalia.

Until he departed Dhubalia for his leave on the twenty-second he was a busy man; he wasn't immune from assignments pertaining to either the conversion from Liberators to Dakotas or the recovery from 215 Squadron's weather-related burdens.

Though he was tour-ex, his practical experiences as a seasoned W/Op were of exceptional value in a flying unit that continuously took on replacements, and that also was switching from bombing to transport duties. Radios, after all, were standard on Dakotas, the squadron's next aircraft – not just on Liberators.

Roy's help, unrelated to his wireless skills, was also greatly needed to assist in the cleanup and rebound after the 10 April storm and to the restoration of satisfactory living and flying conditions at Dhubalia.

The steady and deliberate preparatory work for the squadron's relocation from Dhubalia to Tulihal, in Imphal, India, didn't commence until around the time when Roy departed the squadron for his leave, and his brawn and brains were used on other tasks at Dhubalia.

ROY: In an intense training scheme the squadron converted to C-47 Dakotas at Dhubalia in April. Although I have little recall of events, other than that of imparting my wisdom upon young airmen, I do vividly remember one incident of note. I was sitting in the rear of this Dakota while it was practicing circuits and landings. After setting down for good while taxiing back to dispersal one wheel went off the taxi strip, the nose went down and the tail went up. After crashing against a bulkhead and lying in a heap with a very sore back I smelt petrol.

I hammered with my fist on the bulkhead door, but no one responded. The smell grew stronger, and I was sure that I'd burn. Yelling at the top of my voice, I tried to climb up towards the tail to get out of the exit door on the port side of the fuselage – if I could open it. For maybe twenty seconds I was out of control. I thought they'd forgotten I was there, because silence, other than my own utterings, was all I heard. Eventually – probably sooner than I remember – the door opened and two men appeared, quite unconcerned, but surprised that I, white with rage, was raving at them. However, I got over it in due time.

A Darjeeling leave begins

MATT: As previously mentioned, Roy received word on 20 April of his next assignment – a 'rest' posting – to the Communication Flight at the Headquarters of 231 Group, based in Calcutta. A 'rest' posting, which followed the completion of an airman's operational tour, was non-operational. In theory this was safer than operationally flying over enemy territory. However, a non-operational assignment could still be injurious or worse, such as if an aircraft crashed, but this wasn't Roy's fate. And with the war versus Japan drawing to a conclusion Roy hopefully wouldn't face a return to active combat flying on a second tour six months later.

Before his duty with the Communication Flight at 231 Group Headquarters began Roy was initially given a fourteen-day leave, but this was later doubled to twenty-eight days. Roy would have to report back to Dhubalia to administratively 'finish' this leave before he could move on to his next posting.

ROY: Travelling by bus and train, a friend named Bill and I went on leave to the gloriously refreshing Darjeeling, a 'hill station' located in the Eastern Himalayas at an average elevation of 6,709 feet. Darjeeling's climate was such a relief from the dreadful heat and humidity of Dhubalia and Calcutta, and the vistas were incredible. I was nervous about the bus journey, because we were the only white men on a vehicle overflowing with Indians, including some with chickens – called 'chooks' – in cages. At this time there was a 'Quit India' campaign of disobedience being conducted to try to rid the country of the British and to gain independence, and there had been a small number of violent incidents that we'd heard of in the press, where one or two whites had been killed.

Before I review this travel tale, here's one that preceded it.

On leave in Calcutta, by taxi I planned to collect a nurse working at a local hospital, and with whom I'd made a date. Having caught a taxi outside the Grand Hotel, I said to the driver, 'Chungi Hospital', or whatever it was called. He didn't seem to know what I was saying, so I repeated it a couple of times. *'Theek hai, Sahib,'* ('It's okay' in Hindi) said the driver.

He started driving, but soon we were getting into smaller and smaller streets, crowded with people, so I banged him on the back and again said, 'Chungi Hospital.' Once more from the driver I heard, *'Theek hai, Sahib.'*

Onward we went. Then suddenly we were in a street not much wider than the taxi itself, with tiny shops on either side and a flow of people passing the car. An enormous crowd looked curiously at me, then the driver. Stopping the taxi, he then stood up to harangue the crowd. In Hindi. I presumed that he was asking for directions, but I didn't know what he was actually saying.

This went on for some time. His antics included shouting and also waving his arms.

I started to get worried about my safety. Here I was, sitting in this taxi, absolutely at the mercy of those Indians surrounding me.

I sat imperiously in the back of the cab, trying not to show the slightest concern, because I knew that if anything was going to set them off it would be me looking frightened. Realising that I had to do something, I banged this fellow on the leg until he looked around, and then I uttered 'Howrah Station,' the main railway station serving Calcutta – a location any taxi driver would have known. He stopped for a moment and then continued on with his antics, so I banged his leg again and repeated my command in a much sterner voice.

Eventually he sat down, and off we went. I dumped that car when we got to where I could see other taxis, hired another and turned up very late to meet my date. Phew!

That was the lead-in to my other story about taking a journey with my friend Bill to Darjeeling.

We were sitting in the back row as the only whites on a bus crowded beyond capacity with Indians. On the way to Darjeeling the bus pulled into a clearing and halted. After some discussion in Hindi everybody started to exit the bus. There was shouting and more talking, and pretty soon Bill and I were the only ones left aboard. Those who exited moved away from the vehicle.

As Bill and I looked warily at each other, the driver returned, and, with a lot of sign language and broken English, asked us to follow him. 'Come *Sahib*, come *Sahib*,' he urged. At first, thinking of our well-being, we refused, but in the end we went, not at all convinced we were doing the right thing. After a little way, we saw the Indians from the bus assembled in a group, and we felt this intermittent thumping. We could see that the Indians were looking down into a pit at an elephant. The hole was big enough for it to back up and then charge the end of the pit in an effort to batter its way out, but it was hopeless.

Poor thing! Even now I get a rotten feeling in my stomach. I didn't at the time, but I'm more emotional nowadays. I don't like remembering it.

Apparently, the elephant had been wrecking crops. Its back was about two feet below the edge of the pit that had been dug to trap it. To a local I asked, 'What is going to happen to it?' In reply came, 'Oh, we kill, *Sahib*...We kill.'

These fairly basic people, just villagers, were very cruel by my cultural standards. I wondered how they were going to kill the animal. Would they throw timber into the pit and set light to it? Stab the creature with knives? I couldn't bear to think about it, yet we airmen dropped bombs all over the place!

Bill and I just went back to the bus.

Eventually the driver and the Indian passengers returned, and off we went up into the lower Himalayas to Darjeeling. There Bill and I were billeted with fellow officers.

A sign at the Darjeeling railway station said it was the highest station in the world at 6,801 feet. I certainly felt a bit of oxygen deprivation, and walking up and down the street was accompanied by huffing and puffing.

I'd not realised what a spectacular view I had from my room until the following morning, having checked into my accommodations in the dark, but that morning when I opened the bedroom curtain I experienced one of the rarest moments of mesmerising splendour in my life. Before me was the most incredible sight, one I'll never forget. I was looking up at these snow-covered Himalayan mountains. The highest I could see was Kangchenjunga, the world's third-highest mountain. A small plume of wind-borne ice and snow, looking like smoke, could be seen extending out from the 8,586 metre (28,169 foot) tip, almost like a flag flying in a stiff breeze. I could see other peaks and valleys around it, and the sight was so awe-inspiring that I just stood there gawking at it for a long time. I didn't even go down to breakfast. For a 20-year-old not to go to breakfast, it had to have been out of this world...and it was!

Fortune telling

Another incredible thing occurred while I was there. While playing cards with fellow officers we heard a voice at the door. This Indian fellow on the other side said, 'I tell fortunes, *Sahib*.' One of our group asked, 'How much?' and the reply was ten rupees – a seemingly exorbitant price.

Though most of us said we weren't interested, one chap said he was willing to pay, and the fortune teller and his client went upstairs to the officer's room. Eventually they returned, Abdul, or whatever the fortune teller's name was, and the officer, who looked as white as a sheet. That captured everybody's attention, especially when the officer wouldn't tell us anything about what transpired, so, intrigued and willing to gamble that the fortune teller had something to offer, one by one the others had their fortunes told.

I went last, but feeling somewhat sceptical, I was determined that the fortune teller wouldn't get me. I figured that he was reading the moods of the others and inferring what their minds really felt. In order to expose him as a phony when we went up to my room, I made him look out the opened window, where there could be no reflection for him to see, while I wrote things down using a small pencil. I opted for a small pencil so that he couldn't discern thoughts based upon the movement of the top of a longer pencil.

Imagine an Indian voice saying to me, '*Sahib*, write down your name.' This was followed by requests to also record where and when I was born, where I lived back home and the names of my girlfriend and my parents. Upon completion I had to fold up the paper until it was very small and throw it several times onto a board bearing numerals, which he wrote down. Then began his interpretation.

He told me every single thing that I'd written down. 'Your name is Roy,' he said, 'and you were born in Hong Kong.' He was spot-on accurate with my parents' names...and almost everything! The only small detail that he got wrong was in regard to my girlfriend's name. I'd written down 'Audrey', and he said it was 'Andry'.

I'd tried to trick him earlier by writing my birth date but thinking of another date. Eventually, I could tell by his voice that he'd got it. And he repeated the correct date. Absolutely amazing! Don't ever try to tell me that there is no such thing as mind reading!

Those of us who'd experienced this fortune teller all got talking about things, and one of the fellows said that at some formal function some of them witnessed an Indian who impressed them with his magic tricks. The highlight of that night was when the magician dug a small hole in the garden ground, showed everybody a seed, dropped it into a hole, covered it with earth and watered it. After covering the small area with a cloth, he danced around, and then suddenly a small bulge in the centre of the cloth steadily grew, and grew, and grew, until after some time the cloth resembled a tent with a pole inside. He whipped off the sheet to reveal a small tree. The fellow relating this story to us swore that it took three men to pull the tree out of the ground! India!

MATT: The above is reminiscent of another recollection, by an ex-159 Squadron and 99 Squadron Liberator navigator/bomb aimer (name withheld at the behest of his offspring) in his unpublished memoir:

> There was a time when people who had lived in India were regularly asked if they had ever seen the Indian Rope Trick... I saw the next best thing – the peach tree.
>
> One evening, there were about 10 of us officers sitting on the patio after dinner – it was still daylight...
>
> An adult Indian male and a young boy of 8 or 9 presented themselves and asked if they might perform some famous tricks, and the general opinion was that nobody minded providing it did not cost very much, as we were all very 'poor' people. And so an area in the centre of the floor was cleared. The old man then sent the boy to bring a bucket of soil which was tipped out onto the concrete floor. He then took a peach

stone from his pocket and asked everybody to handle it and confirm that it was a fairly fresh peach stone. This was done, and all agreed that it was a real peach stone.

He wore a traditional white cotton garment, and, while talking to us, he put the stone in the middle of the pile of soil. He then stood over the pile making some gestures and uttering 'magic' words. After a minute he stepped aside and revealed a beautiful little peach tree about six inches high – very green and fresh looking. We were amazed – the boy was nowhere near the soil – and talked about it among ourselves. After another two or three minutes he again stood over the heap of soil with the small tree growing out of it and went through the same rigmarole. Stepping back very carefully, he again revealed the peach tree, although now it was about three feet high and comparatively wide – it just did not appear possible that he had such a large object concealed under his *dhoti*. At no time was he more than ten feet from all ten of us.

Roy is granted a second Darjeeling leave

ROY: Towards the end of my first two-week leave I met a charming, very quiet and attractive Anglo-Indian woman – a hill, not city, type of girl. She was actually a half-caste, and quite white in colour. She lived in a nice house with her father, an Indian. While I was over to their house for dinner one evening, she said that if I could get a leave extension I could stay at their house.

I phoned the 215 Squadron people back at Dhubalia – those from the squadron who remained – and asked them if I could have another fortnight's leave, because it was due to me. Finishing up their relocation to Tulihal, India, and not caring to have another body to worry about, they said yes, I could extend my leave, so I stayed at the house. It was very pleasant living there, and we could use the bar at the Officers' Mess.

When I returned to Dhubalia to check in at the end of my leave extension, 215 Squadron had completed its move to the new location, with the exception of the odd administrative officer or two to handle last-minute issues, like my return from a leave.

Back before my tour of ops had completed I witnessed 215 and also 99 Squadron Liberators returning from ops I didn't fly. Later, on 20 May 1945, as a tour-ex airman at a location where 215 no longer operated Liberators, in watching twelve 99 Squadron Libs coming home to land at Dhubalia after an op to Jumbhorn, Thailand, I was reminded of scenes in those films when the characters went down to the strip to see returning aircraft. After recognising the distant hum of engines, in such a scene somebody would say, 'They're coming.' This likely doesn't happen now because of technology, but in the war years, especially in India, one didn't have the sophisticated electronic equipment that is now commonplace. Back then everybody would rush outside to hear the telltale whir of returning engines, and an aircraft would come in, then a second would land, then a third, etc. Before my tour was finished when this occurred, whenever I wasn't on ops, we'd count them all in...one... two...three and so on. Just like Clark Gable, or whomever, in the movies. I still counted returning Liberators, though after 8 April they were from 99 Squadron, not 215.

Chapter 23

In India a new assignment (in Calcutta), recollections of time off, the end of the war and awaiting the trip home: MAY 1945 *(Part 2)* into OCTOBER 1945 *(Part 1)*

Communication Flight, Headquarters, 231 Group in Calcutta *(Roy's next posting after 215 Squadron)*

On 21 May 1945, at the end of my leave extension I travelled from Dhubalia to Calcutta to report to my new, and non-operational, assignment with the Communication Flight at Headquarters, 231 Group in Calcutta, the town where I'd be based until a few weeks before I departed India in mid-October.

Occasionally taking to the air, my three-man crew transported Lord Richard G. Casey, then the Governor of Bengal, and other VIPs, in addition to delivering mail. Australian Flight Lieutenant Ted Coulin, who'd flown a 215 Squadron tour of ops, was the usual (but not only) pilot, I was the W/Op, but the name of the third crew member, a navigator, escapes me now. Lord Casey, also from Australia, rarely flew.

I liked the small twin-engine monoplanes we were assigned – a Beechcraft C-45 Expediter and a Lockheed Model 10 Electra. The pilots mostly let me fly, but they'd land. We were based at the Royal Calcutta Turf Club, located in the Maidan, a large Calcutta park. In my time in the Communication Flight I totalled only nine hours and forty minutes on the Expeditor and seven hours on the Electra. The flights were short junkets, and so the hours I amassed aloft were small in comparison to my multi-hour 215 Squadron ops.

Those Communication Flight hours were, in part, indicative of how little flying I actually did during my three or so months on the assignment. With more free time on this assignment than ever before I was able to enjoy Calcutta's delights quite frequently.

One day while at the controls flying our aircraft up to a nearby aerodrome I entered the circuit, called up for landing permission and was told which runway to use. After acknowledging the instructions I turned onto the final leg and lost height when approaching the airfield for the landing, per normal procedures. I called out to the sleeping pilot in the cockpit seat next to me, 'Come on, John, we're here. Wake up, we're here. Wake up.'

He didn't respond, so I thought, 'I can land this thing!' Coming in, closer and closer to touchdown, I was doing beautifully. When about ten feet off the ground I heard a stream of invectives and shouting from the pilot. He yelled that he was going to kill me when we got down, that I was a stupid idiot, etc., and with wings wobbling he forcibly took control and safely landed the aircraft.

He cooled down by the time we'd taxied to the caravan used for a flight office. I told him that I'd comfortably flown all around the place and knew what I was doing, and, anyway, there we were, right on target and only just off the ground. I wouldn't have tried a landing had I not felt confident.

Although I went on flying, I never attempted to land again.

Roy is granted another fourteen-day leave

MATT: In his final leave in India (7 to 20 June 1945) while he was on the Communication Flight, Headquarters, 231 Group Roy partook once again of the splendours of Darjeeling.

An incident in Calcutta in 1945

ROY: Being stationed in Calcutta I made the most of this golden opportunity to have fun. Having met a nice girl at Calcutta's Grand Hotel, I remember that we went out quite a few times.

On one memorable occasion after I'd finished flying with 215 Squadron a friend of mine was sitting in the lounge drinking with this girl and me when it became necessary for my air force mate and me to go and get our pay.

To this girl I asked, 'Will you come with us?'

In reply she responded, 'No, I'll wait here for you.'

I said, 'If alone, you're going to get a lot of attention.'

She replied, however, that she could handle it, so off we went. I might add that she was a very attractive girl, and white girls of European or mixed

Anglo-Indian stock, even those who weren't particularly attractive, were a rarity in Calcutta, a town bursting at the seams with young white men in uniform.

My male friend and I raced away in a taxi to the paymaster's office, and because his name and mine were different alphabetically we were directed to different locations. I said that I'd meet him after we'd been paid, and then we'd go back to the hotel together.

When I returned he wasn't there. I waited and waited, but he didn't appear, so in the end I returned to the Grand on my own. You guessed it...he was back there trying to get this lovely woman away from me! However, I soon cleared that up with no lasting damage to friendship.

More remembrances from Calcutta in 1945

While on the Communication Flight I got to know Thea, a very nice girl who was married but separated from her husband. She was dressed in an army uniform. As a pretty cozy couple we took at least two trips up the wide Hooghly River. I hired a native boat, something like a sampan with oars at the rear, and the owner would row or sail up the river for two or three hours. Taking sandwiches, a bottle or two of champagne and a rug, away we'd go. On some river outings my female companion and I were joined by other RAF blokes and their dates, if they had them.

Every night there was an Officers' Mess dance. To my great delight and surprise I learned that one of my old girlfriends from school in Hong Kong was there, someone who'd been writing to me ever since I'd joined up. Said to be staying nearby, she was asking after me, and now she was at the same dance. Enid Watson was her name, a redhead I knew well in school. I walked across the room, found her and chatted amiably with her. I thought then that, absolutely, I had to take Enid out to dinner – something I wanted to do, too.

Then I wondered how I'd handle this with Thea. I went ahead and told Thea that I wanted to take this girl out to dinner. Enid, I explained, was a very old friend, and I owed her a lot for the letters she'd been writing me, too. I got the usual feminine response from Thea, but I decided that I just had to spend time with Enid.

I didn't have enough money to go out to dinner, but the guys rallied round and loaned me the money. Enid and I taxied to a very nice Calcutta restaurant, and then we returned to base. I dropped her off at the women's barracks and went to the Officers' Mess. I've always felt ashamed about that. I should have taken her in for a drink afterwards, but I didn't, because I knew that had I done so, it would have been the end with Thea!

When entering the Mess I found a squadron leader with Thea who thought he was doing well. He treated me coldly, and it took some time to move him out.

He even invited me to meet him outside, but I ignored that, and he finally left. In retrospect, had I fought him trouble could have followed, because of rank differences. Besides, I wasn't interested in bruises, broken bones or worse problems – his or mine!

I soon lost touch with Enid. She returned to Hong Kong and married, becoming Enid Whitely. After her husband's death she went to England and was living with Peter Smith, another Central British School classmate in Hong Kong. Audrey Nash, my dear friend from the olden days, resided not far away from Enid, so it was a little Form 5 there in England.

I mentioned that back at 1673 HCU in September 1944 my clothing was washed by an Indian *dhobi wallah*. Here is one such example of the loss of elasticity in my underwear's waistband, due to the laundering process. When I was in Calcutta following my tour of ops, my billet and the Officers' Mess were separated by a railway line. One night I decided to return to my billet from the Mess early, because I had already imbibed too much liquor. To cross the line to get from the Officers' Mess to my room I had to first negotiate a barbed wire fence separating the Mess from the railway right of way.

After getting hooked up a couple of times I succeeded in making it through the wire, and I faced the next obstacle, the rail line. On this particular night there were two side by side flatbed railway cars in my path. Having crawled under the first one, I stopped to reconsider. 'Suppose the train moved off while I was under that car,' I wondered. To avoid this potential predicament I decided to climb onto the first flatbed, run hard, jump the gap between the two trains and land on the adjoining flatbed. Then I'd continue onward to another barbed wire boundary fence and then to my billet. I knew I could do it; perhaps alcohol had foolishly stoked my courage.

Away I flew!

When I tried to open my legs wide to clear the space I realised that they wouldn't spread properly. My underwear had fallen down and was at the level of the crotch of my pants, thanks to the elastic waistband having been ruined by the repeat beatings by *dhobi wallahs.*

I flew through the night air briefly before crashing to the stones of the rail line. I have no recall, but I got past the second railway car and then through the barbed wire fence on the other side, and somehow I made it back to my billet. I did myself some physical damage, but I healed quickly; my cuts and bruises were minor.

The war with Japan ends, and Roy's India experiences continue *(AUGUST into OCTOBER 1945)*

The two days when the war with Japan was declared over were times of great celebration. Let me explain what I mean by two. It was generally accepted that the war ended with the armistice of 14 August 1945 (V-J Day), when Japan's capitulation was announced, but the formal surrender – when the Instrument of Surrender was signed on the deck of the USS *Missouri* in Tokyo Bay – wasn't until 2 September 1945. The latter officially ended hostilities.

Honestly, I can't remember much about either day; they were each joyous, though perhaps the first one had a bigger effect upon my psyche – and my liver. I'm amazed that such momentous days weren't firmly and permanently etched into my brain! The celebrations followed five-plus years of a dreadful war that even back in 1940, before hostilities versus the Japanese, Winston Churchill had called 'blood, toil, tears and sweat'.

After 14 August, Aussies in the air force were posted to Dhubalia, my former squadron's base during the second half of my Liberator tour, to await a posting home. Officially my stint with the Communication Flight concluded on 30 August. The RAAF honchos told us that they weren't wasting time in bringing us home…or so we were led to believe, but I didn't embark from Calcutta for Australia until 17 October.

About a month before I departed India forever my twenty-first birthday arrived; the special date was 20 September 1945. I received the usual marvelous congratulations that went with somebody's milestone birthday. Then I received a telephone message that some of my 215 Squadron mates were heading to Dhubalia to fly me over to Calcutta for a celebration. I told them that the runway was closed, but they said not to worry and to be at the end of the strip at 1400. Two or three of us got down there and hid in the trees. In time we heard a plane approaching, but instead of landing quietly and then taking off swiftly, it proceeded to beat up the aerodrome.

We were 'packing death' – an Aussie slang term for being deathly afraid – at the end of the strip, waiting. Eventually the aircraft popped down and taxied up to where we were crouched. We piled into the kite and screamed at the pilot to get going. While passing over trees after taking off we saw the base CO's car on its way down. Phew!

I was given a great party in Calcutta. However, halfway through the night I found myself trapped by a mumbling drunk, and it was hard to get away. Then he asked, 'Know any Liberator guys here?' I cautiously asked him why he'd enquired. His reply: 'I'm going to kill them like they killed my mates.' He'd been in one of the railway cars that we'd strafed on the Thailand-Burma Railway, before we changed to attacking only locomotives. I raced around telling everybody not to mention having been on Libs.

At the end of the night's revelry we returned to the railway station to catch the first morning trains to take me back to Dhubalia and my mates back to their aircraft. We grabbed some sleep. Thankfully we weren't pestered by police or beggars – or angry former Thailand-Burma Railway PoWs.

That was almost the end of my Indian adventure, and it sure was an adventure. I waited at Dhubalia just a short while longer before my postings back to Australia was announced.

Chapter 24

Roy's Indian sojourn's conclusion and the voyage home: OCTOBER 1945 *(Part 2)*

Roy's final railway journey in India

In preparation for my return sail to Australia, and having been ensconced at Dhubalia with my fellow Aussies since late in August 1945, I travelled with them to Calcutta in October of that year. Our fairly short but slow rail trip, making many local stops, was aboard Third-Class carriages. Part of the journey was at night. We just sat with our gear on wooden seats and dozed. At some point in the darkness I watched the moonlight-caused shadows on the windows; there were no lights in the carriage. I noticed that the shadows were still moving when there were no trees beside the railway line, so I borrowed a torch and played it on the window sills. I let out a horrified yell that woke up a lot of guys in the carriage; there were cockroaches over everything. Some men even had insects right up next to their faces, and it was disgusting. Confusion reigned, with fellows stomping roaches on the floor. I couldn't sit there.

Eventually everything quieted down again, but the fundamental problem still hung heavily on some minds. The reader who well remembers when I burned down the toilet at Digri in December 1944 will understand why I stood in the open carriage door with a nice cool breeze blowing in my face.

Upon reaching the docks we boarded the ship that would take us home. It was the SS *Sontay*, a well-known name among those who attend reunions, because it transported the first large draft of Australians from South East Asia Command back home after the Japanese capitulation. 'Were you on the *Sontay*?' is typically asked at reunions.

Homeward bound on the SS *Sontay*, arriving in Adelaide

We set sail from Calcutta on 17 October 1945 and steamed down the winding Hooghly River before heading out into the Bay of Bengal and beyond.

Sailing back to Australia was nothing like my trips out, starting in late 1943. No longer was there outright war, accompanied by worry, but aboard ship post-war in 1945 rank had no privileges, except in dealing with lower-ranked uniformed personnel. With war being over, even officers were treated like cattle.

No cabins or bunks were provided aboard ship. I slept on a hammock in the hold. I'd been less comfortable elsewhere in the air force, and being young and easygoing, I was still OK with it.

Some of my new experiences were admittedly good, because we were free from the pressures of war. We sunbathed on deck or atop hold covers while talking most of the time, but I also had a definite uneasiness about what would become of me after my discharge. I'd left school, learned to work a wartime wireless set and I could fire a machine gun. So what?

Upon arrival in Adelaide, not yet at our destination, we were granted a few hours ashore. It was of no surprise that my friends headed for the pub to reassure themselves that they were still true Aussies. It was certainly good to be back. The thing that most staggered us was the barmaid's accent. 'Had a good dye, fellas?' she asked. Of course we were aware of the Australian accent, but the returning lads were wincing. Imagine that! We were all Aussies who spoke in a similar fashion. My Australian accent was much milder, because I'd only arrived in 1940, but, still, even I was recognised as an Aussie by my dialect.

Chapter 25

Roy arrives back home, separates from the air force and is rewarded with a long and successful life: OCTOBER 1945 *(Part 3)* AND BEYOND

Disembarkation in Melbourne, back home at last

I disembarked from the *Sontay* in Melbourne on 25 October 1945, almost two years since I'd departed from the same docks. Assigned to No. 1 Personnel Depot (1 PD) upon disembarkation, I was first given ample leave, from 25 October until 30 November.

My reunion with my family soon after arriving was cause for great celebration. My parents, and I, felt a huge sense of relief that I'd survived. It was marvellous being home! At the time Father was in the process of making arrangements to return to Hong Kong with Mother. Eventually they did return to their beloved Hong Kong. I remained in Australia.

Roy is demobbed, chooses a career path and leads a fruitful life

My RAAF discharge date was 22 January 1946. I'd flown 579 hours and fifty minutes in training, on ops and in pursuing other aerial endeavours. Although there were more than a few moments of trepidation and anxiety during my uniformed years, I'm glad to have had such varied experiences. Talk about growing up fast! About finding the secret to learning! About comprehending the value of hard work! About developing deep camaraderie! I am extremely grateful for my good fortune in emerging unscathed! Those three-plus RAAF years shaped the rest of my life in the most wondrous way.

One day not long after my return home I went into Melbourne. While coming out of Flinders Street railway station I ran into an old friend. Eventually we discussed what we were going to do, now that the war was over. He told me about the Government scheme for ex-servicemen to study at Melbourne

University if one could qualify for a specific study course. I did, and six years later I graduated with a Dental Science degree.

I retired in 1991 after forty years as a dental surgeon in Box Hill, Melbourne. It had been a most satisfying career, and I've been blessed with a family that has supported me and also made it possible to flourish happily and contentedly.

I must acknowledge my personal friends, with whom I spent so much time in the war:

Pilot (aircraft captain)	Reg 'Jackson' Grouse
Wireless operator/air gunner	Frank 'Ned' Kelly
Navigator	John 'The Boong' Campbell
Wireless operator/air gunner	Bill Wright
Pilot (aircraft captain) and Flight Commander	Roy Williams
Wireless operator/air gunner	Les Marsh
Pilot (aircraft captain)	Athol Graham
Pilot (aircraft captain)	Bill Waddington
Pilot (aircraft captain)	J.D. 'Bing' Bingham
215 Squadron Medical Officer	Dr Tom Steele-Perkins
Pilot (aircraft captain)	D.F. 'Dizzy' Neville
Fighter pilot	Roy Bennell
Bomb aimer	Freddy 'Pissy' Houghton
Bomb aimer	John 'Smokey' Williams (died 13 March 1945)
Pilot (aircraft captain)	Murray 'Mac' Gardner (died 13 March 1945)

Epilogue

Born in Hong Kong on 20 September 1924, Roy Stuart Andrews, 86, died in Melbourne, Australia. His obituary, printed in the 24 March 2011 edition of Melbourne's *The Herald Sun*, stated that he 'passed away peacefully Mar. 22, 2011.'

It included these heartfelt words from his kin: 'You meant the world to us all. Your love, integrity and humility were admired and will never be forgotten.'

Appendix I

Roy's wartime operational flights aboard 215 Squadron Liberators, 1944-1945, plus two long non-op flights in 1944 while on 215 Squadron

Times of Roy's thirty-five ops and two long non-op flights, listed below, were mostly taken directly from 215 Squadron's ORB or derived from figures found in ORB documents. Because his flight logbook was no longer accessible a precise count of his actual times aloft on a small number of these thirty-seven flights required educated guesses.

Specifically, in the ORB actual times aloft were noted on twenty-seven of his ops and one of his two long non-op exercises. For these twenty-eight flights his individual Liberator's 'time up' and 'time down' figures are known. However, for each of his eight other ops and one long non-op exercise either:

1. The time aloft was an average of recorded flight times of all 215 Squadron Liberators on that sortie, and these flights (seven) are each identified with an asterisk (*) in the DURATION OF THE FLIGHT column below,

or else:

2. The duration aloft on a particular group flight (same starting point) was the first take-off time of an unknown 215 Squadron participant until the last landing – at the same starting point – of an unknown 215 Squadron participant, but this time range only included Liberators that had set down at the same base. The durations of only two of Roy's flights were calculated in this manner: one non-operational 30 October 1944 exercise and one 21 December 1944 bombing op, each of which is identified with two asterisks (**) in the DURATION OF THE FLIGHT column below.

A document in Roy's RAAF personnel file noted a total operational flight time of 319 hours. Possibly his statement that he flew 319 operational hours came from that same file; with his logbook no longer at his disposal, he was unable to see for himself, so perhaps he couldn't remember the precise number. The 319 value is remarkably close to an estimate of 319 hours and eight minutes of operational flying, based on what was available in 215 Squadron's ORB.

Roy's bombing or bombing/strafing flights were designed to reach the targets in daylight (and sometimes in low light conditions), with only one exception, the op of 2-3 March 1945, when the target in Bangkok, Thailand, was attacked, by design, at night. (The squadron only flew three other Liberator night ops, each without Roy.) Targets attacked in daylight sometimes required some flying in darkness due to the distances involved in reaching the destinations from India bases. On exercises all bombing or mock bombing took place in daylight.

OPERA-TIONAL SORTIE NUMBER	DATE	TARGET, OR NATURE OF FLIGHT IF NOT A BOMBING SORTIE	LIBERATOR SERIAL NUMBER & LETTER CODE	PILOT (aircraft captain)	DURATION OF THE FLIGHT (hrs & mins) (see the text above for an explanation of * and **)	ROY'S CREW POSITION
1	11 Oct 44	Near BURMA: Air-Sea Rescue search	KG831 'B'	Grouse	14hrs 15mins	2nd W/Op (mostly manning a beam gun)
NON-OP	30 Oct 44	INDIA: Exercise GLAXO	KG830 'A'	Grouse	13hrs 10mins**	2nd W/Op
2	4 Nov 44	Insein, BURMA (Rangoon area): Insein locomotive workshops	KG831 'B'	Grouse	9hrs 41mins*	2nd W/Op
3	26 Nov 44	Pyinmana, BURMA: railway station & sidings	KG831 'B'	Grouse	8hrs 32mins*	2nd W/Op
4	28 Nov 44	Mandalay, BURMA: marshalling yards	KG831 'B'	Hadaway	7hrs 18mins*	2nd W/Op
5	1 Dec 44	Mergui, BURMA: jetties, docks & adjacent stores areas (the secondary target in Mergui), after an unfruitful search for the primary target (a naval convoy near Mergui)	EW285 'C'	Hadaway	15hrs 20mins*	2nd W/Op
6	5 Dec 44	Imphal, INDIA: Exercise EARTHQUAKE II	KG831 'B'	Grouse	7hrs 15mins*	1st W/Op (the primary wireless operator)
7	10 Dec 44	THAILAND: Thailand-Burma Railway locomotives & rail wagons at 3 sites – Milestones 174, 175 & 176¾	KG831 'B'	Grouse	14hrs 17mins*	2nd W/Op
NON-OP	18 Dec 44	INDIA: Exercise GUINNESS, Round Two	KH324 'B'	Bingham	11hrs 50mins	2nd W/Op
8	21 Dec 44	Taungup, BURMA: storage dump, Area '3'	KH324 'B'	Grouse	7hrs 44mins**	2nd W/Op
9	23 Dec 44	Taungup, BURMA: storage dump, Area '7'	KG830 'A'	Bingham	7hrs 48mins*	2nd W/Op
10	8 Jan 45	BURMA: Thailand-Burma Railway, Milestone 54, road & rail cutting	KH324 'E'	Bingham	12hrs 00mins	2nd W/Op
11	13 Jan 45	Mandalay, BURMA: Area '2', concentration of troops & supplies	KH324 'B'	Bingham	6hrs 35mins	1st W/Op

OPERA-TIONAL SORTIE NUMBER	DATE	TARGET, OR NATURE OF FLIGHT IF NOT A BOMBING SORTIE	LIBERATOR SERIAL NUMBER & LETTER CODE	PILOT (aircraft captain)	DURATION OF THE FLIGHT (hrs & mins)	ROY'S CREW POSITION
12	16 Jan 45	Zayatkwin, BURMA: airfield	KH324 'B'	Bingham	8hrs 50mins	1st W/Op
13	18 Jan 45	Meiktila, BURMA: main airfield	KH320 'D'	Bingham	6hrs 31mins	1st W/Op
14	21 Jan 45	Ramree Island, BURMA: Mount Peter	KH398 'H'	Bingham	6hrs 55mins	1st W/Op
15	25 Jan 45	Amarapura, BURMA: railway & industrial installations	KH398 'H'	Bingham	6hrs 32mins	1st W/Op
16	28 Jan 45	Kangaw, BURMA: troops & fortifications	KH324 'B'	Bingham	6hrs 15mins	1st W/Op
17	31 Jan 45	Kyaukse, BURMA: Japanese administrative HQ & stores	KH324 'B'	Bingham	7hrs 23mins	1st W/Op
18	3 Feb 45	Jumbhorn, THAILAND: railway yards	KH324 'B'	Bingham	14hrs 23mins	1st W/Op
19	5 Feb 45	Madaya, BURMA: stores, barracks and administrative HQ, Area 'B'	KH324 'B'	Bingham	6hrs 56mins	1st W/Op
20	11 Feb 45	Rangoon, BURMA: supply dump, Area 'F'	KH324 'B'	Bingham	8hrs 24mins	1st W/Op
21	12 Feb 45	Near Myinmu, BURMA: Area 'A', gun positions	KH372 'H'	Bingham	7hrs 31mins	1st W/Op
22	15 Feb 45	Nyaungwun, BURMA: administrative HQ	KH324 'B'	Bingham	6hrs 43mins	1st W/Op
23	18 Feb 45	Yenangyaung, BURMA: concentration of vehicles & troops	KH324 'B'	Bingham	5hrs 50mins	1st W/Op
24	21 Feb 45	Myittha, BURMA: stores buildings & personnel, Area 'D'	KH372 'H'	Bingham	6hrs 46mins	1st W/Op
25	23 Feb 45	Mahlaing, BURMA: Japanese-held Area 'D'	KG830 'A'	Bingham	6hrs 29½mins	1st W/Op
26	24 Feb 45	Myingyan, BURMA: stores & HQ, Area '3'	KH372 'H'	Gardner	6hrs 39½mins	1st W/Op

OPERA-TIONAL SORTIE NUMBER	DATE	TARGET, OR NATURE OF FLIGHT IF NOT A BOMBING SORTIE	LIBERATOR SERIAL NUMBER & LETTER CODE	PILOT (aircraft captain)	DURATION OF THE FLIGHT (hrs & mins)	ROY'S CREW POSITION
27	2–3 Mar 45 (ROY'S ONLY NIGHT-TIME ATTACK)	Bangkok, THAILAND: Makasan railway workshops	KH352 'M'	Gardner	14hrs 17mins	1st W/Op
28	7 Mar 45	Martaban, BURMA: railway jetties & sidings, Area 'C'	KH352 'M'	Gardner	9hrs 28½mins	1st W/Op
29	11 Mar 45	Rangoon, BURMA: supply dump near Victoria Lake, Area 'E', within Area 'B'	KH118 'G'	Gardner	8hrs 30mins	1st W/Op
30	22 Mar 45	THAILAND: Thailand–Burma Railway targets between Milestone 50 & Milestone 100	KH372 'H'	Waddington	13hrs 27mins	1st W/Op
31	24 Mar 45	Pa-auk, BURMA: one of the 3 dump areas, & railway locomotive & rolling stock dispersal areas	KH372 'H'	Waddington	9hrs 14mins	1st W/Op
32	27 Mar 45	Bangkok, THAILAND: Klong Bhang Chak supply dump	KH372 'H'	Waddington	13hrs 52mins	1st W/Op
33	29 Mar 45	Rangoon, BURMA: HQ, Burma Area Army	KH372 'H'	Waddington	8hrs 17mins	1st W/Op
34	5 Apr 45	Rangoon, BURMA: dump near Victoria Lake, Area 'K'	KH372 'H'	Waddington	7hrs 45mins	1st W/Op
35	8 Apr 45	Bilin, BURMA, area: road bridges & railway rolling stock	KH372 'H'	Waddington	10hrs 45mins	1st W/Op

Appendix II

Roy's key air force dates, 1942-1946

All names below were as they appeared at the time of Roy's postings, movements and attachments.

*Roy wasn't called up – when his Royal Australian Air Force service actually began – until 6 November 1942.

**Some Indian state boundaries and names changed postwar due to either Indian independence from England, Partition or just administrative decision-making. Double asterisks mark those wartime spellings/locations pertaining to Roy Andrews that are different today.

***When Roy was posted to RAF Filey it was located in the UK county of East Riding of Yorkshire. However, because of administrative changes this former camp's site is now in a different county.

Key events plus Roy's postings, movements and attachments (not including leaves or special courses)	**Locations**	**Dates (mostly when Roy began his duty, sometimes when a posting was learned)**
*Signed 'Oath or Affirmation' papers at No. 1 Reception Centre (1 RC) (to join the RAAF, one day after his eighteenth birthday)	Melbourne, Victoria, Australia	21 September 1942
*No. 1 Reception Centre (1 RC) (called up, Roy's official RAAF enlistment began)	Melbourne, Victoria, Australia	6 November 1942
No. 4 Initial Training School (4 ITS)	Victor Harbour, South Australia, Australia	6 November 1942
No. 1 Wireless Air Gunners School (1 WAGS)	Ballarat, Victoria, Australia	4 February 1943
No. 3 Bombing and Gunnery School (3 BAGS)	West Sale, Victoria, Australia	26 July 1943
No. 1 Air Observers School (1 AOS)	Cootamundra, New South Wales, Australia	2 September 1943
No. 1 Embarkation Depot (1 ED)	Melbourne Cricket Ground (MCG), Melbourne, Victoria, Australia	28 October 1943

Key events plus Roy's postings, movements and attachments (not including leaves or special courses)	Locations	Dates (mostly when Roy began his duty, sometimes when a posting was learned)
Departed Australia by ship bound for the USA	Melbourne, Victoria, Australia	17 November 1943
Disembarked in the USA	San Francisco, California, USA	(unspecified date)
Departed on a train journey across the USA, bound for New York City	San Francisco, California, USA	(unspecified date)
Arrived in New York City	New York, New York, USA	(unspecified date)
Departed New York City by ship	New York, New York, USA	(unspecified date)
Disembarked, in the UK	(unspecified port)	8 January 1944
No. 11 Personnel Despatch and Reception Centre (11 PDRC)	Brighton, Sussex, UK	9 January 1944
Attachment to RAF Filey (also known as RAF Hunmanby Moor)	***Near Hunmanby, East Riding of Yorkshire, UK	22 February 1944
No. 11 Personnel Despatch and Reception Centre (11 PDRC)	Brighton, Sussex, UK	19 March 1944
No. 6 (Observers) Advanced Flying Unit (6 (O)AFU)	RAF Staverton, near Gloucester, Gloucestershire, UK	21 March 1944
No. 5 Personnel Despatch Centre (5 PDC)	Blackpool, Lancashire, UK	29 May 1944
Departed the UK by sea, bound for Bombay, India, transferred to South East Asia Command (SEAC)	Glasgow, Lanarkshire, Scotland, UK	8 June 1944
Disembarked in India, Bombay	Bombay Presidency, India	11 July 1944
Worli Transit Camp, India, Bombay	Bombay Presidency, India	11 July 1944
No. 1673 Heavy Conversion Unit (1673 HCU)	**Kolar, Mysore, India	18 July 1944
No. 215 Squadron	**Digri, Bengal, India	8 September 1944
No. 22 Armament Practice Camp (22 APC)	**Amarda Road, Orissa, India	21 September 1944
No. 215 Squadron	**Digri, Bengal, India	9 October 1944
No. 215 Squadron	**Dhubalia, Bengal, India	27 December 1944
Communication Flight, Headquarters, No. 231 Group	**Calcutta, Bengal, India	20 April 1945
Transit camp for Australians being returned to Australia (unknown unit number/name)	**Dhubalia, Bengal, India	August 1945
Departed India by sea aboard the SS *Sontay*, bound for Australia	**Calcutta, Bengal, India	17 October 1945
Disembarked in Australia	Melbourne, Victoria, Australia	25 October 1945
No. 1 Personnel Depot (1 PD)	Ransford, Victoria, Australia	25 October 1945
Discharged from the RAAF		22 January 1946

